D1027084

TONY HAWK'S PRO SKATER 4
OFFICIAL STRATEGY GUIDE

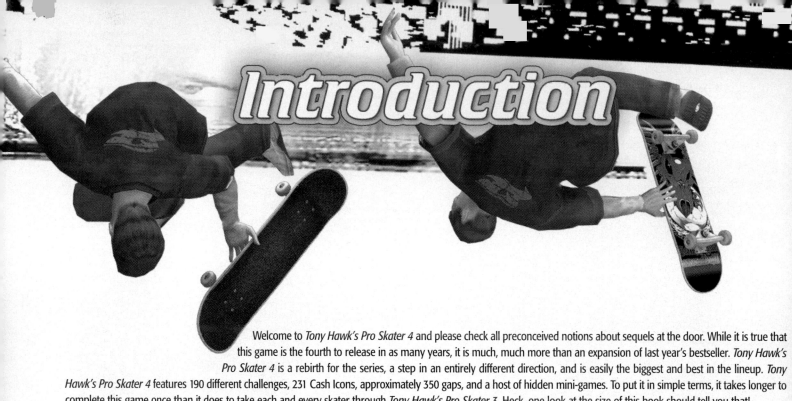

Introduction

Welcome to *Tony Hawk's Pro Skater 4* and please check all preconceived notions about sequels at the door. While it is true that this game is the fourth to release in as many years, it is much, much more than an expansion of last year's bestseller. *Tony Hawk's Pro Skater 4* is a rebirth for the series, a step in an entirely different direction, and is easily the biggest and best in the lineup. *Tony Hawk's Pro Skater 4* features 190 different challenges, 231 Cash Icons, approximately 350 gaps, and a host of hidden mini-games. To put it in simple terms, it takes longer to complete this game once than it does to take each and every skater through *Tony Hawk's Pro Skater 3*. Heck, one look at the size of this book should tell you that!

If you're a newcomer to the series and the above-mentioned numbers seem intimidating, you've got good reason to relax. Not only has Neversoft designed the game with a learning curve that makes it possible for first-timers to gradually work their way through the game, but the book in your hands describes how to complete each and every objective in great detail. Additionally, veteran Pro Skaters will likely find plenty to learn as well. *Tony Hawk's Pro Skater 4* contains, by my approximation, over 100 goals that are more difficult than the very hardest one in *Tony Hawk's Pro Skater 3*.

Fortunately, even when the last Pro Challenge has been completed, there are still hundreds of hours of enjoyment to be had thanks to the game's online multiplayer mode (PS2 only). Significant upgrades have been made from last year's online capability. Not only can up to 8 skaters take to a course at once, but *Tony Hawk's Pro Skater 4* supports numerous team-based games including the highly anticipated Capture the Flag! Lastly, skaters can now upload their own course designs and host their own tournaments! Multiplayer games don't get any better than this!

As an avid fan of the series ever since a demo of the original fell into my hands back in 1999, it has been an honor for me to author the Official Strategy Guides for both *Tony Hawk's Pro Skater 3* and *Tony Hawk's Pro Skater 4*, as well as all the rest of the games in the Activision O2 lineup. During this time, I've gained a greater understanding of what makes these games tick, and what tactics lead to success in the online arena. Great effort was put into the walkthrough portion of this book to not only instruct the player on how to complete the given task, but to *train* the player to ultimately be a better contender online. It is my hope that this book helps you to not only master the single player Career Mode, but also become worthy of playing with the big boys on the Pro-level server. Look for me, I'll be there waiting for you.

Doug Walsh
"el Guide/Dude"

In keeping with the trend set by the earlier games in the series, *Tony Hawk's Pro Skater 4* is bigger, better, and more challenging than any action-sports game in existence. Not only do the courses dwarf those in earlier games, but the tricks are more outrageous and the objectives more challenging. New features like the Spine Transfer and Skitchin' on cars help make this the deepest Pro Skater game to date.

Whether you're a complete newbie just learning how to ollie, or a seasoned veteran looking to learn how to Spine Transfer, this section of the guide has you covered.

CONTROLS

CONSOLE FRIENDLY

Each of the main buttons used in the game are referred to by their main function. For example, instead of specifying the PS2's X Button, the Gamecube's A Button, and the Xbox's A Button when mentioning an ollie, the term Jump Button is used instead.

CHOOSE YOUR WEAPON

The choice between using Directional Buttons (or Directional Pad, or + Control Pad) or the Analog Stick is truly a matter of personal preference. Some enjoy the fluid control the Analog Stick affords, while others feel that inputting trick commands is easier with the Directional Buttons.

BUTTON NAME	XBOX	GCN	PS2	DESCRIPTION
Steer				Use to steer the skater and to rotate left or right when airborne. Also used in conjunction with the buttons to perform tricks.
Steer	LT		LT	Use to steer the skater and to rotate left or right when airborne. Also used in conjunction with the buttons to perform tricks.
Rotate the camera	RT	C	RT	Press to lock/unlock the camera in a particular position.
Jump Button	A	A	X	Hold to gain speed and to set up for tricks. Release the button to Ollie.
Grind Button	Y	Y	△	Grind, and lip tricks. Press along with the Directional Pad when approaching a ledge or rail on an angle to perform a grind. Approach perpendicular to the lip of a ramp or elevated rail to plant. Examples are the 50-50 Grind, Nosegrind, and Footplant.
Flip Button	X	B	□	Press in conjunction with the Directional Buttons after an Ollie or jump.
Grab Button	B	X	○	Press in conjunction with the Directional Buttons after an Ollie or jump. Some tricks can be held for additional points.
Rotate	R	R	R1	Rotate to the right while in the air. Tap to rotate 180 degrees while in the air (optional).
Rotate	L	L	L1	Rotate to the left while in the air. Tap to rotate 180 degrees while in the air (optional).
Revert Button	R	R	R2	Tap to have your skater slide into or out of the Switch stance when on the ground. Also used to perform the Revert maneuver when landing on a vert ramp.
Revert Button	L	L	L2	Revert Button. Tap to shift the skater's stance into or out of the Nollie position when on the ground. Use to perform the Revert maneuver when landing on a vert ramp.
Spine Transfer	R+L		L2 or R2	Spine Transfer when leaping off a vert ramp or spine
Pause	●		▶	Pause the game and bring up the Pause Menu screen.

GAMEPLAY MODES

Tony Hawk's Pro Skater 4 includes a totally revamped Career Mode, and it features numerous multiplayer games for both online and offline play. For those who can't get enough of skating solo, a High Scores list tracks everything done in Single Session mode from the duration a lip is held to your best combo!

FREE SKATE

Free Skate Mode allows skaters to session any of the courses unlocked in Career Mode (or designed in the Park Editor) for as long as they see fit. There are no goals or timer involved and the score received for one combo is instantly replaced by the next. This is the perfect mode to come to when trying to learn how to navigate a newly unlocked course, for practicing the ultimate combination, and for checking off gaps! Ultimately, Free Skate mode is perfect for those times when you just want to hang out and skate.

SINGLE SESSION

Single Session Mode is a blend of Free Skate and Career Mode. While there might not be any objectives to complete, the clock is ticking. Skaters are given two minutes to score as many points they can and statistics are kept for each course in the following categories: High Score, Best Combo, Longest grind, Longest manual, Longest lip, and Longest Combo.

Single Session Mode is perfect for getting in some warm-up runs before going online. The addition of the High Scores table helps reinforce which courses are your strengths and which are not.

CAREER MODE

Dreamt of becoming a pro skateboarder but don't like the idea of having a "frequent visitor" card at the local ER? If so, this is your lucky, er, break. Career Mode gives skaters the chance to increase the Pro's abilities, unlock new decks and courses, and even compete against the world's best skaters; all the while laughing at the injuries your virtual skater endures.

The Career Mode in *Tony Hawk's Pro Skater 4* is unlike any of its predecessors. When first taking to the street, there is neither a timer nor a list of objectives to complete. The player is free to skate around at his leisure, soaking in the sights and scoping out potential scoring lines. When ready to begin tackling some objectives, simply skate up to one of the many people with the arrows over their heads and press the Grab Button to hear what they have to say.

START, DOWN, JUMP BUTTON

Yep, the Retry Last Goal option in the Pause Menu. There's no need to talk to the NPC each time you wish to try again. Just select this option from the Pause Menu and the skater will be whisked away to the starting point immediately. Similarly, the End Current Goal option allows the player to exit out of the current challenge and resume "free skating".

Each of the main courses contains 21 objectives, of which there are four different classes: amateur challenges that are available at the start of the level ("Unlocked"), amateur challenges that are unlocked by completing a corresponding amateur challenge ("Locked"), the Pro challenges and Pro Specific Challenges. Pro-level objectives are essentially Neversoft's gift to veteran virtual skaters and are, for the most part, an order of magnitude more difficult than anything ever before seen in the series. These pro challenges become available after completing 90 amateur challenges and one of the Pro Specific Challenges.

SHINY HAPPY PEOPLE

The non-player characters (NPC's) that offer up the various objectives throughout the game come with two colors of arrows on their heads. Those with blue arrows represent amateur challenges and those with red arrows hovering above them coincide with pro challenges. When on the course with a skater's Pro Specific Challenge, look for the NPC with an elaborate red and gold arrow above them—that's the guy you're looking for!

Once a goal has been successfully completed during the allotted time limit, the NPC disappears. Nevertheless, so long as the challenge has been offered, it can be selected from the View Goals list in the Pause Menu and  attempted again, whether it has been previously completed or not. In fact, the View Goals screen keeps a running tally of high scores and best times for every objective in the game so there's a reason to replay past challenges.

One of the new and exciting features of *Tony Hawk's Pro Skater 4* is the inclusion of Pro Specific Challenges. After completing 90 amateur challenges, select any skater and go to the site of his or her specific challenge. These specialized objectives play on the skater's unique abilities and past performances and are among the most difficult in the game. Completing one of these lengthy tasks unlocks the 5 pro-level objectives on each course and that skater's highlight movie.

SKATER SELECTION

You are free to choose between any of the Pro Skaters at any point during the game and continue on with the same Career Mode game file. This is strategically important at two times during the game. The first is in the beginning when differences in the skaters' inherent abilities are most pronounced. Some objectives are best tackled with vert skaters, and others become more doable with street skaters.

The second time that switching skaters can be helpful is when trying to complete your first Pro Specific Challenge. Some of these challenges are very difficult (Rune Glifberg's), whereas others are less taxing (Steve Caballero's).

When selecting a different skater, be sure to redistribute the Stat Points (if necessary) and assign tricks to any slots that may be vacant. This last point is important—the trick selection assigned to one skater does not transfer to the other skaters. Although you can configure each skater to have the same trick set, they each have different default tricks.

Each time an objective is completed, the skater is awarded a Pro Point, cash, and sometimes even a Stat Point! Pro Points serve as a measure of progress and are used to unlock other courses and, ultimately, the Pro Specific Challenges. Cash, on the other hand, is used for purchasing everything from secret skaters to new decks and clothing. With the exception of unlocking the Carnival and Chicago courses, money is primarily used for collecting goodies!

Although it's not quite an award, certain objectives involve special ramps that the NPC brings along. These ramps are called ProSets and become unlocked once its corresponding objective has been completed. ProSets can be turned on or off via the Options screen in the Pause Menu.

TWO PLAYER

The following gameplay modes are available on all consoles, provided there are two controllers plugged in. See the Online Multiplayer chapter at the end of this guide for details on playing online (PS2) or via a system link (Xbox). Also, those who will not be playing online or via a System Link are encouraged to check out the Multiplayer Chapter as well, as winning tactics are provided for each of the nine courses in the game.

Trick Attack

This is a Two Player version of the Single Session mode. Here, skaters compete against one another to see who can earn the highest score in the chosen time limit (30 seconds to 10 minutes). Put a lengthy scoring run together and set to the task of toppling your opponent. The number of points isn't what matters, only that you have more than the other guy.

Score Challenge

New to *Tony Hawk's Pro Skater 4*!

This mode is similar to Trick Attack, but instead of specifying a time limit, players choose a point goal to reach (100,000 to 100,000,000). The game continues until someone reaches the pre-determined score. Be sure to take both players' skill levels into account before selecting a point total, as all but the absolute best players will likely not reach scores over 10,000,000 points in a reasonable amount of time (without cheating).

Combo Mambo

New to *Tony Hawk's Pro Skater 4*!

Combo Mambo is a lot like Trick Attack, but only combos count here. Select a time limit (30 seconds to 10 minutes) and set to the task of assembling a bigger scoring line than your opponent. Each player's highest combo is listed at the top of the screen and remains there until a higher combo is landed. Be the one with the bigger combo when time runs out to win!

Slap!

Choose a time limit (30 seconds to 10 minutes) and get ready for some brawlin'! In Slap Mode, it's not the points that matter, it's how much momentum your skater has that counts. Trick off of rails and ledges to build up the Special Meter and to gain speed. Seek out opponents and crash into them. Whoever has the most momentum gets credited with a "Slap" while the other person is left picking up teeth. Whoever has the most Slaps at the end of the game wins.

King of the Hill

Some try to be "king of the world" but for others, being King of the Hill is where the real glory is! Follow the arrow at the top of the screen to the crown and try holding onto it the longest. Instead of keeping track of points, the amount of time a player holds onto the crown is recorded. Once that person reaches the designated time limit (30 seconds to 10 minutes) the game is over.

Graffiti

Graffiti mode tests the player's ability to perform completely awesome tricks on terrain found throughout the course. Each player is assigned a color of "paint". Go big off of a particular ramp or grind a lengthy rail to "tag" it in your color.

Ramps, rails, ledges, etc. display the color of the person who incorporated it into the higher scoring line of tricks. Steal tags from other skaters by scoring more points on a piece of terrain. Whoever has the most tags at the end of the time limit (30 seconds to 10 minutes) is the winner.

Horse

Similar to the backyard basketball game of the same name, Horse gives players the chance to take turns trying to one-up each other. Each player has 10 to 30 seconds to begin a scoring attempt that ends when the skater either bails or touches down on all four wheels. Players alternate trying to outscore one another. Should someone fail to top a score that has been "set", that person gets a letter. Whoever spells out the chosen word (maximum of 15 letters) first is the big loser.

Free Skate

Grab a buddy, grab a controller, and get skating. This timeless mode of play allows for skaters to cruise the course, working on scoring lines simultaneously. This is a great mode for warming up before heading online or to one of the other game modes.

PARK EDITOR

Even when every movie, course, and secret skater has been unlocked, and it seems like the offline portion of the game has been played to an end, there's still the Park Editor to keep you coming back for more. Like the Create-A-Skater mode, the Park Editor has received some incredible enhancements since *Tony Hawk's Pro Skater 3*. Rather than discuss the controls, which are listed in the User's Manual, this section of the guide provides a brief overview to the newest elements of this wonderful feature.

There's no denying it, the biggest enhancement to the Park Editor mode is the ability to upload and download user-created parks to the Internet for online play. In fact, players can pre-assign items such as crown locations for games of King of the Hill as well as base locations for Capture the Flag. Parks that get the most attention online will be placed on a "Best Parks" list so there's plenty of incentive to make a good one.

While not necessarily a new feature, the Park Editor has received countless new terrains, including many of the pieces from the ProSets found throughout the game. Players can now choose between large environmental structures such as the demolished building from Alcatraz or even the stage at the EMB in San Francisco! Many of the funboxes used in *Tony Hawk's Pro Skater 3* have been included as well, giving players a chance to combine their favorite elements from courses like Suburbia, Tokyo, and Rio all into one large course.

BUILDING TIPS

Designing a park that enough people find fun to play (and possibly to even hold online tournaments on) is quite a challenge and takes a good deal of trial and error. Consider the following tips when trying to build the next great skatepark.

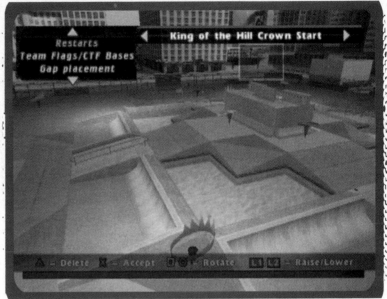

1. Study the pre-made parks. Open up these parks in the editor and look closely at what their designers did in terms of elevation, rails, and even the placement of starting positions and gaps. Try making slight changes to the original design and testing it out. After dissecting the pre-made parks that were included in the game, try downloading some of the "best" ones online and see what it is that makes them so popular.

2. Once you're ready to design a park from scratch, decide on what style of skater the park is going to cater to. Although each park should likely have something for every type of skater, it should also have a distinct personality. Perhaps it will consist of lots of bowls or lengthy grinds? Either way, think about it ahead of time and design those elements into the park first.

3. In addition to deciding on a style of park, it's important to decide ahead of time on the both the size of the park and its ground elevations. Although the Park Editor in this year's game allows the designer to increase the width and length of the park on the fly, beginning designers will likely find it easier to design a medium-sized park as it reduces the chance of clutter. With respect to raising and lowering the ground, doing so after most of the ramps are in place could make for a big headache. Decide early on if some areas are to be elevated or sunken and use large structures such as those from the 'Big Pool' category to raise and lower the ground.

4. One of the most common mistakes in newbie park design is adding too much clutter. There's a fine line between building a park that has loads of scoring opportunities and one that prevents the skater from ever getting a good line started. Be sure to think twice about adding loads of plants and signs; just because no ramp is there doesn't mean a skater won't be trying to manual past.

5. The most important, and difficult, thing in park design is adding flow. A well-designed course has scoring lines that seem to materialize where you'd least expect them. Continue tweaking and testing your design until there are at least two or three scoring lines that can be hit for big points. Afterwards, adjust the terrain placements as necessary to keep those lines fresh and interesting.

6. Get creative! Give the park a memorable name, add some fun gaps, and show it off to your friends. Or, if you have your PS2 online, add some CTF bases and King of the Hill locations and upload the park to the Internet. Invite some of your "Homies" to test it out over a friendly game of Trick Attack. Either way, enjoy the Park Editor and good luck!

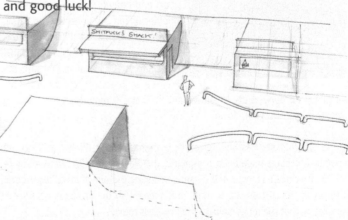

CREATE-A-SKATER

Creating your own personal Pro Skater has never been more fun than with the Create-A-Skater mode in *Tony Hawk's Pro Skater 4*! Not only are there hundreds of clothing, tattoo, and accessory items available to choose from, but players are even given precision control the size of the skater's head, foot, biceps, calves, you name it! Additionally, these custom skaters can be outfitted with a wealth of Secret Gear as well!

Although the Create-A-Skater has always been a fun tool to play with, its importance in the game has grown by leaps and bounds with the increasingly popular online component of the game. Players are encouraged to utilize this mode to make personalized, distinct skaters to use them online. Oh, sure, the Pro Skater characters also work online, but this is an opportunity to show the Pro Skater community your personal style. Don't let everyone down!

The Create-A-Skater has been given its own Pro Specific Challenge. Once 90 amateur objectives have been completed, the player is free to attempt any of the Pro Specific Challenges in the game, including the one at the Shipyard that is reserved the custom skater. And, in keeping with the Pro Skater tradition, completing that challenge unlocks the Pro Bails movie.

Of all the ways in which to customize the Created Skater, none are as important to the gameplay as the Stats. Each Created Skater begins with a rating of "5" in each of the various abilities. However, unlike the Pro Skaters, you are free to redistribute these Stat Points any way you like. Consider not pushing any one ability past a rating of 7 for the time being so as to not get too out of balance. Also, Lip Balance is most likely the one ability that can be skimped on early in the game. Boost the Rail and Manual Balance abilities, as well as Ollie and Speed to enable the Created Skater to have a chance at some decent scoring lines right off the bat.

SAVE IT!

Be sure to save your Created Skater. This way, he or she is ready to embark on his or her own Career next time you play the game.

PRO-SPECIFIC CHALLENGE

Movie Stunt Double

Create-A-Skater's Pro Challenge takes place at the Shipyard.

REQUIRED SPECIAL TRICKS

None

Time	2:00
Awards	$1250 and Pro Bails Movie

Movie Director
"We only have a couple minutes of light left and we have to get these shots, people! You have to hit all of the detonators and the only way to dodge the enemy fire is to be in a combo... ready, set, ACTION!"

It's up to the wily and oh-so-cool skater to navigate the Shipyard from one helicopter to the other while triggering all the detonators and avoiding enemy fire. The green detonators have been placed sporadically on the railroad tracks and must be cleared in a single combo. To make matters more difficult, there's a boatload of TNT sitting on the track as well. Dodge the red stuff, hit the green stuff, and lip trick on the far helicopter to end the scene.

ALL SHOOK UP

Each time a detonator is hit, its accompanying batch of TNT explodes. Although the skater won't be harmed by the explosions, the screen shakes violently. Since it's going to be hard to see the skater's lean, be sure to focus solely on the Balance Meter. It doesn't hurt to memorize the detonator placement, either!

Drop off the chopper and through the roof below to start the run. Keep a straight line and hop into a grind on the right-hand rail. Grind through the first three detonators while following the tracks down to the left. Quickly hit the **Track 2 Track** gap by ollieing into a grind on the left-hand track just after clearing off the third detonator. Grind through the fourth detonator and manual towards the ramp directly ahead. Air off the ramp and Revert back into a manual to keep the string alive.

Manual down the center of the tracks and hop into a grind on the left-hand rail just after passing the TNT. Grind around the bend to the left, take out the detonator, and immediately jump to the right-hand rail to escape sudden death. Only two detonators remain. Grind through the first detonator and keep grinding until the skater is about to pass the TNT on the left. Ollie over the TNT on the left and grind on the rail to hit the final detonator. Hop off the rail into a manual and leap off the quarter pipe at the end of the road to lip trick on the helicopter's landing skid. That's a wrap!

Trick Lists

Each Pro Skater begins their career with their own personalized assortment of Flip, Grab, Grind/Lip, and Special Tricks. The player is free to swap any of these tricks with others of the same type, including Special Tricks. Not only that, but there are four empty slots in both the grab trick and flip trick groupings in which the player is free to assign tricks to the special double-tap commands. Although the skater begins the game with just four Special Trick slots, additional slots can be earned by completing specific challenges throughout the game.

The tables in this section outline all of the tricks in each group, including the number of points that are earned for successfully pulling them off . Many tricks can be linked directly to another trick via a second or third press of a button, or via a combination of button presses. The point values represent both the number awarded for "tapping" a trick for the first time in the Normal and Switch stances. The Scoring section of this chapter explains the point scoring system in much greater detail.

OLLIE TRICKS

An Ollie is the most fundamental trick in skateboarding. The skater leaps into the air, simultaneously tapping the tail (or the nose in the case of a Nollie) to the ground to kick the board upward against the skater's feet. Doing so enables the skater to leap higher on ramps, onto rails to grind, and to do a host of other maneuvers. Simply put, it all begins with the Ollie. The following variations of the Ollie not only add style to a scoring line, but also in the case of the Fastplant or Boneless, can help add extra height to a jump.

All of the skaters have the entire assortment of Ollie Tricks at their disposal and, to make things easier, the commands are identical. The only difference is the name assigned to the trick in the case of the Beanplant, Boneless, and Fastplant. These names are used interchangeably throughout the book and are synonymous with one another.

NO LOVE FOR OLLIE

The Ollie alone is not worth any points, as it is nothing more than a means to an end. Add some rotation or a Kickflip to start earning the points.

NAME	COMMAND	POINTS (NORMAL/SWITCH)
Ollie	Jump	0/0
Nollie	Jump while in Nollie position	200/NA
Fakie Ollie	Jump while in Switch position	NA/240
No Comply	Up + Jump	100/120
Beanplant Boneless Fastplant	Up, Up + Jump	250/300
Wallie	Jump while in a Wallride	250/300

PLANTS

Plants are more of a bonus than an actual trick. When skating around the courses, keep an eye out for cars or conspicuous people and animals and try to Ollie onto them. Hit the top of these objects and people with at least one pair of wheels to successfully plant. Not everything awards a plant bonus, but getting one is always a nice surprise.

MANUALS

The Manual is essentially a wheelie. The skater balances either on the front or rear wheels as a means of continuing a trick. Oftentimes the Manual is used as a means of "linking" a grind on one object to a grind on an object too far away to Ollie to. By tapping Up, then Down on the controls the as the skater is about to land from a jump or an Ollie, the skater leans back on the tail and manuals along on the rear wheels. Tap Down, then Up on the Directional Pad to Nose Manual. Both the Manual and the Nose Manual have initial point values of 100 points, but points continue to accrue throughout the duration of the manual. While in a manual, press the Revert Button to have the skater Pivot or Nose Pivot. Pivots are not only worth 250 points, but can be used to dramatically increase the multiplier.

Manuals may be a great way to link tricks over great distances, but they require incredible balance. Pay attention to the Balance Meter that appears alongside the skater, as it indicates whether the skater is leaning too far in one direction. Tap Up and Down on the Directional Pad to keep the needle in the center.

There are numerous Special Manual tricks in *Tony Hawk's Pro Skater 4* that not only help to link tricks, but earn huge points in the process. Regardless of the type of manual trick you attempt, use them in between jumps and grinds as a way of chaining lengthy combinations together.

SKITCHIN'

One of the new abilities in *Tony Hawk's Pro Skater 4* is that the skater can now ride up to the back of a moving car or motorcycle and grab onto it to Skitch a ride around town. Simply skate to the rear of a vehicle and press Up on the controls to latch on. Once the skater has a firm grasp, switch your attention to the Balance Meter. Tap Left and Right to keep the needle centered.

Skitchin' isn't just a good way to earn points (initial score of 500 points just for grabbing on), but it's a fast way to get around town, too! Finally, tapping Down on the controls during a Skitch causes the skater to release the Skitch and gain a speed boost. Since the skater takes off past the vehicle, this is best done when Skitching on the corner of the vehicle so as to not plow into it!

FLATLAND TRICKS

Flatland tricks are extensions of the Manual and Nose Manual. These impressive maneuvers can best be described as dancing. Rather than just keeping the skater's feet on the grip tape, he or she works around the board, balancing on everything from the sides of the wheels to the underside of the trucks. Flatland tricks require a great deal of balance and skill, but once mastered can drastically improve the skater's overall scoring ability.

Flatland tricks bear a similar Balance Meter to manuals. Although the points they award are high, watch the meter and ollie out of the trick before bailing.

NOT SO FAST!

Flatland tricks are best performed while the skater is as close to stationary as possible. Try tacking a quick succession of flatland tricks onto the end of a lengthy chain right when the skater appears to be losing steam. Even if it appears that the skater has plenty of speed as he slides across the ground on rail, avoid trying to ride it up a ramp or over a funbox. The resulting drop in speed and balance will likely ruin what could have been a valuable scoring line.

Flatland tricks can be performed once the skater is in a Manual or Nose Manual. Once in a flatland trick, the skater can transfer seamlessly in and out of tricks by pressing the commands listed below. All modifiers can be performed by double-tapping the Flip Button. Pressing the Revert Button performs rotations. Finally, points accrue during the entire time in which the flatland trick is held. The scores below represent just the base score awarded for beginning the trick.

TRICK	COMMAND	POINTS	MODIFIER	POINTS	ROTATION
Anti Casper	Flip, Grab	350	Anti Casper Flip	500	Anti Casper Spin
Casper	Flip, Grind	350	Casper Flip	500	Casper Spin
One Foot Manual	Grab, Grind from a Manual	200	360 Fingerflip	450	Pivot
One Foot Nose Manual	Grab, Grind from a Nose Manual	200	Half Cab Impossible	450	Nose Pivot
Pogo	Grind, Grind	250	Wrap Around	500	Pogo Spin
Switch Foot Pogo	Grind, Grab	300	Half Wrap Truck Transfer	500	Switch Foot Pogo Spin
To Rail	Grab, Flip	500	Rail Flip	500	NA
Truckstand	Grind, Flip	250	Truckstand Flip	500	Truckspin
Handstand	Grab, Grab	250	Handflip	500	NA
Half Cab Impossible	Flip, Flip from Nose Manual	450	360 Fingerflip	450	Nose Pivot
360 Fingerflip	Flip, Flip from Manual	450	Half Cab Impossible	450	Pivot

REVERT

The Revert is nothing more than a landing trick. By tapping the Revert Button as the skater touches down on a vert ramp, the skater powerslides 180 degrees. And while it may not look like much, this little maneuver buys just enough time to transition into a manual or another vert trick! Go big off a quarter pipe, tap the Revert Button as the skater touches down and quickly execute a new trick. Keeping the controller's vibration function active helps, as the controller rumbles during the 'window' in which to perform the follow–up trick.

The key to using the Revert effectively is to understand its limitations. For starters, the Revert will not allow a skater to link endless half pipe routines into one lengthy combination. The reason for this is speed. Every time the Revert is used, the skater suffers a significant drop in speed. No speed equals no height, which together means

skater fall down and go boom. This isn't to say that one or two hits in the half pipe can't be linked together. They can, just be sure to mix in a grind so as to regain the speed that was lost.

In addition to the 100/120 points earned by landing a FS/BS Revert, it serves as a very convenient Multiplier to end scoring lines. Consider beginning and ending lengthy scoring chains with big jumps off vert ramps followed by a Revert. Sandwich lengthy grinds and manuals with these jump-to-Revert combos to really milk the courses for all the points they're worth!

Although the most common, and safest, follow-up to a Revert is a manual, it's far from the only option. After reverting off a ramp, the skater has a brief period in which he or she can quickly ollie into a grind, tap into a manual, or even perform a flip trick. Additionally, the skater can Revert directly to a second aerial maneuver if on a narrow halfpipe. This is especially true when on a mini-halfpipe, such as the one in Kona.

GRINDS

Grinds are a set of tricks that take place completely on objects or surfaces other than the street. In a grind, the skater slides the trucks or deck of the board along a rail, curb, ledge, or any other narrow object. Grinds not only make for a good source of points, but they enable the skater to cover distance during a trick. However, like the manual, a grind

requires a mastery of balance to pull off over significant distances. Pay attention to the Balance Meter and aim to keep the needle in the center!

The points earned for grind tricks are based on the distance the trick was held. Grinding a ledge from one side of a building to another earns more points than simply grinding the length of a park bench. Incorporate grinds into each scoring line, along with manuals and Reverts, to really build up the score.

A long, fast grind on a curving ledge can be difficult to ollie out of safely, especially if there's water nearby! Well, you're in luck. With a press of the Left or Right Revert Buttons, the skater can drop out of a grind on a moment's notice. Not only does the skater safely touch down and end the combo, but 100 points are awarded in the process!

Each of the grinds listed in the table can be performed either frontside (FS) or backside (BS). To know the difference, the skater should be in their favored stance and facing a ledge for FS grinds. Face away from a ledge while in the skater's favored stance to perform a BS grind.

The column "Point Incrementer" shows the amount of points by which the score for a trick increases over the time that trick is held.

TRICK	COMMAND	POINTS	POINT INCREMENTER
50-50	Grind	100	7
Boardslide	Press Grind while perpendicular to ledge	200	14
Lipslide	Press Grind while perpendicular to ledge	200	14
Tailslide	Left or Right + Grind	150	11
Noseslide	Left or Right + Grind	150	11
Nosegrind	Up + Grind	100	7
5-0	Down + Grind	100	7
Crooked	Up/Right or Up/Left + Grind	125	9
Overcrook	Up/Right or Up/Left + Grind	125	9
Smith	Down/Right or Down/Left + Grind	125	9
Feeble	Down/Right or Down/Left + Grind	125	9
Bluntslide	Down, Down + Grind	250	18
Nosebluntslide	Up, Up + Grind	250	18

A new feature to the *Tony Hawk's Pro Skater* series is the ability to seamlessly transfer from any grind or slide, whether it be FS or BS, to another with just two button presses. By linking multiple grind styles together during a single grind, it's possible to boost the multiplier significantly without having to ever ollie off the rail! Input the commands in the following table to transfer to the specified grind. Be warned, however, that it becomes harder to maintain balance with each successive grind combo.

TRICK	COMBO COMMAND
50-50	Grind, Grind
Noseslide	Grind, Flip
Nosegrind	Grind, Grab
Crooked	Grab, Grab
Bluntslide	Grab, Flip
Nosebluntslide	Grab, Grind
Smith	Flip, Flip
5-0	Flip, Grab
Tailslide	Flip, Grind

If the skater attempts to grind on an object that is too short, or if the grind is initiated too close to the end of the rail, the skater gets points awarded for having 'Kissed the Rail.' Kissing the rail awards 50 points while in the normal stance and 60 for a switch stance.

LIP TRICKS

Lip tricks are similar to grinds, except the skater pauses on the rail instead of sliding horizontally across it. Lip tricks not only require approaching the rail at a 90-degree angle (from below, typically), but they also demand incredible balance and strength on the part of the skater. Avoid trying to hold lip tricks for more than a second or so

until the skater significantly increases his or her Lip Balance rating. Finally, monitor the Balance Meter and tap Up or Down as necessary.

AIR TRICKS

FLIP TRICKS

Flip tricks are one of the most commonly used tricks in the game, as they can be used in combination with a simple ground level ollie or when skying eight feet out of a half pipe. Flip tricks take place when skaters use their hands or feet to flip the board while in the air. Some flip tricks, like the Kickflip and Heelflip, can be done so quickly that their use is pervasive throughout nearly every scoring line. Other, more intricate, tricks (such as the Sal Flip or Varial) require much greater height than a simple ollie affords.

Thanks to the relative simplicity of the Kickflip and Heelflip, there is seldom a reason for a plain ollie. And while the 'Variety Enforcing Points System' may reduce the Kickflip's value to nearly nothing over the course of a run, Kickflipping into a grind will boost the Multiplier, something an Ollie will never do. On big 7-figure scoring lines, each extra Kickflip or Shove-It could be worth over 50,000 points!

As was the case with the lip tricks, players are free to assign whatever flip tricks they desire to the 12 trick slots. Study the trick slot assignments and the tables to learn which tricks are the most valuable and what their combos are.

CUSTOMIZATION!

The commands for lip tricks, flips and grabs, and Special Tricks can all be customized to fit the player's preference. Because of this, there will be no command inputs listed for the individual tricks.

As was the case with grinds and flatland tricks, lip tricks can be seamlessly transferred into and out of, provided they are the same style. For example, all tricks that are performed on the lip of the ramp or on the rail with the board touching the surface can be linked together through the commands listed in the Lip Extras table. Similarly, all tricks that are performed upside-down can be linked together via the commands in the Invert Extras table. The one exception to this is the Andrecht Invert, which has its own special link to: The Switcheroo. Once the transfer is made to The Switcheroo, however, all of the available Invert Extras are open for comboing into and out of it.

TRICK	POINTS (NORMAL/SWITCH)	COMBOS TO	
Nose Stall (default)	300+/360+	Lip Extras	
Andrecht Invert	550+/660+	Andrecht Extra	
Axle Stall	400+/480+	Lip Extras	
Blunt to Fakie	500+/600+	Lip Extras	
BS Boneless	550+/660+	Lip Extras	
Disaster	600+/720+	Lip Extras	
Eggplant	550+/660+	Invert Extras	
Gymnast Plant	575+/690+	Invert Extras	
Varial Invert to Fakie	450+/540+	Invert Extras	
Invert	500+/600+	Invert Extras	
FS Noseblunt	550+/660+	Lip Extras	
FS Nosepick	550+/660+	Lip Extras	
One Foot Invert	500+/600+	Invert Extras	
Rock to Fakie	500+/600+	Lip Extras	
The Switcheroo	600+/720+	Invert Extras	

LIP EXTRAS			INVERT EXTRAS	
TRICK	**COMBO COMMAND**		**TRICK**	**COMBO COMMAND**
Axle Stall	Grab, Grab		Gymnast Plant	Grab, Grab
BS Boneless	Grab, Flip		Varial Invert to Fakie	Grab, Flip
Disaster	Flip, Flip		One Foot Invert	Flip, Flip
Rock to Fakie	Flip, Grab		Eggplant	Flip, Grab
FS Noseblunt	Grind, Grind		Invert	Grind, Grind
FS Nosepick	Grind, Flip		Andrecht Invert	Grind, Grab
Blunt to Fakie	Grind, Grab			

ANDRECHT EXTRA	
TRICK	**COMBO COMMAND**
The Switcheroo	Grind, Grind

GRAB TRICKS

Grab tricks represent the most difficult skateboard maneuvers, as the skater must be going big off a ramp or out of a bowl to even consider attempting one. As the name implies, grab tricks occur when the skater reaches down and grabs hold of a part of the skateboard. This concept has led to a lengthy list of highly stylized tricks, first created by many of the pros featured in this very game!

The great thing about grab tricks is that they can be held for additional points. The dangerous thing about grab tricks is that they can be held for additional points. Although it's definitely okay to hold on to the board to squeeze some extra points out of an Airwalk or Method, just make sure you let go before the skater begins to land. Holding on to the Grab Button for even a split-second too long can send the skater headfirst into the pavement!

WALLRIDE

Wallrides are similar to grinds in execution. When approaching a wall, ollie and hit the Grind Button to skate across the wall horizontally. Don't come in at a right (90 degree) angle or the skater becomes a pile of pain on the ground. Wallrides are worth 200 points (240 points in Switch stance).

FLIP TRICKS

TRICK	POINTS (NORMAL/SWITCH)	DOUBLE-TAP TRICK	POINTS	TRIPLE-TAP TRICK (NORMAL/SWITCH)	POINTS (NORMAL/SWITCH)
Kickflip	100/120	Double Kickflip	500/600	Triple Kickflip	1000/1200
Heelflip	100/120	Double Heelflip	500/600	Triple Heelflip	1000/1200
Impossible	100/120	Double Impossible	500/600	Triple Impossible	1000/1200
Pop Shove-It	100/120	360 Shove-It	500/600	540 Shove-It	1000/1200
FS Shove-It	100/120	360 FS Shove-It	500/600	540 FS Shove-It	1000/1200
Back Foot Kickflip	150/180	Double Back Foot Flip	500/600	NA	NA
Backfoot Heelflip	150/180	Double Back Foot Flip	500/600	NA	NA
Varial Kickflip	300/360	360 Flip	500/600	NA	NA
Varial Heelflip	300/360	360 Heelflip	500/600	NA	NA
Hardflip	300/360	360 Hardflip	500/600	NA	NA
Inward Heelflip	350/420	360 Inward Heelflip	500/600	NA	NA
Front Foot Impossible	400/480	Double Front Foot Impossible	800/960	NA	NA
Ollie Airwalk	500/600	Ollie Airwalk Late Shove-It	1000/1200	NA	NA
Ollie North	500/600	Ollie North Back Foot Flip	1000/1200	NA	NA
Fingerflip	700/840	Double Fingerflip	1000/1200	NA	NA
180 Varial	700/840	360 Varial	900/1080	NA	NA
Heelflip Varial Lien	800/960	NA	NA	NA	NA
Sal Flip	900/1080	360 Sal Flip	1000/1200	NA	NA

GRAB TRICKS

TRICK	POINTS (NORMAL/SWITCH)	POINT INCREMENTER	DOUBLE-TAP TRICK	POINTS (NORMAL/SWITCH)	POINT INCREMENTER
Japan	350/420	NA	One Foot Japan	800/960	25
Crail Grab	350/420	NA	Tuck Knee	400/480	NA
Wrap Around	450/540	25	Body Wrap	600/720	25
Cannonball	250/420	15	Fingerflip Cannonball	500/600	15
Stalefish	350/420	NA	Stalefish Tweak	400/480	NA
Benihana	300/420	NA	Sacktap	1500/1800	NA
Crossbone	350/420	NA	CrookedCop	400/480	NA
Airwalk	400/480	NA	Christ Air	500/600	NA
Indy Nosebone	350/420	NA	Del Mar Indy	400/480	NA
Tailgrab	300/360	NA	One Foot Tailgrab	500/600	NA
Madonna	600/720	40	Judo	800/960	NA
FS Shifty	500/600	NA	BS Shifty	500/600	NA
Melon	300/360	NA	Method	400/480	NA
Nosegrab	300/360	NA	Rocket Air	400/480	NA
Mute	350/420	NA	Seatbelt Air	500/600	NA
Indy	300/360	NA	Stiffy	500/600	NA

TRIPLE-TAP?

While the Flip Tricks screen in the game shows the Double Tap tricks (tap the Flip Button 2x to perform these extra tricks), the screen doesn't show the available triple tap tricks. Each of the five basic flip tricks (Kickflip, Heelflip, Impossible, Pop Shove-It, and Shove-It) can each be performed three times in one leap by tapping the Flip Button 3x after the initial directional press.

INDEPENDENT

No, not the brand of trucks—the scoring! When it comes to 'Variety Enforcing Point System' each of these tricks are tracked separately. This means that even once a Double Kickflip is only netting 25% its original value, a Triple Kickflip performed for the first time will earn the full 1000 points!

SPINE TRANSFER

Making its debut in *Tony Hawk's Pro Skater 4* is the Spine Transfer. This simple but powerful move makes it possible for the skater to extend a scoring line over a spine. By tapping the Revert Button while lifting off the top of a spine or vert ramp, the skater automatically transfers to the other side of the ramp or to a ledge or rail beyond the lip of the ramp.

The Spine Transfer can be used to transfer up and down ramps that aren't even adjacent, as long as they're lined up with one another. Ultimately, when combined with the manual and the Revert, the Spine Transfer makes it possible to extend a scoring string through most any situation.

SPECIAL TRICKS

When it comes to scoring big points with a single trick, look no further than the collection of Special Tricks available to your skater. The player can assign and use any of these multiple-command tricks–provided the Special Meter glows a bright red. It's possible to earn additional Special Trick slots throughout Career Mode, bringing the total for the game to 11! Use the additional slots to assign any of these technical tricks to use at a later time.

FAST TRICKS

Although all of the Special Tricks are elaborate and make a good addition to any scoring line, some Air Tricks are performed at a faster speed than the rest. These high-speed tricks colored red can be used more often during lengthy scoring lines without the larger risk of bailing. Read 'Special Trick Management' for additional tips on making the most out of the Special Tricks.

SPECIAL AIR TRICKS

TRICK	POINTS (NORMAL/SWITCH)
1-2-3-4	1400/1680
360 Varial McTwist	5000/6000
540 Flip	1450/1740
540 Tailwhip	2000/2400
Barrel Roll	5000/6000
Slamma Jamma	1750/2100
Bodywrap 540	4500/5400
Double Kickflip Varial Indy	1100/1320
Fingerflip Airwalk	1500/1800
FS 540	4500/5400
FS 540 Heelflip	4500/5400
Gazelle Underflip	3500/4200
360 Ghetto Bird	3500/4200
Hardflip Late Flip	1500/1800
Heelflip Handflip	1200/1440
Indy 900	11000/13200
The Jackass	1500/1800
Kickflip Backflip	3000/3600
Kickflip Underflip	1000/1200
McTwist	5000/6000
Misty Flip	5000/6000
Nollie Flip Underflip	1050/1260
Quad Heelflip	1200/1440
Semi Flip	1450/1740
Stalefish Backflip	4500/5400
Stalefish Frontflip	4500/5400
The 900	9000/10800

SPECIAL GRAB TRICKS

TRICK	POINTS (NORMAL/SWITCH)	POINT INCREMENTER
Double Kickflip Madonna	1750/2100	30
Casper Flip 360 Flip	2500/3000	30
Assume the Position II	1000/1200	30
Backfoot Nosegrab	1200/1440	30
BigSpin Shifty	1500/1800	30
Chomp On This	1000/1200	30
Judo Madonna	1600/1920	30
Kickflip Superman	1500/1800	30
Kickflip One Foot Tail	1100/1320	30
Might as Well Jump	1750/2100	30
Samba Flip	1400/1680	30
Sit Down Air	1200/1440	30

SPECIAL LIP TRICKS

TRICK	POINTS (NORMAL/SWITCH)
Bigspin Flip to Tail	3500+/4200+
BS Nose Comply	3000+/3600+
Burntwist	3000+/3600+
Dark Disaster	3000+/3600+
Heelflip FS Invert	3200+/3840+
Ho Ho Sad Plant	3500+/4200+
One Foot Blunt	3000+/3600+
Russian Boneless	3000+/3600+

SPECIAL GRIND TRICKS

TRICK	POINTS
5-0 Fingerflip Nosegrind	500+
American Tribute	500+
B-Ballin Slide	500+
Big Hitter II	500+
Ghetto Blastin	500+
Cartwheel 50-50	500+
Coffin	500+
Crail Slide	500+
Crook BigSpinFlip Crook	500+
Daffy Grind	500+
Darkslide	400+
Double Blunt Slide	500+
Falcon Slide	500+
Fandangle	500+
Layback Sparks	500+
Ferret Fight	500+
Flip Kick Dad	500+
Froggy Grind	500+
5-0 Overturn	500+
Faction Guitar Slide	500+
Handstand 50-50	500+
Hang Ten Nosegrind	500+
Human Dart	500+
Hurricane	400+
Muska Beatz	500+
Nosegrind to Pivot	500+
Noseslide Lipslide	500+
One Foot Smith	500+
Rocket Tailslide	500+
Rowley Darkslide	500+
Salad Grind	500+
Ghetto Tag Grind	500+
Tailblock Slide	500+

SPECIAL MANUAL TRICKS

TRICK	POINTS
One Wheel Fireworks Show	1500+
Ahhh Yeeah!	1400+
Handstand 360 Hand Flip	1400+
Handstand Double Flip	1400+
Lazy Ass Manual	1500+
No Comply 360 Shove-It	1500+
One Wheel Nose Manual	1400+
Primo	1200+
Reemo Slide	1300+
Rusty Slide Manual	1400+
Sproing	1500+

Scoring

The ability to score lots of points is an integral part in succeeding at *Tony Hawk's Pro Skater 4*. However, completing those Sick Score goals requires more than simply repeating the Sal Flip over and over. Not only are tricks worth progressively less each time they are performed, but many other factors such as riding "Switch," linking tricks for multipliers, spinning, etc. all affect the number of points earned. This section breaks down each of the different factors that control how many points are earned.

SICK SCORING SECRETS

Check out the 'Special Trick Management' portion of this chapter for tips on making the most out of the Special Tricks. With these tips, you'll be dropping 7-figure scoring lines like mad!

RIDING SWITCH

Unlike decks from the 1980's and earlier, today's skate decks are bi-directional. This means they can be ridden nose or tail first. Although riders are always stronger in their "Normal" stance, whether it be Regular-footed (left foot forward) or Goofy-footed (right foot forward), expert riders can perform nearly all of the tricks in their repertoire in what's called a "Switch" stance. A rider is said to be riding Switch when he or she has the tail end of the board pointed in the direction in which he or she is traveling. The word "Switch" appears in the upper left-hand corner of the screen whenever the skater is in the Switch stance. Since this is more difficult, performing tricks while in the Switch stance is worth an additional 20% in terms of points.

MULTIPLIERS

No matter how many times the skater lands a 900, the Sick Score objectives will forever remain out of reach without the ability to link tricks and gaps together for multipliers. Simply put, for every trick that is done without the board touching down, an additional multiplier is added. Every time another trick is done or another gap is hit, the multiplier grows by one. Should the skater eventually touch down without bailing, the total points (base score) for the string of tricks are multiplied by the number of tricks and gaps completed.

The ability to link tricks with manuals, Reverts, and grinds is of extreme importance in building up a huge multiplier. Practice incorporating a couple of gaps into each combination and scoring hundreds of thousands, if not millions, of points per chain will be a common occurrence.

SPINNING

One of the easiest ways to ramp up the points is to add rotation. Granted, a 720 Rocket Air is significantly more difficult to land than a straight Rocket Air, but the opportunity to increase the points earned by a factor of four is hard to ignore. Although the bonus increases for every 180 degrees of rotation, make sure you come out of the spin before striking the ground.

Adding rotation to a trick isn't the only way to milk some extra points out of an aerial. If after performing at least 180 degrees of rotation the skater lands on the ramp at a perfect right angle, a 1,000-point "Perfect Landing" bonus will be awarded. On the other hand, a really ugly landing will be deemed "Sloppy" and 500 points is deducted from the base score.

SPINNING MULTIPLIERS	
180	1.5x Trick Score
360	2x Trick Score
540	3x Trick Score
720	4x Trick Score
900	6x Trick Score

SPINNING IN CIRCLES

There are two ways to rotate while in the air. Spin to the left or right by pressing in the chosen direction on the controller. Another option is to use the Rotate Right and Rotate Left Buttons. Using the specified Rotate Buttons is the preferred method, as there is less chance of the spin interfering with the trick inputs.

GAPS

Each course in *Tony Hawk's Pro Skater 4* has roughly 40 gaps to find and check off the in-game checklist. Gaps are bonuses that are awarded for completing a specific type of trick involving a piece of the environment. Many gaps require the skater to transfer between two ramps, grind a particular series of rails, or manual along a set ledge. Gaps not only add points to the score, but can be used to build the multiplier as well. Complete each course's gaps checklist to unlock a special prize!

VARIETY-ENFORCING POINTS SYSTEM

The percentages in the following table are based on the original point value for the trick. All tricks performed more than five times are worth 10% of the original score. The points for tricks decline independently between those performed in a Normal stance versus thus done while riding Switch.

First time landing a trick	100%
Second time	75%
Third time	50%
Fourth time	25%
Fifth time	10%

SPECIAL TRICK MANAGEMENT

Newcomers to the series may feel overwhelmed when trying to select a small handful of tricks from the list of more than 100 Special Tricks available. Furthermore, the whole issue of remembering the commands for each of them can be somewhat difficult as well. If you fall into this category, or just want some extra pointers, continue reading. This section is going to break down the ins and outs of choosing Special Tricks that make million-point scoring lines as common as a Rail-2-Rail gap.

Each player will develop his or her own style of gameplay, but for those still seeking a style, it is recommended to always have at least two Special Grinds and a Special Manual assigned to the Special Trick slots. Once more spots become available, work on giving each type of trick equal representation, as this allows for a much greater balance. Consider mimicking the following setup once all 11 Special Trick slots have been made available(three Special Grinds, two Special Manuals, two Special Lip Tricks, 2 slow Special Airs, and two fast Special Airs).

What to consider when selecting these tricks is discussed shortly. First, the issue of remembering all of the various commands needs to be addressed. A very user-friendly method of keeping 11 Special Tricks straight is to use the Up, Down and Down, Up directional commands for 10 of the 11 tricks. Assign the Special Manuals, Special Lip Tricks and two of the Special Grinds to the Up, Down + Grind Button and Down, Up + Grind Button commands. Assign the two fast Special Airs the Up, Down + Flip Button and Down, Up + Flip Button commands and do the same for the slower Special Airs, but with the Grab Button. Organizing the Special Tricks in this manner makes it harder to forget a command, and also makes remembering to alternate between tricks somewhat easier.

Now that you know what commands to use and how many tricks of what type to select, the time has come to pick them. Although this decision should be based largely on personal taste, it's a decision that can be changed at any time by entering the Edit Tricks menu. There are essentially three things to consider when selecting Special Tricks: 1) the point value; 2) whether or not the trick is easy to land; and 3) whether or not you think it's cool.

Judging by point values is an excellent way to decide which Special Manuals, Grinds, and Lip Tricks to select, but it becomes a bit less reliable with Special Air Tricks. The reason for that is because some of the higher scoring tricks are just too hard to land consistently. For example, the Indy 900 is a very valuable trick, but it's very difficult to land without maximum speed and even then it's still hard to land while performing any sort of ramp-to-ramp transfer or gap. On the other hand, tricks such as the Kickflip Underflip don't offer nearly as many points but can be incorporated into a lengthy scoring line much easier. Take note of the tricks marked in red in the Special Air Tricks table, as those are ones that are performed at a faster rate and can be worked into scoring lines more readily.

The last point to address with regards to selecting Special Tricks is "style". While it may not matter during Career Mode, having a fresh looking skater who can perform all the coolest moves is part of the fun of playing online. Select tricks that ultimately make you smile or say "Wow!" After all, this is all for fun, enjoy yourself!

Tony Hawk

Age
33
Hometown
Carlsbad, CA
Stance
Goofy
Push Style
Never Mongo
Trick Style
Vert

STARTING STATS

Air	7	Switch	4
Hangtime	5	Flip Speed	4
Ollie	3	Rail Balance	5
Speed	5	Lip Balance	6
Spin	8	Manual Balance	3

SIGNATURE TRICKS

360 Varial McTwist
Froggy Grind
Indy 900
Barrel Roll

1. Falcon Egg
2. Hawk Emblem
3. Tony Ape
4. Pterodactyl – Black
5. Skele-Hawk
6. Tony Photo
7. Birdman Crest
8. Water Photo
9. Birdhouse Logo
10. Pterodactyl - White

THE PRO SKATERS

HAWK / Burnquist / Caballero / Campbell / Glifberg / Koston / Lasek /
Margera / Mullen / Muska / Reynolds / Rowley / Steamer / Thomas

PRO-SPECIFIC CHALLENGE

Sky High Transfer

Time	4:00
Awards	$1250 and Tony's Movie

Tony's Pro Challenge takes place at the College.

REQUIRED SPECIAL TRICKS

Barrel Roll   360 Varial McTwist
Indy 900

Atiba Jefferson

"Man, that ramp is huge! Are they really going to move that scaffolding further out as you go? I'll get the photos, while you concentrate on nailing the tricks across the gap. Good luck man, and don't look down!"

Tony's Pro-Specific challenge takes place on the roof of the Fine Arts building. A large halfpipe has been constructed atop the undulating roof. Tony is going to have to transfer from this pipe to an identical one resting on top of a mountain of scaffolding nearby. Although he will get to warm up with some easy grab tricks across a narrow channel, it won't be long before he's letting loose with a handful of Special Tricks across a 24ft gap—three stories up!

There are three distances that will need to be tricked across. The first gap is very short and the three tricks that need to be performed are the most basic of grab tricks (provided you didn't alter the button assignments). In fact, although they can be each done individually, the Tailgrab, Nosegrab, and Indy can all be performed in one monstrous leap across the gap. Each successful transfer will score the **Tony's Pro Challenge** gap. Also, look for each of the **Tony's Pro Challenge Trick** bonuses to appear. Not only do these boost the score for the leap, but they serve as confirmation that credit was given for the trick and transfer

SPLAT!

Nobody wants to see Tony's carcass lying in a heap on the ground below, not even in a videogame. Fortunately, you don't have to. Although missing the ramps on occasion is all but guaranteed, Tony will be resurrected atop the roof right before impact. This saves you from having to waste time riding the elevator back to the roof.

Things start heating up a bit after the first three tricks are performed across the gap. The scaffolding slides further away from the rooftop halfpipe and the tricks get slightly harder to pull off. The second batch of tricks is all grab tricks again, but each requires a diagonal press to perform. Get the feel for the

distance by gapping back and forth while performing just one of the tricks at a time. To help prepare for the final batch of tricks, try holding the grab as long as possible, or even rotating while gapping across the channel. These skills will come in handy momentarily. The default tricks needing to be performed at this distance include the Benihana, Japan, and Madonna.

Once the first two trick groups have been completed, the ramps slide apart once again—this time to a jaw-dropping 24 ft! Now comes the hard part. Tony has to gap across this amazing distance three times while performing a different Special Trick with each jump. And these aren't simple tricks like the Semi-Flip; Tony must do a Barrel Roll, Indy 900, and a 360 Varial McTwist.

The key to completing this incredible challenge is to work the halfpipe to keep the Special Meter lit. Be sure to stay in a straight line when tricking out the Special Meter, as it's quite easy to drift off the roof! Also, take some trial jumps across the gap before trying to perform the Special Tricks. Approach the ramp on a hard

angle towards the gap, but not too close to the edge, else the skater may not get enough height.

The hardest part about completing this challenge is landing the tricks cleanly. Although there is enough time after the Barrel Roll and 360 Varial McTwist to straighten the skater out for landing, this is not the case for the Indy 900. In order to have the best chance of landing this trick, it's important to not take off from the ramp on too much of an angle—this trick requires plenty of height! Be sure to input the commands for the Special Trick as soon as Tony lifts off the ramp.

Bob Burnquist

Age
36
Hometown
Sao Paulo, Brazil
Stance
Regular
Push Style
Never Mongo
Trick Style
Vert

STARTING STATS

Air			
Hangtime	4	Switch	8
Ollie	5	Flip Speed	4
Speed	4	Rail Balance	5
Spin	4	Lip Balance	5
	6	Manual Balance	5

SIGNATURE TRICKS

Burntwist
Sit Down Air
One Foot Smith
Samba Flip

1. Burnquist – BB Black
2. Burnquist – BB Green
3. Liquid Helium
4. Hands
5. Puppet Icon
6. Ace
7. Burnquist Space Ace
8. Rocket Man
9. Air Mocca
10. Roulette

THE PRO SKATERS

Hawk / *BURNQUIST* / Caballero / Campbell / Gllfberg / Koston / Lasek /
Margera / Mullen / Muska / Reynolds / Rowley / Steamer / Thomas

PRO-SPECIFIC CHALLENGE

Broken Loop Gap

Bob's Pro Challenge takes place at the Zoo.

REQUIRED SPECIAL TRICKS

Samba Flip
Sit Down Air

Time	4:00
Awards	$1250 and Bob's Movie

Atiba Jefferson
"Yo Bobby, wasn't that loop at your house big enough? See this time, they're making the gap bigger and bigger as you go. Oh, oh, yo, I'm on it, but try not to land on your freakin' head."

Just when you think you've seen everything, along comes Bob Burnquist and his roof-less loop. Bob's Pro-Specific challenge is very similar to Tony Hawk's but instead of gapping between elevated halfpipes, Bob must trick across an enormous gap at the top of a loop! This challenge takes place in three different stages. Each successive stage requires the skater to perform more complex tricks across an even bigger gap than before.

Bob's broken loop isn't the only ramp that's been constructed for this challenge. Large vert ramps have been set up on both ends of the loop to give the skater a way to max out the Special Meter and to gain the speed needed to clean the gap. The ramps are aligned with the lead-in parts of the loop. Stick to the center of the vert ramps and land the tricks cleanly to be in a good position for attacking the loop. There is no substitution for a perfect approach when the third stage of this challenge rolls around, so practice getting it right early.

During the first stage of the challenge, the loop is simply missing its top and the skater only needs to follow the white x's on the ramp to be properly lined up. Trick off the vert ramp to gain some speed and then charge the center of the loop. Follow the x's and ride straight off the edge of the ramp while upside-down. Quickly perform one of the flip or grab tricks specified in the top right corner of the screen, and ride out the landing on the other side of the loop. Each successful trip through the loop scores the **Loop Hole** gap. Also, look for each of the **Bob's Pro Challenge Trick** bonuses to appear. These not only boost the score for the leap, but they serve as confirmation that credit was given for the trick and transfer. Continue going back and forth through the loop until all three of the tricks have been landed. Consider selecting the 'Retry Last Goal' option from the Pause Menu if this first stage takes much longer than 50 seconds.

The second stage of the challenge features tricks that require diagonal presses of the controls. As if that wasn't bad enough, the two halves of the loop have been moved further apart from one other. Although it's even more important to build speed on the vert ramps than before, a small adjustment to the angle

of approach must be made as well. Be sure to angle the skater slightly to the right before hitting the gap. Continue to follow the x's on the ramp to make sure the skater is in good position, but bear to the right when leaving the first ramp.

The third and final stage of the challenge maxes out the difficulty by expanding the loop gap to an incredible distance and by forcing Bob to perform Special Tricks across the gap. Trick off the vert ramp to gain some speed and push towards the ramp. Take off from the ramp to the right of the white x's and input the double-tap trick command immediately. Allow Bob to drift to the right while upside-down and release the grab just as soon as it begins—this is no time for squeaking out extra points!

Now that the Special Meter is fully lit, it's time to attempt some Special Tricks. Start with the Samba Flip, as it is the more difficult to land of the two. Attack the loop just as before, but now it's even more important to input the trick command as fast as possible. The Samba Flip requires considerable hangtime to pull off and that other ramp is closing in fast! Once the Samba Flip has been landed, go about doing the Sit Down Air in the same manner. Fortunately, the Sit Down Air can be landed cleanly while the skater is in the process of getting back to his feet. In other words, if you can land the Samba Flip, you should have no problem with the Sit Down Air.

FINGER TAPPING GOODNESS

It may not be necessary, but if you're having trouble getting the Samba Flip off fast enough, try rehearsing those Special Trick button presses on the vert ramps. Don't mess around with rotation, just ride up the ramp and practice inputting the button presses as fast as possible.

Steve Caballero

Age
36
Hometown
Campbell, CA
Stance
Goofy
Push Style
Never Mongo
Trick Style
Street

STARTING STATS

Air		Switch	4
Hangtime	5	Flip Speed	5
Ollie	6	Rail Balance	6
Speed	5	Lip Balance	5
Spin	4	Manual Balance	5
	5		

SIGNATURE TRICKS

Kickflip Superman
FS 540
Faction Guitar Slide
Daffy Grind

1 Chinese Dragon
2 Face Series – 2000
3 Shoe Dragon
4 Ape
5 Cab Guitar
6 Dragon 2000
7 Classic Dragon – 1999
8 Cab Skull – Orange
9 Cab Inkblot
10 Ban This

THE PRO SKATERS

Hawk / Burnquist / *CABALLERO* / Campbell / Gllfberg / Koston / Lasek /
Margera / Mullen / Muska / Reynolds / Rowley / Steamer / Thomas

PRO-SPECIFIC CHALLENGE

BMX Doubles

Steve's Pro Challenge takes place at Kona.

REQUIRED SPECIAL TRICKS

None

Time	2:00
Awards	$1250 and Steve's Movie

Rick Thorne

"Ah, that's my dog! What's up Cab? You ready to bust these doubles? The kids are gonna be stoked. We're gonna go over and under each other. I'm gonna start off with a flip, you're gonna go over me, and then I'm gonna signal you, you so some lip tricks, then I'm gonna go over you."

When it comes to riding the halfpipe, things can get pretty hairy with two people in the pipe at the same time—and if one of them is riding a bike, it can get downright ugly. Well, Steve and Rick have mastered this dangerous form of doubles riding and they're ready to give the crowd what they came to see. The only way to pull off a stunt like this is with great communication. Look for Rick's signals and follow his lead. The run is going to have a total of 12 over-and-under tricks and the trick will only count if it's done while Rick and Steve are transferring over one another.

The remaining six tricks come as three more "overs" followed by three "unders". Although the tricks are slightly more complex in that they require diagonal button presses, the second half of the challenge is otherwise just like the first. Air over Rick while performing the specified air tricks and then take up residence on the coping in each of the required lip tricks to complete the challenge.

The first three tricks are going to be done up high while transferring over Rick. Watch for the trick signal in the upper right corner and perform the trick while leaping off the wall over Rick. Time the jump well to score the **Air Over** bonus and to get credit for the transfer.

Rick is sick of going low and wants to start busting some airs over his skating compadre; Steve has to go low for the next 3 tricks. Perform each of the lip tricks that appear in the corner of the screen and balance it long enough for Rick to transfer overhead. Look for the **Lip Under** bonus to signal a successful pass and drop back down the wall. Make certain to perform the lip tricks on the coping of the halfpipe near the orange arrows and not on the overhead cable—Rick's got some ups, but he doesn't get *that* high.

Kareem Campbell

Age

30

Hometown

N.Y/L.A

Stance

Regular

Push Style

Never Mongo

Trick Style

Street

STARTING STATS

Air		Switch	5
Hangtime	6	Flip Speed	5
Ollie	3	Rail Balance	7
Speed	6	Lip Balance	2
Spin	5	Manual Balance	4
	7		

SIGNATURE TRICKS

30 Ghetto Bird
Kickflip Backflip
B-Ballin Slide
Double Blunt Slide

1. City Stars 1
2. City Stars 2
3. Campbell 1
4. Campbell 2
5. B-Ball
6. Database Overload
7. Beat Box
8. Campbell 3
9. Chicken Heads
10. City Stars DJ

THE PRO SKATERS

Hawk / Burnquist / Caballero / **CAMPBELL** / Glifberg / Koston / Lasek /
Margera / Mullen / Muska / Reynolds / Rowley / Steamer / Thomas

PRO-SPECIFIC CHALLENGE

Roof Gap Challenge

Kareem's Pro Challenge takes place at San Francisco.

REQUIRED SPECIAL TRICKS

None

Time	2:30
Awards	$1250 and Kareem's Movie

Atiba Jefferson

"Yo Yo Reemo baby, it is time to take it to the rooftops. Use your entire bag of flip tricks – bust the tricks across the roof gaps or they won't count. Survive long enough and we'll want to see you do some combos."

Meet up with Atiba on the roof of the Slam Brothers warehouse at Pier 18 for the ultimate falling tricks challenge. Here Kareem must perform a bevy of flip tricks while gapping across the rooftops of the warehouses on the waterfront. Although the entire challenge consists of performing the specified tricks while gapping between the three nearby rooftops, it is actually broken into three stages. During the first 1:00, the tricks are listed individually. Survive the first minute to reach the second stage—combos! The following 1:00 consists of pairs of tricks that must be performed over the roof gaps in a combo. Finally, those who make it to the final 0:30 have that much time to perform a 5-trick mega combo!

The first stage of this challenge requires the skater to stay on top of the ever-growing list of individual flip tricks by performing them between the rooftops. Tricks can be cleared off the list only by being performed while gapping between either of the two rooftop gaps near Atiba—it doesn't have to be over the **TC's Roof Gap Too** gap. Trick onto the white building and turn around. From here, go back and forth to the third building, getting in two rooftop gaps, and tricks, before having to turn around again. Concentrate on clearing off the tricks that are listed multiple times to keep the list short and continue going back and forth across the two gaps until this stage of the challenge is finished.

After the first minute is over, the challenge becomes literally twice as hard. The second minute of the challenge features two tricks that must be performed in a single combination. Since it's virtually impossible to land an Inward Heelflip to Pop Shove-It from a simple ollie, Kareem must rely on the pipes sticking out of the roofs to aid in linking two separate rooftop gaps together. As the timer begins nearing the 1:30 mark, dash over to either end building and turn and face the gaps. As soon as the first combo appears, perform the easier of the tricks in the combo while gapping into a grind on the pipe. Balance across the

middle building while in the grind and tack on the other flip trick while gapping onto the other building. Continue going back and forth from building to building while using the pipe on the center building to link up the two rooftop gaps.

STAYIN' ALIVE

It's important to remember that the goal of this challenge isn't to complete *every* trick that gets listed, but just to make it to the end. Along those lines, seek out tricks that are duplicated or have the easiest combos. Often a combo itself will be duplicated further down in the list. Seek those duplicates out and nail two combos with one pass. This entire goal comes down to how you do in the final thirty seconds, everything up to then is just a warm-up.

One last 5-trick combo is listed once thirty seconds are left on the clock. Quickly head to the roof of the white building and begin the combo towards Slam Brothers warehouses. Perform the first two tricks while gapping across the roofs and land in a manual on the building at the far end. Hit the quarter pipe, Revert the landing, and manual back towards the roof gap. Trick back onto the pipe and then across the final gap on the other side if necessary.

It is very rare for this mega-combo to not feature at least one duplicate trick, but if it should happen, Kareem is forced to travel back across the gap between the white building and the warehouse where Atiba is. To do so, land in a manual on the white building and quickly turn and slide into a grind on the pipe back towards the warehouse. Drop the final trick into the trick string while gapping back onto the center rooftop.

Rune Glifberg

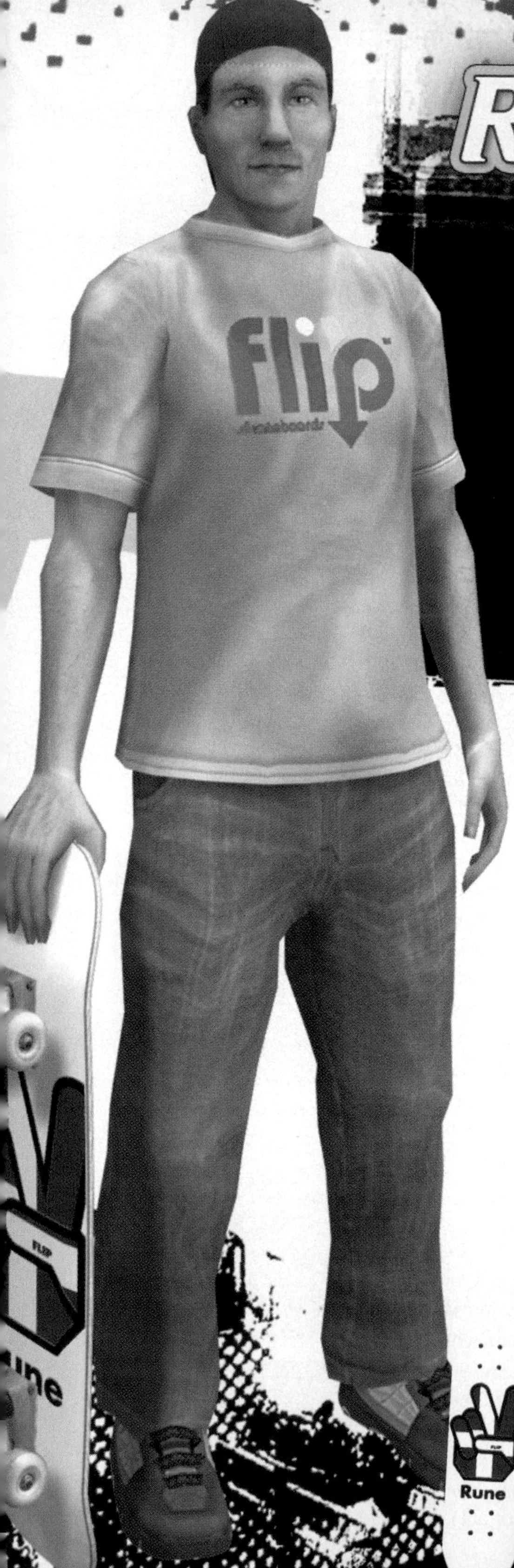

Age
27
Hometown
Copenhagen, Denmark
Stance
Regular
Push Style
Never Mongo
Trick Style
Vert

STARTING STATS

Air	7	Switch	6
Hangtime	7	Flip Speed	5
Ollie	5	Rail Balance	4
Speed	4	Lip Balance	5
Spin	5	Manual Balance	2

SIGNATURE TRICKS

Backfoot Flip Nosegrab
Heelflip Handflip
Crail Slide
One Foot Blunt

1. Victory – Denmark
2. TV Logo 1
3. Buzz Bomb
4. Sorry Logo – Red
5. Pixelated
6. HKD
7. Mask
8. Sorry Logo – Blue
9. TV Logo 2
10. Sprite Bomb

THE PRO SKATERS

Hawk / Burnquist / Caballero / Campbell / **GLIFBERG** / Koston / Lasek /
Margera / Mullen / Muska / Reynolds / Rowley / Steamer / Thomas

PRO-SPECIFIC CHALLENGE

Rune's Pool Party

Rune's Pro Challenge takes place at Alcatraz.

REQUIRED SPECIAL TRICKS

Heelflip Handflip   One Foot Blunt
Backfoot Flip Nosegrab

Time	5:00
Awards	$1250 and Rune's Movie

Atiba Jefferson
"Pool Party! Session these pools and do the tricks that the kids call out!"

Atiba might be calling for a pool party, but Rune's Pro Challenge is anything *but* relaxing: welcome to the most difficult Pro-Specific Challenge in the game! The group of kids hanging around Alcatraz sure know how to be demanding—they've assembled a laundry list of 8 super-tough stunts that challenge Rune to do everything from bust a potent combo to lip tricking on the roof of the cell block.

The first stunt is to perform a Heelflip Handflip while spine transferring between the pools for the **Pool Change** gap. Drop into the pool and go big into the air with several tricks and rotation to max out the Special Meter in one leap. Spine Transfer into the other pool and quickly input the command for the Heelflip Handflip while airborne.

The second stunt requires a lip trick (Down/Left + Grind Button) to be performed on the railing of the watertower. Leap up from the center of the pool and stall on the rail long enough to get the **Watertower Lip** gap.

Drop down from the rail and Spine Transfer back to the other pool. The kids have pushed a plank out over the pool and want to see you transfer over it  while doing a grab trick (Left + Grab Button). Gather up some speed and air up and out of the pool on an angle to clear their plank safely. Landing this trick cleanly earns the **Rune's Plank Gap** bonus.

Stick to the pool under the plank, as now the kids want to see a lip trick (Up + Grind Button) on top of the cellblock. Line Rune up to the left side of the pool to avoid the plank and work the pool back and forth in a straight line to gain speed. Boneless out of the pool straight into the air and input the trick command on the way up to have Rune lock in on the rooftop. Hold the lip trick until the **How'd you get up THERE?** gap triggers.

Hope you're not afraid of heights! Now that the kids know you have some ups, they want to see a Spine Transfer out of the pool and through the roof of the watertower to the bowl inside. Build up a ton of speed and Boneless out of the pool below the watertower and initiate the Spine Transfer while soaring into the air past the railing. Transfer over the uppermost ledge and into the bowl for the **Super-high Watertower Spine** gap.

Get used to that watertower, all of the remaining stunts are either performed in it or over it! The kids' sixth request is to see a 50,000-point combo inside the bowl. Start the string by linking together a couple of quick grabs and flips to get the multiplier started. Revert the landing, leap into the air across the bowl and perform an aerial Special Trick. Follow this up by reverting into another Special Trick. Keep the chain alive with another Revert and put whatever momentum Rune has left to use with a couple of extra flip tricks to guarantee the 50k.

The Special Meter is no doubt completely lit after that combo, and the kids know it. Give them they want to see—Spine Transfer back out of the watertower to the pool below while performing a Backfoot Flip Nosegrab during the fall.

The final, and most challenging, stunt is to sky up out of the pool and do a One Foot Blunt Special Lip Trick on top of the skater standing on the roof of the watertower—what's left of it, anyway. Well, actually, the skater is holding his board above his head and that's where the lip trick must be done. Enter the pool nearest the watertower and line up just to the left of the slimy stain on the side of the pool below the tower. Work the pool to max out the Special Meter and Boneless out of the pool and into a lip trick on the watertower's roof, right at the feet of the skater for the **Watertower Roof Lip** gap. From there, ollie up and rapidly tap the commands for the One Foot Blunt to lip trick on the grommet's raised skateboard. Hold the stall long enough for the **Rune's Grommet Gap** to trigger and jump down to safety!

TIMING IS CRITICAL

In order to ollie off the watertower lip into a stall on the grom's skateboard, the Grind Button must be pressed at the highest point in the ollie. If the second lip trick is right back on the watertower, it's because you're either pressing the Grind Button too early or too fast. Adjust accordingly.

Eric Koston

Age
: 25

Hometown
: San Bernardino, CA

Stance
: Goofy

Push Style
: Mongo When Switch

Trick Style
: Street

STARTING STATS

Air		Switch	7
Hangtime	4	Flip Speed	6
Ollie	3	Rail Balance	6
Speed	7	Lip Balance	3
Spin	4	Manual Balance	6

SIGNATURE TRICKS

Fandangle
Slamma Jamma
Falcon Slide
Chomp On This

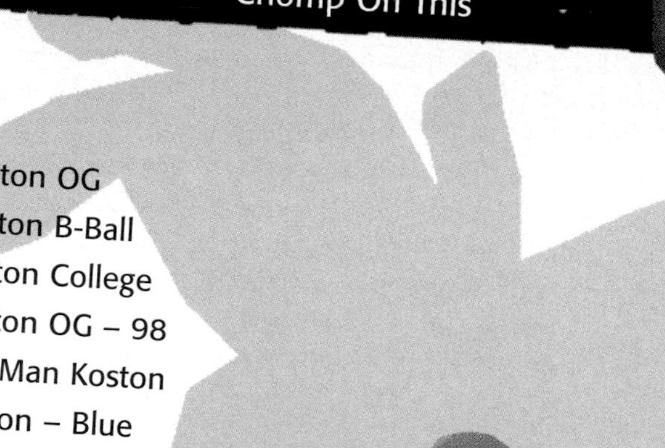

1. Koston OG
2. Koston B-Ball
3. Koston College
4. Koston OG – 98
5. Old Man Koston
6. Koston – Blue
7. Dog
8. Super Cock
9. Flag Deck
10. Flow 2

THE PRO SKATERS

Hawk / Burnquist / Caballero / Campbell / Glifberg / **KOSTON** / Lasek /
Margera / Mullen / Muska / Reynolds / Rowley / Steamer / Thomas

PRO-SPECIFIC CHALLENGE

K-Grind Cables

Eric's Pro Challenge takes place at the Shipyard.

Time	6:00
Awards	$1250 and Eric's Movie

REQUIRED SPECIAL TRICKS

None

Atiba Jefferson

"Koston, are you sure you want to chomp on this? It can definitely make a sick photo, but you could get wrecked, man. All right, if you want to grind these cables, I'll get the photos."

Eric is known as one of the sickest long-distance grinders in skating—a reputation that's about to be put to the test. Atiba is ready to photograph the three gnarliest grinds ever dreamt up. Each grind takes place high above the oil-stained ground of the Shipyard on various cables stretched taught between the cranes and warehouses. Maximum Grind Balance is a must!

50-50

The grinds featured in this challenge are very long and should be first attempted with a basic 50-50 grind as it is the easiest to balance. Also, The record that gets recorded within the 'View Goals' listing is for the fastest completion time, not points—there is no benefit to grinding the cables with a more elaborate grind.

The first of the grinds begins atop a crane over the water near catwalk and extends out over the water near the three-sided bowl then turns to the left and circles all the way past the barges to the docks. The skater gains a lot of speed during this downhill grind and managing it through the turns is difficult. Although the skater's balance is still pretty stable for the first two 90-degree turns, the left-hand turn after the second barge can be tricky. Get the Balance Meter as centered as possible going into the turn and be ready to tap to the Left and Right to keep the skater upright till the docks. Make it off the cable to score the **Run 1!!!** gap.

The second cable grind only features one turn—an extremely tight U-turn! The skater must hop into a grind on the cable from atop the crane near the barges and grind across the yard to the main warehouse near the starting point. The cable then wraps tightly around the large smokestack and descends gradually to the awning of the warehouse below the crane. Tap opposite of the skater's lean while rounding the smokestack and continue to gingerly balance the skater all the way back across the yard towards the barges to earn the **Run 2!!!** bonus.

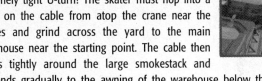

The third and final grind is not nearly as straightforward as the previous two. This grind is on a cable that is stretched between three different cranes and descends steeply towards the buoy. What makes this cable grind difficult isn't the turns or even the steep descent, it's the fact that the grind must travel uphill to get past the two other cranes. Trick into the initial grind with a 360 Shove-It to get the Special Meter maxed out quickly and 50-50 grind towards the crane near the barge. As soon as the skater starts slowing down due to the incline, ollie into another 50-50 grind to gain some speed. Repeat this as necessary to gain enough momentum to climb over the hill. It will likely take two of these "hop-n-grinds" to get past the first crane, and one more to summit the second crane. From there, it's just a matter of staying upright while making the lightning-quick descent to the rooftop near the buoy. Make it all the way to the end of the cable without bailing before time runs out to score the **Run 3!!!** gap.

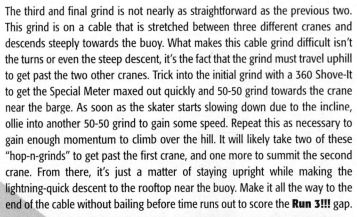

Bucky Lasek

Age
: 28

Hometown
: Baltimore, MD

Stance
: Regular

Push Style
: Never Mongo

Trick Style
: Vert

STARTING STATS

Air	7	Switch	5
Hangtime	7	Flip Speed	5
Ollie	3	Rail Balance	3
Speed	5	Lip Balance	6
Spin	7	Manual Balance	2

SIGNATURE TRICKS

Bodywrap 540
Heelflip FS Invert
Misty Flip
Big Hitter II

1. Gambler
2. Designer Lasek
3. Rooster
4. Bucky Photo
5. Birdhouse Logo
6. Race Car Logo
7. Bucky Sequence
8. Bucky Stripes
9. Birdhouse Toy Logo
10. Red Throttle

THE PRO SKATERS

Hawk / Burnquist / Caballero / Campbell / Glifberg / Koston / **LASEK** /
Margera / Mullen / Muska / Reynolds / Rowley / Steamer / Thomas

PRO-SPECIFIC CHALLENGE

Rusty Old Ramp

Bucky's Pro Challenge takes place at the Shipyard.

Time	4:00
Awards	$1250 and Bucky's Movie

Atiba Jefferson
"See if you can nail 5 big combos on this busted up old ramp.

REQUIRED SPECIAL TRICKS

None

Most skaters have ridden nasty old ramps at one time or another, but none have ever dropped in on a decrepit tanker ship that has been gutted and turned into a floating skatepark-of-death. Well, thanks to this Pro Challenge, Bucky Lasek is about to find out what's it like. This challenge tests the skater's ability to perform five separate combos (10,000, 20,000, 50,000 100,000, and 250,000 points) all in one 4:00 span. If only it was that easy. The ramps slowly begin breaking apart and huge holes in the bottom of the ship eventually open.

Since many of the ramps on the ship disappear as the combo requirements get larger, it's important to not grind the rails that run the perimeter of the ship until the last combo. Similarly, get through the first two or three combos without the use of aerial Special Tricks. Each trick is worth fewer points each time it is used and having the full value of the Special Tricks is key to laying down the final 250,000-point combo.

CONSERVATION EFFORTS

Not only is it wise to leave the Special Tricks and grinds until the last combo so as to get their full value, but it's also a good idea to land a combo as soon as the points meet the requirement. Avoid the impulse to add additional tricks to the combo if the score has already been met—doing so only makes it harder to complete the combos that follow.

Tackle the very first combo in just one leap off the spine in the center of the ship. Drop in off the balcony and let loose with a quick Ollie Airwalk to 720 Japan. Revert the landing for the extra multiplier and ride it out to move on to the next combo.

The moment the 10,000 point combo has been finished, the middle of the spine disappears, creating a large channel which can be gapped for the aptly named **Rusty Old Ramp Channel Gap**. Cruise through the center of the ship and go big off the vert ramp with another 720 flip and grab combo, preferably with one of the double-tap tricks. Revert the landing and launch immediately into another grab trick while transferring over the Spine. Roll out the landing to move on to the next combo.

The next combo requirement is 50,000 points and not only do more pieces of the spine break apart, forcing Spine Transfers, but sections of the vert ramps also disappear. Start the combo off by launching a rotation-heavy grab trick off the spine, reverting back towards the vert ramp for a multiplier-boosting series of flip tricks. Revert into a manual and head through the channel to the far side of the ship and ride up the wall and into a Special Lip Trick. Release the lip as soon as enough points have been scored.

The challenge starts getting much harder with the onset of the 100,000 point combo challenge. Not only are there only four staggered pieces of the spine left, but now there are four large panels missing from the vert ramps. Line the skater up between a solid piece of vert and one of the remaining scads of spine and treat the two ramps like your own private mini-pipe. Start the combo off with a big ol' air-based Special Trick to elevate the base score and Revert the landing. Perform multiple grabs on each successive leap. Add a 540 with each jump and continue going back and forth between the two ramps until a quick calculation shows the string to be worth over 100,000 points.

The final combo is worth 250,000 points and as if that wasn't bad enough, large pieces of the ship's floor have rusted completely through and are now open to the toxic soup below. There's no reason to hold back now—it's all or nothing from this point!

Come to a halt in the center of the ship (the only place it's safe) and face either of the directions that allow for a transfer off the white vert ramps, over the water, and directly at one of the remaining pieces of the spine. Charge the vert and trick across the hole in the floor for the **Big Hole Gap** bonus and immediately Revert towards the spine. Launch into an aerial Special Trick, Revert back towards the vert and go straight into the air with another Special Trick. Revert into a manual and head carefully towards the railing on the edge of the ship. Hop into a Special Grind on the handrail and go for a spin around the edge of the ship. Once on the long straightaway on the other side, ollie out of the grind and onto the floor to end the combo.

Bam Margera

Age
22

Hometown
Philadelphia, PA

Stance
Goofy

Push Style
Never Mongo

Trick Style
Street

STARTING STATS

Air	4	Switch	6
Hangtime	4	Flip Speed	5
Ollie	6	Rail Balance	7
Speed	6	Lip Balance	3
Spin	5	Manual Balance	4

SIGNATURE TRICKS

One Wheel Fireworks Show
The Jackass
Flip Kick Dad
Russian Boneless

1. Animalism
2. Heartogram
3. Squared
4. Ecotone
5. Arbor
6. Manimal
7. Letterman
8. Trophy
9. Instinct
10. Welcome

THE PRO SKATERS

Hawk / Burnquist / Caballero / Campbell / Glifberg / Koston / Lasek /
MARGERA / Mullen / Muska / Reynolds / Rowley / Steamer / Thomas

PRO-SPECIFIC CHALLENGE

Shopping Cart Slam

Bam's Pro Challenge takes place at Alcatraz.

REQUIRED SPECIAL TRICKS

None

Time	4:00
Awards	$1250 and Bam's Movie

"Welcome to the shopping cart Olympics! Now in four minutes, you gotta pass all 3 trials of shopping cart skill! Race, Hurdles, and Slalom. Now let's see what you got, man!"

Bam's had enough skating for one day—it's time to race a shopping cart down the switchbacks at Alcatraz! The three race courses must all be completed within the time limit and any crashes cause Bam and the cart to restart that particular run from the top. Although each course is made different by the barriers that are set up, all three races begin at the top of the road near the lighthouse and end on the dock by the ferry.

Barreling down the hill in a shopping cart is a unique experience. Although the cart has rather responsive steering and allows for jumping via the Cart Air, the lack of any way to slow down or stop makes tackling hairpin turns and a slalom course very difficult! One saving grace is that if the cart gets sideways while airborne, it's possible to recover by pressing the Revert Button. Ultimately, success at this challenge comes down to each player's personal ability to handle the speed and react to the numerous hurdles and slalom gates. Warm up on the traditional Race and study the position of the hurdles and gates on the above maps so as to know what to expect.

The first race is just that, a flat out race to the dock. Practice getting used to the incredible speed that is gained while exiting the second turn towards the powerhouse. During the first race, both the tunnel and the sewer routes are open. Take multiple runs down the hill, alternating between the swinging wide into the tunnel (the preferable path for the slalom course) and taking that turn tightly towards the sewer (mandatory for the hurdles race).

Above all else, practice launching out of the sewer area and onto the balcony of the building beyond the walkway. Keep the cart straight and it will land cleanly on the either the upper or lower balcony. Continue straight ahead towards the docks and pull a Cart Air over the railing to land on the dock. Launch off the kicker and into the water to start the next race.

The second race is the Hurdles race and it features a bevy of barriers that must be leaped over via the Cart Air jump. Proceed as before, but be sure to stick to the center of the road after the first turn. Hit the ramp in the middle to clear all four of the barriers that follow it. Continue following the centerline after the second turn as well, as the barriers leading down to the powerhouse have blockers rising up on either side—you must hurdle their center. Once at the powerhouse, take the turn tightly and immediately jump to hurdle the barrier. Hug the left side of the sewer and sky up and onto the balcony of the building and leap down to the docks from above.

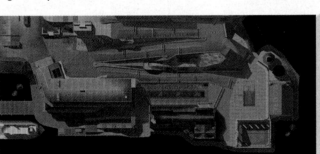

The final race is the most difficult—the Slalom race. Navigate the four gates on the upper stretch and take the first turn as tight as possible to be in good position for the second leg of the course. Things get a lot tougher after the second turn as the gates are no longer in a convenient S-pattern, but much more random. Take the third turn wide and cruise right into the tunnel for the easier of the two routes to the finish line. Weave between the final S-turns and out onto the dock to complete the objective.

Rodney Mullen

Age
32

Hometown
Gainesville, FL

Stance
Regular

Push Style
Never Mongo

Trick Style
Street

STARTING STATS

Air		Switch		
Hangtime	2	Flip Speed	7	
Ollie	2	Rail Balance	7	
Speed	6	Lip Balance	5	
Spin	3	Manual Balance	2	
	8		8	

SIGNATURE TRICKS

Gazelle Underflip
Semi Flip
5-0 Fingerflip Nosegrind
Rusty Slide Manual

1. Saint
2. Paper Circles
3. Blocks
4. Minimal
5. Quack Quack
6. Former Brigader
7. Camaro
8. Thumbs Up
9. Art
10. Sinner

THE PRO SKATERS

Hawk / Burnquist / Caballero / Campbell / Glifberg / Koston / Lasek /
Margera / **MULLEN** / Muska / Reynolds / Rowley / Steamer / Thomas

PRO-SPECIFIC CHALLENGE

Trick Inventions

Rodney's Pro Challenge takes place at Kona.

REQUIRED SPECIAL TRICKS

Semi Flip
Rusty Slide Manual

Time	5:00
Awards	$1250 and Rune's Movie

"Hey Rodney! You've invented a ton of tricks over the years. Can you still remember them all? Hit all of the tricks in each list in a single combo."

In a test of memory as much as reflexes, Rodney is challenged to lay down three lengthy combos that each feature tricks of his own creation. Although Rodney is best known lately for his jaw-dropping flatland maneuvers, the first two combos involve numerous flip tricks so getting plenty of speed and air are key.

The first combo features three easy flip (Left + Flip Button, Right + Flip Button, and Up + Flip Button) tricks, followed by Rodney's signature air trick, the Semi Flip. Hit the nearby quarter pipes to trick out the Special Meter ahead of time and line the skater up with the low-angled funbox in the middle of the park. A lot of manualing is needed during these combos and the steeper boxes interrupt manuals. Once in a good spot, charge the quarter pipe on either bank of ramps and perform all three flip tricks in one quick sequence. Revert the landing, manual across the box to the ramps on the other side, and perform the Semi Flip.

The second combo contains more tricks, some of which are double-tap flip tricks, and require three leaps off the quarter pipes. Take care of the first pair of flip tricks during the initial leap (Left + Flip, Flip Button and Right + Flip, Flip Button) and Revert into a manual back across to the other ramps. It's a little tight, but another double flip trick (Up, Up + Flip Button) and the grab (Down + Grab Button) can be performed during this jump so long as speed isn't a problem.

Carefully balance back over the low-angled box to the ramp across the way and perform the last flip trick (Down/Left + Flip, Flip Button).

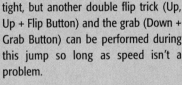

The third and final combination features a plethora of Rodney's different flatland tricks. So long as Manual Balance is at a rating of 9 or higher and the trick commands are input one after the other, this last combo shouldn't pose too much difficulty. From a standstill, tap into a manual then perform the Casper (Flip + Grind Button), Casper Flip (Flip + Flip Button), Anti Casper (Flip + Grab Button), Handstand (Grab + Grab Button), and Handstand Flip (Flip + Flip Button).

After flipping the handstand, tap into Rodney's Rusty Slide Manual and quickly ollie out of it to land the combo and to complete the challenge.

Chad Muska

Age
24

Hometown
Loraine, OH

Stance
Regular

Push Style
Never Mongo

Trick Style
Street

STARTING STATS

Air Hangtime	4	Switch	5
Ollie	4	Flip Speed	5
Speed	8	Rail Balance	8
Spin	5	Lip Balance	3
		Manual Balance	3

SIGNATURE TRICKS

Muska Beatz
BS Nose Comply
Ghetto Tag Grind
Ghetto Blastin

1. Red Muskalade
2. Black Muskalade
3. Gold Muskalade
4. Silver Muskalade
5. Green Muskalade
6. Muska Sporty
7. Red Silhouette
8. Candyland
9. Yellow Silhouette
10. Pearl Muskalade

THE PRO SKATERS

Hawk / Burnquist / Caballero / Campbell / Glifberg / Koston / Lasek /
Margera / Mullen / **MUSKA** / Reynolds / Rowley / Steamer / Thomas

PRO-SPECIFIC CHALLENGE

Trick Out the Beatz

Chad's Pro Challenge takes place at San Francisco.

REQUIRED SPECIAL TRICKS

None

Time	5:00
Awards	$1250 and Chad's Movie

"So, you want to make an album with us. Well, we're gonna have to hear some beats first. Nail tricks and combos to increase your beat meter. Don't bail! Nail 8 beats, and we got us a deal!"

PROSET SETUP

Be sure to turn on ProSet1 so that the wooden spines right below the Hubba ledge will be there for some quick halfpipe action with the ramp against the wall.

It's time to lay down some tracks for Chad's next album. The Music Producer wants to see 8 full beats, to the count of 1000 each, and the only way to do it is to perform numerous tricks and multiple combos. The key to this challenge is innovation, dropping the same tired tricks over and over won't get the Beat Meter thumping fast enough. Also, the Beat Meter resets to 0 after a bail —don't wipeout.

A good song consists of numerous instruments and sounds. Well, in order to 'Trick Out the Beatz' Chad must lay down multiple sounds as well. Think of each type of trick as a different instrument, such as a bass line, drums, guitars, vocals, and scratching. Few people will find a song consisting of just a bass line to be that entertaining. Similarly, a skating judge isn't going to look too fondly at a routine consisting of just grab tricks. Although the Beat Meter continues to rise steadily no matter what tricks are performed, linking together a variety of tricks such as flip tricks, lip tricks, grinds, grabs, and even pivots, will really get the Beat Meter hopping.

The initial beats are at a slower tempo and thus a good time to perform aerial-heavy combinations. These tricks, especially the grabs, are less hyperactive by nature than many of the street tricks and fit the beats better. Hit the **Rampin' Up** and **Hubba Spine** gaps while rotating through multiple grabs and flip tricks. Toss in some Reverts and manuals to build up combos in the 50,000 to 75,000 point range and keep it up until the first few beats are recorded.

Once the Beat Meter starts thumping at a faster tempo, shift focus away from the quarter pipes to include more flatland. Trick between some of the manuals and flatland tricks and use the Revert Button to spin through lots of rotation, thereby adding a good dose of scratching to the track.

The tempo of the Beat Meter gets faster with each successful recording. Once 6 beats have been nailed down, start venturing to other parts of the plaza and wharf to include lengthy Special Grinds on the EMB and some air-based Special Tricks on the quarter pipes. Keep laying down tricks and combos like mad without bailing and the Music Producer will want to sign you in no time!

Andrew Reynolds

Age
25

Hometown
Lakeland, FL

Stance
Regular

Push Style
Never Mongo

Trick Style
Street

STARTING STATS

Air		Switch	7
Hangtime	4	Flip Speed	5
Ollie	2	Rail Balance	8
Speed	8	Lip Balance	4
Spin	4	Manual Balance	3
	5		

SIGNATURE TRICKS

Dark Disaster
BigSpin Shifty
Noseslide Lipslide
Quad Heelflip

1. OG Baker
2. Drawing
3. Andrew 3000
4. Swashbuckle – White
5. Swashbuckle – Black
6. Choice Brand – Blue
7. Choice Brand – Green
8. Pirate Flag
9. Red Baker Logo
10. Pirate Scene

THE PRO SKATERS

Hawk / Burnquist / Caballero / Campbell / Glifberg / Koston / Lasek /
Margera / Mullen / Muska / **REYNOLDS** / Rowley / Steamer / Thomas

PRO-SPECIFIC CHALLENGE

Drop the Hammer

Time	3:30
Awards	$1250 and Andrew's Movie

Andrew's Pro Challenge takes place at San Francisco.

REQUIRED SPECIAL TRICKS

None

"Hey Yo Drew! We're all set up for these photos. These could be the biggest gaps you've ever hit, man. Warm up ollieing the gap, and then we'll get a photo of each trick. If your knees don't blow out, your back definitely will."

When it comes to hitting huge gaps, no one does it quite like Andrew Reynolds. Whether it's doing a fakie Nollie down a 10-set or a Heelflip over an embankment, if it's a gap then there's a good chance he's done it. Well, here's your chance to take it up a notch and clear the most incredible gaps in all of San Francisco. Atiba has placed a set of kickers throughout the city and wants to see Andrew gap over everything from the pier to the fountain to the street! Each gap is going to be done three times, first with an ollie, then a Double Kickflip, and finally a Triple Heelflip over each of the gaps before moving on to the next.

The first gap is from the overhead walkway, over the water, and onto the pier on the other side. Hop into a grind on the sign in the middle of the walkway to gain speed and ollie straight off the kicker. This is the smallest of the gaps and requires the least amount of speed to clear. Completing this setup scores the **Andrew's Pro Challenge Pier** gap.

The second gap is up and over the overhead walkway from the ground below. Andrew starts facing the L-shaped banked wall outside the warehouse at the corner of the level. Aim for the center of the wall, where the angle is, and trick off the wall to gain speed. Try to land as cleanly and as close to the center of the wall as possible to be lined up with the kicker. Charge the kicker and go big off the end to clear the walkway for the **Andrew's Pro Challenge Walkway** gap.

BOMB DROPPING

If timed properly, it's possible to gap the overhead walkway and land in a grind on top of the bus as it cruises down the street. It won't help in completing Andrew's challenge, but switching into some flatland tricks atop the bus looks mighty cool!

The difficulty starts picking up a bit at the next challenge where the skater must gap the fountain. Grind the signs for speed and ollie off the edge of the kicker straight ahead. Although it's all right to hit the bronze sculpture atop the fountain, it will knock the skater around a bit, potentially causing a wicked faceplant. When it comes time for the Triple Heelflip, attempt to Boneless (Up, Up + Jump Button) from the edge of the kicker for a little extra height. Otherwise, brushing against the top of the fountain will likely interrupt the lengthy flipping that is required. Clearing the fountain cleanly will earn the **Andrew's Pro Challenge Fountain** gap.

The fourth gap is from the sidewalk by the EMB ledge, over the grass and walkway, and into the bowl. Skate down the ramped walkway towards the blue rail straight ahead and grind on it to pick up speed. Hopefully no cars are coming and you have a straight shot at the kicker near the ledge. Boneless off the ramp while angling very slightly to the right to gap all the way into the bowl. This is arguably the most difficult of the five gaps, but once you nail it down, it's just a matter of performing the right trick while in the air. Landing cleanly in the bowl will net the **Andrew's Pro Challenge Bowl** gap.

The final gap location takes place on the roof of the Slam Brothers warehouses at Pier 18. Trick across the gap in the roofs for the **TC's Roof Gap Too** gap and head straight for the kicker at the end of the roof. Boneless off the kicker for some extra oomph and do the requisite flip tricks while soaring over the city traffic and onto the sidewalk across the street. Shorten the distance needed to complete the gap by angling slightly to the left, towards the corner, but it's not necessary if the Boneless is well timed. Completing all three leaps across the street not only earns the **Andrew's Pro Challenge Street** gap, but completes this challenge as well!

Geoff Rowley

Age
25

Hometown
Liverpool,
England

Stance
Regular

Push Style
Never Mongo

Trick Style
Street

STARTING STATS

Air Hangtime	5	Switch	5
Ollie	2	Flip Speed	6
Speed	7	Rail Balance	8
Spin	4	Lip Balance	7
	3	Manual Balance	3

SIGNATURE TRICKS

Rowley Darkslide
Casper Flip 360 Flip
Ferret Fight
Sproing

1. Hellcat
2. One Way Logo
3. Spring Heel Jack
4. TV Logo 2
5. Victory UK
6. Script Logo
7. Heshman
8. Sorry Logo – Yellow
9. HKD – Black
10. Pixelated

THE PRO SKATERS

Hawk / Burnquist / Caballero / Campbell / Glifberg / Koston / Lasek /
Margera / Mullen / Muska / Reynolds / **ROWLEY** / Steamer / Thomas

PRO-SPECIFIC CHALLENGE

Flip-Gap-Grind

Geoff's Pro Challenge takes place at London.

REQUIRED SPECIAL TRICKS

Rowley Darkslide
Casper Flip 360 Flip

Time	3:00
Awards	$1250, Pro Set 3 and Geoff's Movie

"Let's see if you can nail these grind gaps! See, we'll start off small then we'll work our way up. The higher we go, the harder the combo gets."

Geoff's Pro Challenge not only involves busting complex flip tricks across huge gaps, but he's got to land them in a grind on some of the narrowest rails and ledges in all of London. There are a total of three gaps to hit, and each one of them must be cleared three times while performing more complex tricks with each pass.

The first gap is over by the South Bank. Skate up the walkway leading onto the bridge, gap across the street, and land in a grind on the right-hand handrail leading down the other side by the river. This is a pretty tough gap to hit even with a fully lit Special Meter, so be certain to Boneless off the walkway before it flattens out. The first run requires a flip trick (Up + Flip Button) followed by a Nosegrind (Up + Grind Button) on the rail. Be sure to ollie off the rail before it turns to the right, as splashing into the river will negate the otherwise successful gap. The second

attempt is similar to the first, with the only difference being a 5-0 (Down + Grind Button) grind instead of a Nosegrind. The third hit on this gap specifies the skater land in a Rowley Darkslide on the railing. Since this is a Special Grind, be sure to trick out the Special Meter on the quarter pipe near Atiba if it's not already glowing. Get the flip trick off as soon as the board lifts off the ground so as to have time to prepare for the Special Grind on the rail.

The second "Insane Grind" is going to begin on the roof of the National Gallery. Drop in off the windowsill, air off the ramp on the balcony and land in a grind on the ledge straight ahead below the trees. Here, the flip trick (Up/Right + Flip Button) is slightly more complex to pull off. Make certain not to drift out of alignment from the ledge below when inputting the commands. Freefall cleanly after performing the trick and land in a FS Crooked grind (Up/Right + Grind Button). The second run at this gap requires the same flip trick, but the landing must be a FS Overcrook (Up/Left + Grind Button). The third pass specifies the same flip trick, but the landing must be in a Rowley Darkslide. Unlike the first gap, there is plenty of time after the initial flip trick to input the commands for the Rowley Darkslide, so be sure to line up with the ledge and press the specified buttons at the right time.

The third gap is from a neighboring rooftop into a grind on the electric wires running through the Square, then down onto the street below. The good thing with this gap is that there's plenty of time to set up for the final flip trick— just balance the grind until you're ready to flip down onto the street. The first pass specifies a flip (Up/Left + Flip Button) to a FS Feeble (Down/Right + Grind Button) on the wire, then one last flip (Left + Flip Button) onto the street. Even if the wrong tricks get performed, be sure to land the string cleanly to keep the Special Meter lit.

LIGHT IT UP

The remaining two runs at this gap both incorporate Special Grinds into the string, so be certain to trick out the Special Meter ahead of time, even if it's by launching off the roof into a 720 Japan. Whatever it takes.

The second run at this gap requires the same initial flip trick, but this time landing in a Rowley Darkslide, and finishing with a double flip (Left + Flip, Flip Button) onto the street. The final run is by far the toughest though. This one requires a Casper Flip 360 Flip to a Rowley Darkslide to a triple flip (Left + Flip, Flip, Flip Button). Keep the skater lined up and straight and get that initial Special Trick performed as quickly as possible, so as to have enough time to get the Rowley Darkslide going. Once in the grind, give a quick glance down below for oncoming traffic, and triple flip out of the grind to end the challenge.

Elissa Steamer

Age
31
Hometown
Fort Meyers, FL
Stance
Regular
Push Style
Never Mongo
Trick Style
Street

STARTING STATS

Air			Switch	5
Hangtime	5		Flip Speed	5
Ollie	5		Rail Balance	6
Speed	4		Lip Balance	5
Spin	5		Manual Balance	5

SIGNATURE TRICKS

Judo Madonna
No Comply 360 Shove-It
Bigspin Flip to Tail
Cartwheel 50-50

1. Dove
2. Steamer Drawing
3. Bootleg – Black
4. Ripoff – Red
5. Bootleg – Blue
6. Censored – Yellow
7. Censored – Orange
8. Real B – Grey
9. Real B – Red
10. Bootleg - Grey

THE PRO SKATERS

Hawk / Burnquist / Caballero / Campbell / Glifberg / Koston / Lasek /
Margera / Mullen / Muska / Reynolds / Rowley / **STEAMER** / Thomas

PRO-SPECIFIC CHALLENGE

Elissa's Super Gaps

Elissa's Pro Challenge takes place at Alcatraz.

REQUIRED SPECIAL TRICKS

Judo Madonna

Time	3:00
Awards	$1250 and Elissa's Movie

"Giz – now I know you all about going big these days. Let's get some photos of you busting on some of these big gaps. OK? Now Yo! The run-up's pretty sketchy, so hit the ramps and rails to help you line up."

Elissa's Pro Challenge is very similar to Andrew's in that she must gap huge distances while performing several tricks. Although there are only three gaps to hit, the trick combinations are more difficult to pull off, and even harder to land! Only one of the gaps has a very clean run-up, as Atiba mentioned, and some quick reflexes are needed just in order to attempt the gap.

ALL IS NOT LOST...

If Elissa fails to clear the gap, or accidentally grinds off in the wrong direction, don't give up. Even if she goes far out of bounds, the Special Meter stays lit for the next attempt so long as blood isn't spilled. Do whatever it takes to keep the skater upright until she is placed back at the starting spot for that gap.

The first gap is from the ramped portion of the guard's walk near the exercise yard, over the wall and onto the sheets of plywood lying on the steps. Although it's not necessary to Boneless over the wall, having a fully lit Special Meter is very important. Trick into a grind on the stone ledge directly ahead, switch up the grind, then trick into a third grind on the railing that curves down the hill to the right. Charge past Atiba and up the angled path to the left of the wall. Ollie just before the path flattens out and soar over the wall to the wood below for the **Guard's Walk 2 Step Planks**. Elissa must repeat this two more times: once while performing a triple flip trick (Up + Flip Button three times), and again while doing her patented Judo Madonna Special Trick. Input the trick commands as soon as the board clears the wall and there shouldn't be any problem.

The second gap is down the **Massie Crumbling Stairset** gap. Hop into a quick grind on the metal barrier that's been set up to gain some speed and ollie right before the steps to clear the gap. Just like before, there's no need to do a No Comply or Boneless, a regular Ollie is all it takes! The gap must be hit two more times, each while performing different tricks. For the second hit, Atiba wants to see a fancy combo of a grab trick (Down + Grab Button) to a double flip trick (Right + Flip, Flip Button). The third and final leap down the crumbling stairs must be done while performing Elissa's Judo Madonna Special Trick.

The final gap is a doozy! Elissa starts on the grass near the lighthouse facing the switchbacks. Charge the metal rail near the cart, ride straight off the end of the rail (don't ollie) and over the ledge towards the wooden kicker that's been set up. Launch from the kicker over the switchbacking path and into the sewer far below for **Elissa's Switchbacks 2 Sewer Pipe** gap. Since this a much larger gap than the previous two, there's more time to pull off more difficult combos. For the second leap into the sewers, Atiba wants to see another pair of grab (Down/Left + Grab Button) and flip (Down + Flip Button) tricks linked together. There's plenty of time to pull off that combo during the freefall, but the same can't be said for the final stunt. The third attempt at this gap requires another triple flip trick (Left + Flip Button three times) with a Judo Madonna tacked on afterwards for good

measure. Begin the flip tricks immediately and begin inputting the commands for the Judo Madonna as the board rotates through the third flip trick.

Jamie Thomas

Age
26
Hometown
Dotham, AL
Stance
Regular
Push Style
Never Mongo
Trick Style
Street

STARTING STATS

Air				
Hangtime	4	Switch		4
Ollie	4	Flip Speed		5
Speed	7	Rail Balance		8
Spin	5	Lip Balance		4
	4	Manual Balance		5

SIGNATURE TRICKS

Crook BigSpinFlip Crook
One Wheel Nosemanual
Might as Well Jump
American Hero

1. Cross
2. Zero or Die
3. Freebird
4. Spikes
5. Thomas Smith
6. Single Skull
7. Jesus
8. Skeleton
9. Priest
10. 3 Skull with Blood

THE PRO SKATERS

Hawk / Burnquist / Caballero / Campbell / Glifberg / Koston / Lasek /
Margera / Mullen / Muska / Reynolds / Rowley / Steamer / **THOMAS**

PRO-SPECIFIC CHALLENGE

A Day in the Life

Time	0:20
Awards	$1250 and Jamie's Movie

Jamie's Pro Challenge takes place at the College.

"Chief, nobody shoots an entire spotlight in one day! OK – all right, all right, if you say so. Do each trick as fast as you can and then we'll break for the next spot. Chief, let's do this man."

REQUIRED SPECIAL TRICKS

None

PROSET SETUP

Make sure all ProSets are on for this challenge.

It's 9:40am and you've got a full day ahead of you. Atiba wants to shoot 10 different tricks at 10 different spots around campus. The tricks are never more complex than a Smith Grind, but that doesn't mean this goal isn't challenging. No other goal in the game requires as much efficiency out of the player as Jamie's Pro Challenge. There will be 15 seconds added to the clock for each successful photo.

ALL SWITCHED UP

Many of the tricks that need to be performed in this challenge are grinds. It is therefore very important to note the skater's stance and select the directional button that applies to that stance and whether or not the skater is facing the ledge/rail.

9:40 AM

The first task is to perform a FS 5-0 grind on the lower school pool lip. Since Jamie is a regular footed skater, approach the ledge on the left side of the pool and ollie into the grind (Down + Grind Button). Ollie off the grind and onto the small patch of grass near the English building.

10:20 AM

Double back towards the tennis courts and perform a double-tap flip trick (Down/Left + Flip, Flip Button) while ollieing over the tennis net.

12:00 PM

Skate up past the kiosks towards the stone bridge while in the regular stance and perform a Noseslide (Right + Grind Button) on the right-hand ledge of the stone bridge.

12:30 PM

Stay in the regular stance (facing right) and loop around the back of the Fine Arts building towards the Philosophy Building. Ollie into a Smith Grind (Down/Right + Grind Button) near the orange arrow and hold it across the steps of the building.

1:10 PM

Slow the board down a bit and approach the rails between the Coliseum and the Engineering building. Hop into a grind and flip (Up + Flip Button) while transferring a grind across the rails.

2:00 PM

It's time to head back across campus to the Woodward School. Special Grind the beige wall for speed and roll up to the blue handrails of the elementary school and Nosegrind (Up + Grind Button) on one of them.

3:15 PM

Head past the security office towards the clock tower and slide into a switch stance. Continue straight ahead and hop into a Tailslide (Left + Grind Button) on the bench that curves off towards the clock tower to the left. This will send the skater back towards the stone bridge.

4:00 PM

Boneless into a grind atop either of the kiosks and flip (Left + Flip Button) out of the grind onto the ground.

6:20 PM

Use the ramp on the back of the pickup truck to grind the Schnitzel's World sign into the frat house and Nosegrind (Up + Grind Button) onto the ledge with the kegs.

7:15 PM

Now for the final trick, a big meaty grab from the roof of the Fine Arts building to the English building. Head past the upper school pool and enter the set of doors to catch a ride on the elevator. Once on the roof, charge the quarter pipe in the far right-hand corner and perform the specified grab trick (Down/Left + Grab Button) while gapping across to the other building.

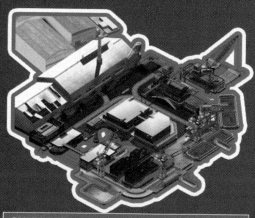

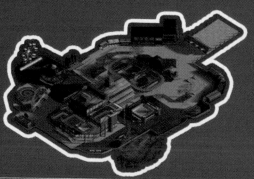

SKATE-THRU

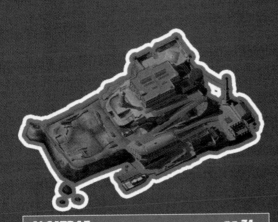

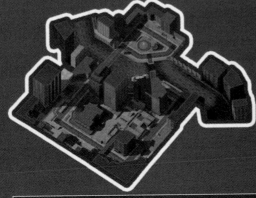

College

Unlocked at the start of the game.

College campuses have historically offered skaters some of the best street terrain of any setting outside of a skatepark, and this one is no exception. This corner of the California College campus not only features lengthy fences, rails, and walls for grinding, but also a pool, several quarter pipes, and a tennis court! That's right, a tennis court! And when battling it out with the jocks and the rent-a-cop gets tiring, you can always go crash the kegger at the frat house!

LEVEL GOALS

Unlocked Objectives

Get a High Score: 40,000 points
Collect the S-K-A-T-E letters
Collect the C-O-M-B-O letters
Race the Inline Skater
Nail the tricks they yell out
Get back at the 5 frat boys
Spine Transfer over the wall
Warn the other skaters
Skitch the Professor's car
Grind down Officer Tom's Banners

Locked Objectives

Get a Pro Score: 75,000 points
Stop all of the Pink Elephants
Medal the High-Combo Competition
Nail a 360 Varial McTwist
Clock 5 jocks in one combo
Gap between floats 10 times

Pro Challenges

Combo the Benches, Stairs and Flag Pole
Get all 4 Master's Lip Gaps
Collect Pro C-O-M-B-O
Beat Bob's 3 best combos
Get a Sick Score: 250,000 points

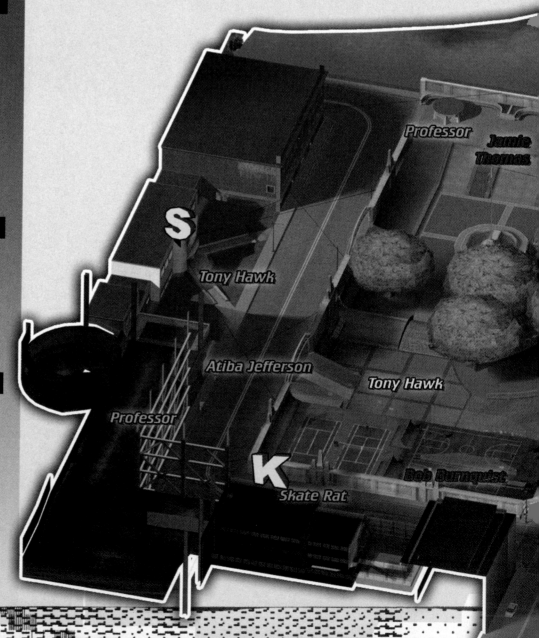

The College level has been designed so as to not only provide a gentle learning curve for newcomers to the series, but it also serves as the perfect introduction to many of the newer features for those who have played the previous games. And while launching Indy 900's from the roof of the Fine Arts building may not be the *higher learning* California College deans have in mind, it will help prepare you for a profitable career as a pro skater. Go through each of the goals as they appear before moving on to another location—the, err, *classes*, get tough mighty quickly!

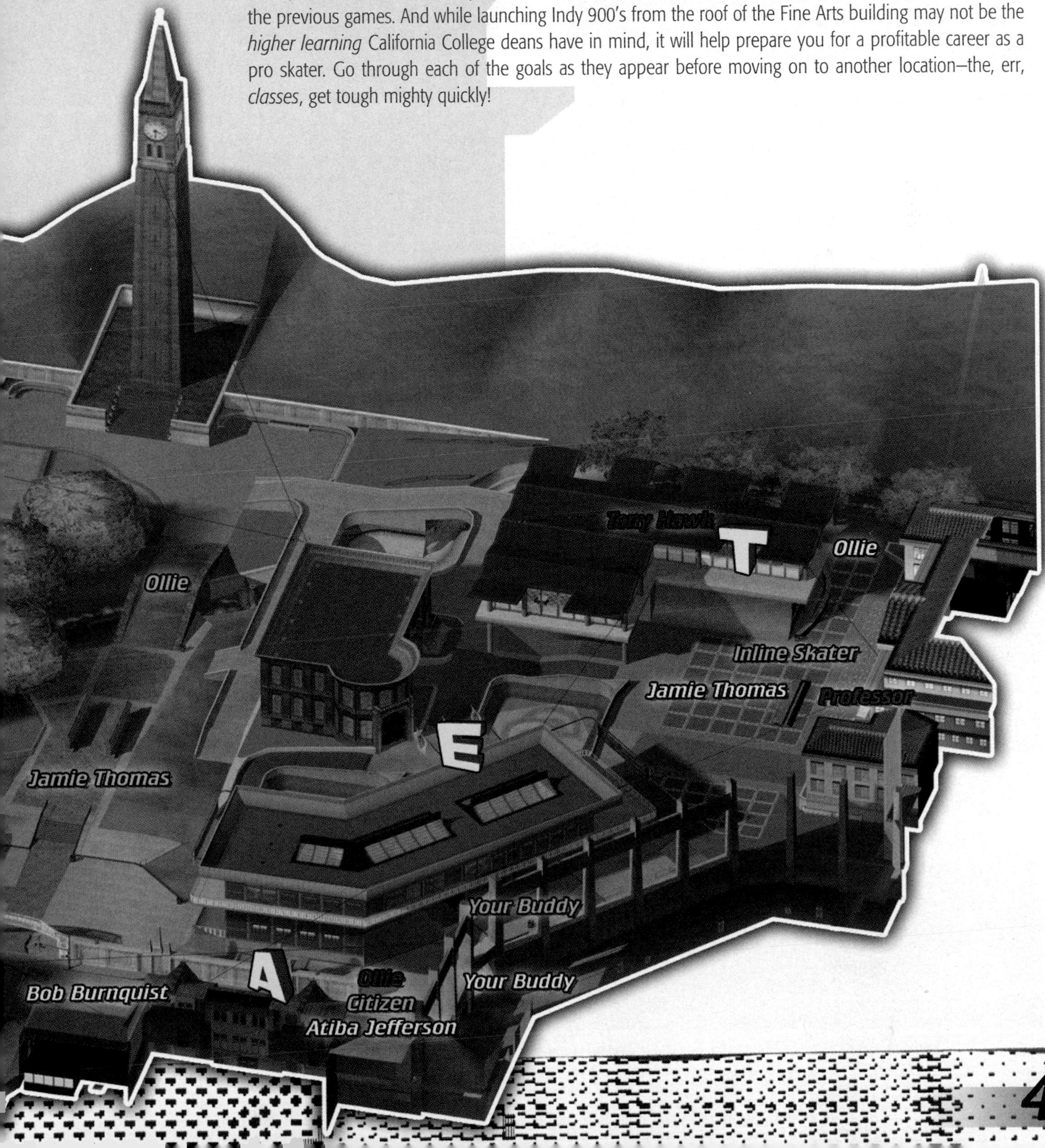

Tony Hawk

T

Ollie

Ollie

Inline Skater

Jamie Thomas

Professor

Ollie

E

Jamie Thomas

Your Buddy

A

Your Buddy

Bob Burnquist

Ollie

Citizen

Atiba Jefferson

Amateur Challenges

GET A HIGH SCORE: 40,000 POINTS

Location	Near the kiosks
Time	2:00
Awards	$250 and a Stat Point
How unlocked	N/A
Unlocks	ProSet3, 'Get a Pro Score: 75,000 points'

Jamie Thomas
"Hey, what's up man? I got lucky with this score. Let's see what you can do."

The handrails and concrete quarter pipes in the College's central plaza make it a great place to practice linking together tricks. Although there is a full 2:00 to score the requisite 40,000 points, it's a good idea to score as many points in one trick string as possible so as to be better prepared for the more difficult challenges ahead.

Turn and face the wooden spine behind Jamie and launch into the air. Quickly link a pair of aerial tricks together and Revert out of the landing. Manual down the slope towards the arch by the street and use the concrete quarter pipe near the wall to leap into a 540 Indy. Revert the landing and immediately Nose Manual up the ramp to the right and stall on top. Pop Shove-It out of the stall and Revert the landing for one additional multiplier.

COLLECT THE S-K-A-T-E LETTERS!

Location	Near the campus security office
Time	2:00
Awards	$250 and a Stat Point
How unlocked	N/A
Unlocks	Nothing

The Professor
"Let's see if you can even spell. Try to collect the S-K-A-T-E letters!"

S — Cross the street towards the Woodland School and grind the blue handrail. Ollie off the handrail to grab the "S" above the door.

K — Grind the rail in the corner near the parking garage and transfer from the raised gate to the power line above for the **High Road Hop!** gap and to score the "K".

A — Spine Transfer into the garbage truck parked outside the frat house and out the other side to snag the "A" hovering above.

T — The "T" is hovering above the concrete quarter pipe in front of the fine arts building.

E — Head up the quarter pipe below the purple and gold "Swallow Pride" banner and slide into a grind on the handrail for the **Bachelor's in Engineering Grind** gap. Grind around the corner and ollie off the rail to get the final letter.

COLLECT THE C-O-M-B-O LETTERS

Location	On the stone bridge
Time	2:00
Awards	$250 and a Stat Point
How unlocked	N/A
Unlocks	Stop all of the Pink Elephants!

Ollie the Bum
"Hey, skater-person! My C-O-M-B-O letters got away from me... Do me a favor and collect the letters all in one combo!"

Hop into a grind on the silver railing curling off to the left by the stone bridge and hold the grind onto the wooden fence near the grass to gather up the first four letters. Ollie over the bridge after rounding the corner in the fence and continue the grind on the other side to claim the final letter and the **Skippin Over!** gap. The skater must land the combo cleanly, so jump down out of the grind onto the walkway beyond the fence.

NEW IN *TONY HAWK'S PRO SKATER 4*!

Veteran players will no doubt welcome this variation of the requisite S-K-A-T-E letters objective. Instead of collecting the letters, Ollie raises the bar and forces the skater to collect C-O-M-B-O in one consecutive trick string. The letters disappear if the trick combination is broken.

RACE THE INLINE SKATER

Location	Near the Philosophy Building
Time	0:30
Awards	$250 and a Stat Point
How unlocked	N/A
Unlocks	Medal the High-Combo Competition

Local Inline Skater
"Hey man, there's NO WAY you're faster than me! Okay then, let's see if you can beat my best time at the ULTIMATE inline route!"

This Inline Skater is forever trying to challenge the skateboarders who cruise his campus, and this time he's set up a race course that snakes around the university and into the parking garage down the street. There are a total of 15 gates to pass through; the red arrow at the top of the screen showing the way. Since the skateboarder is lying down on his or her back, he or she can't do any more than turn left or right and perform a Luge Hop (similar to an ollie).

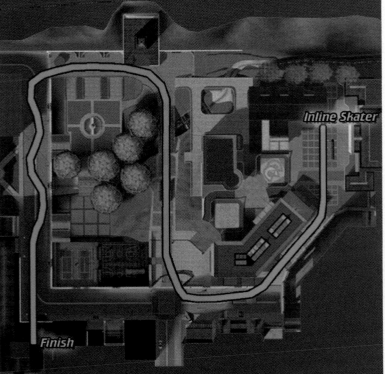

Inline Skater

Finish

It shouldn't take more than a couple of practice runs to memorize the locations of the gates and to complete this objective. Nevertheless, the following tips can help shave some seconds off the finishing time. For starters, keep the Jump Button held down for maximum speed. Drop in on the roll-in and follow the arrow through the first three gates. Luge Hop up the steps leading towards the kiosks to keep from having to swerve around and Luge Hop again when going over the stone bridge to pick up even more speed when rounding the curve near the clock tower. Take the turn by the security office wide to avoid oncoming traffic and to set up for the final few gates. Be sure to make sharp, quick turns when slaloming through the final gates to avoid wasting time.

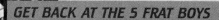

DROPPING IN

Transfer to the rooftop of the school for the **Class Transfer!** gap and gain speed in the halfpipe up there. The added height and speed make it possible to perform three or more tricks at once when transferring back to the ramps at ground level.

NAIL THE TRICKS THEY YELL OUT

Location	In front of the Woodland School
Time	1:00
Awards	$250 and a Stat point
How unlocked	N/A
Unlocks	ProSet4 and 'Nail a 360 Varial McTwist'

Tony Hawk
"Oh man! I bring some ramps to this demo and the kids are out of control! How 'bout if you take over for a while? Try to land the tricks as the kids call them out. You've got to clear all the tricks to finish this one off."

GET BACK AT THE 5 FRAT BOYS

Location	Between the Coliseum and the Engineering building
Time	2:00
Awards	$250 and a Stat point
How unlocked	N/A
Unlocks	Clock 5 jocks in one combo

Your Buddy
"Uh... Arrgh! Hey there... The local frat boys trash-canned me! Can you get 'em back for me?!"

This is the first of the falling trick objectives and contains 19 different tricks that need to be performed. Use Tony's wooden spine and the concrete ramp against the school as a makeshift halfpipe and perform the tricks that appear in the lower right-hand corner of the screen. The order in which the tricks appear is completely random but only the most basic grab and flip tricks are included in this challenge.

Numerous tricks begin to appear on the side of the screen. The list turns red if it grows to 12 or more tricks and the challenge is lost if 15 tricks are left to pile up. Completing 19 tricks in 60 seconds may seem daunting, but it is possible to wipe numerous tricks from the screen simultaneously. The first way is to quickly input the commands for two different tricks during one jump. Although the skater's minimal starting stats may prohibit two consecutive grab tricks, back-to-back flip tricks are possible. Another way to clear out multiple tricks concurrently is to perform a trick that is listed more than once. For example, if Heelflip is listed twice, the skater only needs to perform it once to clear away both instances of the trick in the list.

Those frat boys picked on the wrong dude this time! Show those beer-guzzling apes what happens when they pick on the friend of a pro skater. Seek out each of the five frat boys and knock over the kegs on which they're standing.

Head down the walkway towards the large beige wall across the street from the garbage truck and Wallie into a grind on top of the wall. Balance the grind towards the blue arch to take out the first two frat boys and jump down into the street.

Use the plywood on the back of the pickup truck as a ramp and leap onto Schnitzel World's awning. Leap through the frat house window to take out another frat boy and claim the **Through the Frat Window Ollieing!** gap. Knock over the fourth frat boy on the balcony, then leap through the distant window and land in a grind on the concrete ledge to take out the final frat boy and to snag the **Through the Frat Window Grinding!** gap.

SPINE TRANSFER OVER THE WALL

Location	Across from the parking garage
Time	2:00
Awards	$250 and a Stat point
How unlocked	N/A
Unlocks	ProSet7 and 'Gap between floats 10 times'

Atiba Jefferson

"Yo, you ready to shoot some photos? Then let's start out with some Spine Transfers over the wall."

Atiba Jefferson, the sport's leading photographer, thinks you're ready for a photo shoot. He's a busy man and only has two minutes to spare—so try not to waste his time!

This objective requires the skater to complete three Spine Transfers over the wall across the street from the parking garage. Ollie off the wooden ramp on the sidewalk and Spine Transfer to clear the wall and land on the ramp on the other side. After completing this, Atiba asks that a flip trick be added to the Spine Transfer. Charge the ramp once again, ollie, Spine Transfer, and quickly perform the indicated flip trick while transferring over the wall. Atiba wants to see a grab trick for the third photo. Spine Transfer over the wall just as before, but this time hit the grab trick listed.

WARN THE OTHER SKATERS

Location	In front of Billy's Sporting Goods store
Time	0:16
Awards	$250 and a Stat point
How unlocked	N/A
Unlocks	Nothing

Skate Rat

"Hey dude, Officer Tom is after our buddies again... they are skating at all our favorite spots... You have to warn them before he gets there!"

Officer Tom must have ran out of doughnuts, because he's got nothing better to do than harass your skater friends. Use the red arrow at the top of the screen as a guide and race across campus to warn to them before it's too late.

Skater #1: Philosophy building

It's important to grind on ledges and handrails while darting across campus to gain speed, especially at the start of the challenge. Grind the handrail down into the plaza, then grind the left-hand handrail up the slope towards the purple and gold concrete pool. Grind clockwise around the edge of the pool and trick off onto the brick walkway leading up towards the white Philosophy building. Boneless over the picnic tables to warn the skater. *Seventeen seconds added to the clock.*

Skater #2: Security Office

Head around the back side of the Fine Arts building and grind the logs lying in the grass to pick up additional speed. Continue straight past the concrete culvert and the clock tower towards the Security Office by the street. *Twenty two seconds added to the clock.*

Skater #3: Coliseum

Head over the wooden bridge and ollie up the stairs of the nearby building to cut through the hallway towards the pool. Circle around the pool towards the alley between the Coliseum and the Philosophy building and transfer to the ramp below for the **Coliseum Transfer!** gap. The next skater is right there at the base of the lower ramp. *Sixteen seconds added to the clock.*

Skater #4: Parking Garage

The final skater to be warned is standing on the street corner near the parking garage. Grind the handrails to avoid getting taken out by the football players and head down the street past the frat house and Schnitzel World towards the parking garage at the far end.

SKITCH THE PROFESSOR'S CAR

Location	Second floor of the parking garage
Time	0:02
Awards	$250
How unlocked	N/A
Unlocks	Nothing

Professor
"Goodness gracious! My car! They're stealing my baby! Try to stop them!"

Roll up to the back of the car and press Up to grab hold of the rear bumper; act quick, though, because they're about to get away! Once the skater is Skitchin' a ride on the back of the stolen car, the thieves take off down the street and through the campus in an attempt to shake the valiant skater. Ignore the surroundings and concentrate on the Balance Meter. Tap Left and Right to keep from letting go. Maintain a hold on the car for a complete lap around the College to return the car to the Professor.

GRIND DOWN OFFICER TOM'S BANNERS

Location	Across the street from the frat house
Time	2:00
Awards	$250
How unlocked	N/A
Unlocks	Nothing

Citizen
"Officer Tom is running for chief of security? You've got be kidding! Wallride up the walls, then Wallie up and grind the banners down!"

Officer Tom has proven himself not worthy of the skater vote; it's time to curb his popularity now before things get out of hand. There are a total of 7 banners that need tearing down and they're all hanging on the large beige wall by the street. Wallie into a grind on the wall and carry it straight through the banners to tear them down and to claim the **Banner Gap!** bonus.

The first 4 Banners are all on the wall facing the frat house and can be torn down with one long grind linking together multiple **Banner Gaps** with the **Gateway Gap!**. From there, jump into a grind on the wall leading off to the right at the corner and continue the grind for the fifth banner.

Leap down to the street and use the quarter pipe beyond the next blue arch to slide up and into another grind and maintain it towards the Security Office to snag the final two banners.

GET A PRO SCORE: 75,000 POINTS

Location	In front of the Philosophy building
Time	2:00
Awards	$250
How unlocked	Complete 'Get a High Score: 40,000 points'
Unlocks	ProSet1

Jamie Thomas
"Hey, you're back? You think my score is weak? Let's see what you got!"

The Pro Score requirement is nearly double that of the High Score challenge and serves as a great reason to begin incorporating Special Tricks into the scoring line. Although Jamie has added two wooden quarter pipes and a spine to the course, the following scoring line only utilizes the wooden spine near Jamie.

Begin the combination by linking a flip and grab trick together off the spine while rotating 540 degrees. Revert the landing and manual straight towards the concrete ramp near the Fine Arts building. Throw down a quick flip-based Special Trick and Revert into another manual upon landing. Head to the right and ollie into a Special Grind on the ledge of the pool. Trick off the end of the ledge to end the string.

STOP ALL OF THE PINK ELEPHANTS

Location	Behind the Fine Arts building near the logs
Time	0:10
Awards	$250
How unlocked	Complete 'Collect the C-O-M-B-O letters'
Unlocks	Nothing

Ollie the Bum
"Aaaargghh!!! They're everywhere!... Pink Elephants are everywhere! You gotta help me, Senator!"

Be sure to Revert here to start the combo, else time will run out!

Ollie

Log Hop!

While it might be great for poor ol' Ollie the Bum that his hallucination ends in just 9 short seconds, this certainly doesn't make grabbing all 12 pink elephants any easier! Luckily, the booze-induced pachyderms stick around as long as the skater is in a combo. The pink elephants are all located in the culvert between Ollie and the metal grates near the street across campus.

Covering the length of the river in such a short amount of time requires lots of speed and there's no better way to get it than by grinding on the logs and concrete ledges near the river. Grind the logs near Ollie to collect the first three pink elephants, then manual down the concrete river and into a grind on the lower ledge to grab two more. Spine Transfer over the two valves to get two more pink elephants and make sure to Revert into a manual when going under the stone bridge as time will likely be running out momentarily. Quickly hop into a grind on the log under the bridge and **Log Hop** down the river, collecting the final five pink elephants along the way.

MEDAL THE HIGH-COMBO COMPETITION

Location	In front of Schnitzel World
Time	0:10
Awards	$250
How unlocked	Complete 'Race the Inline Skater'
Unlocks	Nothing

In the high-combo competition, the skater is given 10 seconds to initiate a trick combination and the judges score the run the moment all four wheels touch down on the pavement. Since the local shop sponsoring this shindig didn't have enough money for tons of ramps and funboxes, the course is on the small side. This is actually a blessing in disguise given the time limit, as there's no need to waste valuable seconds scouting out a place to initiate a scoring line—it can be started anywhere! Also, the savvy skater can use the contest's format to gain a second try. Begin the combination as soon as the timer starts. This way, if an impromptu header interrupts the line, there might still be time on the clock to start a second trick string.

Although the judges frown upon skaters who perform the same trick over and over during a single run, they don't mind seeing the same combination used in all three runs.

Bob Burnquist
"Check this out – a local shop is sponsoring a competition! It's all about getting a big combo. You'll get 10 seconds to start one. Best 2 out of 3 runs count. You want to give it a roll?"

NEW IN *TONY HAWK'S PRO SKATER 4!*

Unlike the previous games in the series, competitions in *Tony Hawk's Pro Skater 4* are merely one of the many challenges available on each course. Not only that, many of them are much shorter and more specific than in the past as well. It's important to note that each competition in *Tony Hawk's Pro Skater 4* takes place in a specific area of the course and points scored outside this area will not be tallied.

Start the run by launching into a 540 Kickflip to Japan on the wooden ramp at the starting point and Revert the landing. Manual towards the rail set up on either side of the course and ollie into a Special Grind. Trick across the gap to the rail at the far end and land in another Special Grind. Carry the grind around the U-turn and flip trick onto the third and final rail to head back towards the starting point. Manual up the quarter pipe and boost high off the ramp for a flip-based Special Trick. Revert the landing for an additional multiplier to pound one last nail in the competition.

NAIL A 360 VARIAL MCTWIST

Location	Below the tennis courts
Time	0:30
Awards	$250 and a Special Trick Slot
How unlocked	Complete 'Nail the tricks they yell out'
Unlocks	ProSet5

Tony Hawk

"Hey! Want to try this trick? I just learned it myself. Get your Special Meter full and then nail a 360 Varial McTwist!"

Tony has brought out a series of wooden spines to help teach you a new Special Trick but only one of them is necessary for right now. Go big off the concrete ramp below the fence and Revert the landing to max out the Special Meter. Charge the nearest wooden spine and input the command for the 360 Varial McTwist to complete the objective.

CLOCK 5 JOCKS IN ONE COMBO

Location	Near the coliseum
Time	2:00
Awards	$250
How unlocked	Complete 'Get back at the 5 frat boys'
Unlocks	Nothing

Your Buddy

"The football team is hogging the coliseum for their practice—that ain't right!"

First it was the frat boys, now it's the football team—it's time to stick up for Your Buddy once again! In this objective, use the handrails and the quarter pipes at the end of the corridor to maintain a lengthy trick combination and knock down 5 of the football players in the process. Unlike the frat boys, these guys are bigger, faster, and more aggressive. In fact, they'll clothesline the skater right off his or her board if not tricking when passing by.

Although the skater can knock the jocks down while manualing, it is much easier to maintain good momentum and balance while grinding the handrails. Hop into a grind and hit the **Rail Hop!** gap to continue grinding the length of the corridor while knocking the jocks down. Manual into the ramps at the end of the corridor, perform a basic trick, Revert the landing, and quickly hop back onto the railing on the other side for the **Rail Cross!** gap. It will likely take at least two trips down the length of the corridor to clock them all.

CLOCKED JOCKS TALLY

Completing this objective unlocks the "Clocked Jocks" tally for future runs through the coliseum. See how many you can knock down in one combo—the number turns from red to yellow when you've set a record.

GAP BETWEEN FLOATS 10 TIMES

Location	Near the frat house
Time	2:00
Awards	$250
How unlocked	Complete 'Spine Transfer over the wall'
Unlocks	Nothing

Atiba Jefferson

"Hey we can get some great photos here, the parade just started. Gap between any of the floats 10 times before the parade ends."

The parade around California College may only consist of three floats, but those floats each contain plenty of vert for the skater looking to liven up the party. The floats drive slowly down the street and around the corner by the parking garage during this objective. Although they move slow enough so as to not pose too great a challenge for the gapping skater, the corner does make it much more difficult. With a little practice, this objective can be completed before the parade hits the parking garage.

Each of the floats is slightly different; the first float features two wave-like spines to the rear with a kicker ramp of sorts at the front. It's possible to ollie from the front of this float to gap to the middle one. The middle float is essentially a rectangular pool with vertical walls. Although a Spine Transfer from the middle float to the yellow one leading the parade is possible, jumping to the float at the rear is not. To hit that particular **Float Gap!!!**, ollie while pressing Up. Since falling off the floats is the only real hazard in this challenge, it's a good idea to refrain from rotating.

From the start, Spine Transfer across the blue float and ollie to the middle float. From there, Spine Transfer back and forth between the float in the middle and the yellow one at the front. Although it's possible to ollie back to the blue float, it is a slightly riskier maneuver as the front end of that float is much narrower.

GRIND HAPPY

The **Float Gap!!!** can also be made while grinding, which is especially helpful if the skater happens to fall off the floats. Wallie into a grind on the edge of the middle float and ollie across onto either of the other floats to score another gap and to rejoin the parade.

Pro Challenges

COMBO THE BENCHES, STAIRS AND FLAG POLES

Location	Near the security office
Time	0:10
Awards	$500
How unlocked	Complete a Pro-Specific Challenge
Unlocks	Nothing

Jamie Thomas
"Hey, this is my favorite spot. Let's see what you can get going on the Benches, Stairs and the Flag Pole Ledge."

Hop into a speedy clockwise grind on the bench directly behind Jamie and trick off of it and into a grind on the concrete ledge running down the stairs towards the flagpole for the **Plaza Jump!** gap. Ollie off the end of the ledge and into a Special Grind on the edge of the basin by the flagpole. Carefully balance the skater for a couple of laps around the flagpole and ollie out of the grind to end the string once enough points have been reached.

GET ALL 4 MASTER'S LIP GAPS

Location	In front of the Philosophy building
Time	1:00
Awards	$500
How unlocked	Complete a Pro-Specific Challenge
Unlocks	Nothing

The Professor
"Would you like to be a super-genius like me? Get a Master's Degree in all 4 disciplines! Get all 4 Lip Gaps!"

The Professor wants to see you hold a lip trick on the uppermost railing or ledge of each of the four class buildings. Leap up and hold a lip trick until that building's respective Master's gap is triggered.

Kick off the educational process by skating across the grass to the wooden ramp straight ahead. Launch into a lip trick on the roof of the Philosophy building for the **Masters in Philosophy Lip** gap. Drop down and turn towards the Fine Arts building. Leap from the banked wall where the race with the inline skater had begun and lip trick on the angled roof above for the **Masters in Fine Arts Lip** gap.

PROSET SETUP

This objective requires that ProSet1 be turned on. ProSet 1 was unlocked by completing the 'Get the Pro Score' objective.

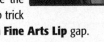

Trick over the wooden spine in the middle of the plaza and sky up to the 'Swallow Pride' banner. Hold a lip trick on the banner for the **Masters in Engineering Lip**. The last degree to get is in English. Roll down the slope towards the brown building with the arch and use either of the quarter pipes against it to leap into a lip trick on the rooftop for the **Masters in English Lip.**

COLLECT PRO C-O-M-B-O

Location	Near the coliseum entrance
Time	2:00
Awards	$500
How unlocked	Complete a Pro-Specific Challenge
Unlocks	ProSet2

Ollie the Magic Bum

"Hello Mr. president! I lost my C-O-M-B-O letters again, sir... Think you can grab 'em for me? Pleeeaaase!"

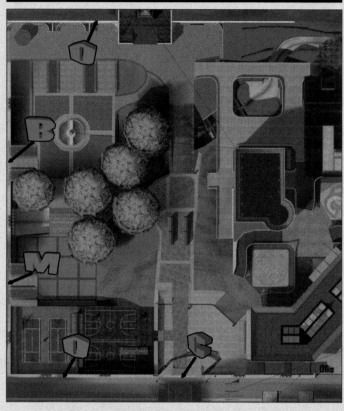

Wallride up into a grind on the right-hand edge of the beige wall near Ollie and carry the grind across the arch to the "C" and the "O". Quickly ollie into a manual near the tennis courts and ride up the quarter pipes near the back wall. Continue the grind off to the right towards the security office. Grind past the "M" and the second "B" all the way to the end of the wall. Ollie out of the grind while angling to the right to land in yet another grind on the cable leading to the wall near the benches. Grind this cable onto the wall to grab the final "O" and ollie off near the clock tower to touch down safely.

BEAT BOB'S 3 BEST COMBOS

Location	At the basketball court
Time	0:30
Awards	$500
How unlocked	Complete a Pro-Specific Challenge
Unlocks	Nothing

Bob Burnquist

"Hey, ready for a tour around College? Let's hit three of my favorite spots. See if you can beat my best combos."

The first combo starts on the basketball court and must be in excess of 20,000 points. Charge the left-hand spine and gap over to the ramp on the right while performing a healthy combo such as a 540 Varial Heelflip to Indy. Revert the landing and manual back through the court towards the Engineering building. Trick down the stairs to another manual tap into a lip trick atop the concrete ramp straight ahead.

The second combo starts from atop the banner above the ramp just mentioned. This time the skater must best Bob's score of 40,000 points in a single combo. Make the drop and skate towards the railing on the left side of the steps. Grind the railing and trick into a Special Grind on the fence behind it for the **Grind Hop to the Fence** gap. Trick into another Special Grind on the tennis net, manual towards the ramp near the wall, and go boost the score some more with a 720 Indy to Revert.

Bob scored 60,000 points in one combo by dropping in from the banner on the opposite side of the Engineering building. Show him what's really possible from that starting spot by hopping into a Special Grind on the ledge in front of the Philosophy building. Grind across the steps and onto the curved ledge to the left. Trick off the end of the ledge and into a Special Grind on the logs lying in the grass for the **Log Hop** gap. Grind the logs towards the concrete "river" and ollie into one more grind, either on the logs to the right or the ledge straight ahead.

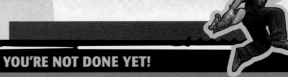

GET A SICK SCORE: 250,000 POINTS

Location	On the roof of the Fine Arts building
Time	2:00
Awards	$500
How unlocked	Complete a Pro-Specific Challenge
Unlocks	ProSet6

Tony Hawk
"All right, check this out. I set up some ramps for some big roof-to-roof gaps. Give it a shot, and see if you can beat my sick score. Oh yeah—don't fall."

YOU'RE NOT DONE YET!

Just because all 21 objectives have been completed doesn't mean there's nothing left to do at the College. In addition to partaking in a friendly game of tennis with Bjorn, there's plenty of dough to collect, as well as 40 gaps to find.

Ride the elevator up to the roof of the Fine Arts building and meet up with Tony to test your skill on the final College objective. He's set up numerous ramps at the edge of the roof and wants to see someone score 250,000 points!

Fire up the Special Meter by tricking heavily between the two ramps right in front of the starting point. Gap across to the left while performing a 540 Heelflip to Airwalk and Revert the landing. Manual across the rollercoaster-like rooftop towards the ramp in the corner and go big with a high-scoring special trick such as Tony's Indy 900—preferably from the Switch stance. Revert back to another manual and head straight across to the ramp used earlier. Tack another valuable Special Trick onto the string, Revert into another manual and use that corner ramp one more time for a pair of quick aerials to boost the multiplier.

SIDE MONEY

RACKETEERING: PLAY TENNIS WITH BJORN

Time	Infinite
Awards	$500

Bjorn
"Hey! Skater-person! You wish to play me in tennis, no?"

Skate up to the tennis racket on the ground near the tennis courts and talk to Bjorn. The skater has nothing to lose when playing Bjorn and money to gain. Manage to beat Bjorn in one service game of tennis (scored 0, 15, 30, 40, game) and skate away with an extra $500. Of course, there is a catch. Bjorn isn't going to let some "skater-person" use his racket, you have to use the skateboard as a racket!

The Jump Button is used to serve the ball and to swing the board. The closer the skater is to the ball when the Jump Button is pressed, the harder the ball is returned. Bjorn can just about return any "slow" or "medium" hit ball, so be sure to get good and close for that "hard" hit—the old man has a bit more trouble with those! Press Left and Right to run down the ball as Bjorn returns it and also to direct the shot. Typical rules of tennis apply; if the ball bounces twice on one side of the net, the person who hit it gets a point. Also, any ball hit out of bounds is a point for the opponent.

GARBAGE DAY

Time	0:40
Awards	Thirty $50 bills

Spine Transfer into the garbage truck parked outside the frat house to trigger the Garbage Day mini-game. Several garbage trucks make their way towards one another from either end of the street. It's up to the skater to try and snag as many of the $50 bills floating above the street as possible. Spine Transfer back and forth between the garbage trucks to pluck the cash out of the air. Another way of getting a lot of the cash is to use a single truck as a halfpipe and repeatedly leap into the air while the truck motors down the street.

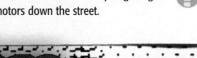

GAP CHECKLIST

[1] PLAZA JUMP!　　　　　　　　　**10 POINTS**

Grind the upper edge of the benches near the security office and leap across the walkway and into a grind on the steps leading down towards the flagpole.

[2] KIOSK HOP!　　　　　　　　　**25 POINTS**

Grind the roof of either kiosk and leap into a grind on the silver handrail by the stairs.

[3] LOG HOP!　　　　　　　　　**25 POINTS**

Grind any of the logs near the river or clock tower and leap into a grind on a different log. The logs cannot be touching.

[4] RAIL CROSS!　　　　　　　　　**25 POINTS**

Grind one of the handrails in the coliseum and ollie into a grind on a parallel rail.

[5] RAIL HOP!   25 POINTS

Grind a handrail and ollie across to another rail and continue the grind.

[6] BACHELORS IN ENGINEERING GRIND   50 POINTS

Ride up the concrete vert ramp and into a grind on the lowermost rail of the Engineering building.

[7] BACHELORS IN FINE ARTS GRIND   50 POINTS

Ride up the concrete vert ramp and into a grind on the ledge of the Fine Arts building.

[8] BANNER GAP!   50 POINTS

In 'Grind Down Officer Tom's Banners' only. Grind across the beige wall near the street, tearing down the large red banners as you go.

[9] BENCH TO BENCH!   50 POINTS

Grind the picnic tables in front of the Philosophy building and ollie into a grind on the benches behind the Fine Arts building.

[10] CLASS TRANSFER!   50 POINTS

Use the vert ramp beside the elementary school to transfer to the roof near the parking garage.

[11] COLISEUM TRANSFER!   50 POINTS

Use the vert ramp at either end of the coliseum corridor to transfer over the wall towards the frat house or the Philosophy building. This gap is bidirectional.

[12] GATEWAY GAP!   50 POINTS

Grind over any of the blue arches on the beige wall near the street.

[13] GRIND HOP TO THE FENCE   50 POINTS

Leap from a grind on either the tennis net or the handrail into a grind on the chainlink fence near the basketball court.

[14] HIGH ROAD HOP!   50 POINTS

Grind up any of the open gates near the parking garage and hop into a grind on the power lines above.

[15] HIGHER LEARNING!   50 POINTS

Transfer a grind from any of the blue handrails near the Woodward elementary school to the roof over the front door of the school.

[16] INTO THE RIVER!   50 POINTS

Use the vert ramps flanking the end of the river to transfer down into the culvert.

[16] INTO THE RIVER!   50 POINTS

Use the vert ramps flanking the end of the river to transfer down into the culvert.

[17] NICE EQUIPMENT!   50 POINTS

Grind the awning of Billy's Sporting Goods Store. Leap from a grind on the bike racks out front.

[18] OFF THE LIL KICKER!   50 POINTS

Air off the tiny concrete kickers at the top of the steps around the edge of campus near the security office.

[19] OVER THE STAIRS!   50 POINTS

Hit the vert ramps near the steps by the basketball court and transfer up and over the staircase.

[20] SCHNITZEL'S FOR ALL!   50 POINTS

Leap from the plywood on the back of the pickup truck into a grind on the ledge below the Schnitzel World sign.

[21] SKIPPIN' OVER!   50 POINTS

Transfer a grind between any two ledges or fence posts.

[22] THROUGH THE FRAT WINDOW GRINDING! 50 POINTS

Break through the window of the frat house while grinding the concrete ledge on the left or the Schnitzel World sign.

[23] THROUGH THE FRAT WINDOW MANUALING! 50 POINTS

Manual across the top of the concrete vert ramp to the left of the frat house and break through the window. Can perform this gap exiting either window also.

[24] THROUGH THE FRAT WINDOW OLLIEING! 50 POINTS

Ollie through either frat house window from the wall to the left or the awning on the right.

[25] BACHELORS IN ENGINEERING LIP 100 POINTS

Leap into a stall on the lowermost rail of the Engineering building.

[26] BACHELORS IN FINE ARTS LIP   100 POINTS

Leap into a stall on the lower ledge of the Fine Arts building.

[27] MASTERS IN ENGINEERING GRIND 100 POINTS

Grind the upper edge of the Engineering building, particularly the rail holding the "Swallow Pride" banner.

[28] MASTERS IN ENGLISH GRIND   100 POINTS

Leap into a grind on the roof of the English building.

[29] MASTERS IN FINE ARTS GRIND   100 POINTS

Grind the roof of the Fine Arts building.

[30] MASTERS IN PHILOSOPHY GRIND   100 POINTS

Grind the roof of the Philosophy building.

[31] ON THE FENCE!   100 POINTS

Leap off the vert ramps between the b-ball court and the river and land in a grind on the top of the chainlink fence near the court.

[32] OUT OF THE RIVER!   100 POINTS

Sky up and out of the river off the ramped grate at the end and land on either of the ramps alongside it.

[33] MASTER'S IN ENGINEERING LIP   150 POINTS

Leap into a stall on the roof of the Engineering building.

[34] MASTER'S IN ENGLISH LIP   150 POINTS

Leap into a stall on the roof of the English building.

[35] MASTERS IN FINE ARTS LIP   150 POINTS

Leap into a stall on the roof of the Fine Arts building.

[36] MASTER'S IN PHILOSOPHY LIP   150 POINTS

Leap into a stall on the roof of the Philosophy building.

[37] TRAFFIC LIGHT GRIND   150 POINTS

Leap into a grind on any of the traffic lights.

[38] CLOCK TOWER GRIND!   200 POINTS

Jump into the black void behind the clock tower and carry a grind on the wire on the other side all the way to the roof of the English building.

[39] OVER THE RIVER!   200 POINTS

Use the vert ramps flanking the end of the river to transfer up and over the culvert.

[40] TONY'S PRO CHALLENGE GAP   500 POINTS

Gap between the moving halfpipes in Tony's Pro Challenge.

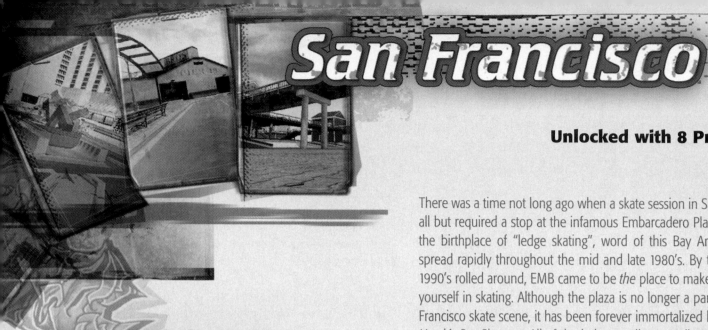

San Francisco

Unlocked with 8 Pro Points

There was a time not long ago when a skate session in San Francisco all but required a stop at the infamous Embarcadero Plaza. Arguably the birthplace of "ledge skating", word of this Bay Area hot spot spread rapidly throughout the mid and late 1980's. By the time the 1990's rolled around, EMB came to be *the* place to make a name for yourself in skating. Although the plaza is no longer a part of the San Francisco skate scene, it has been forever immortalized here in *Tony Hawk's Pro Skater 4*. All of the ledges, walkways, rails, and even the fountain have been faithfully recreated to offer the digital street stylist the chance to tear it up for old time's sake. The trip down memory lane isn't only for Bay Area skaters; the EMB was also featured in the San Francisco "Streets" course in the original *Tony Hawk's Pro Skater*.

LEVEL GOALS

Unlocked Objectives

Get a High Score: 50,000 points
Collect the S-K-A-T-E letters
Collect the C-O-M-B-O letters
Find the Messenger's 5
Missing Packages
Axle Stall the 3 pier signs
Feed the 4 angry sea lions
Manual the Overhead Walkway
Beat Muska's 3 best combos
Darkslide the waterside railing
Medal the Competition

Locked Objectives

Get a Pro Score: 100,000 points
Save Painter Neal
Race the Bike Messenger
Race to get the Camera
Manual, Gap and Manual the setup
Nail the tricks they yell out

Pro Challenges

Get a Sick Score: 300,000 points
Collect Pro C-O-M-B-O
Manual the Pad in both directions
Do the Spine Transfer-Transfer
Grind the Blockers off the Ledges

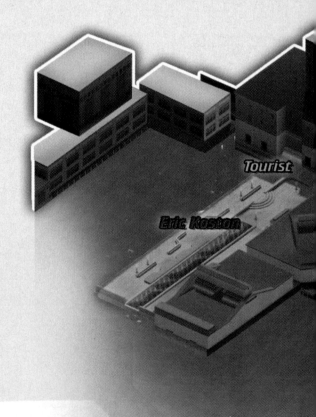

Tourist

Eric Koston

The EMB is a thing of the past, but the same can't be said for the renowned San Francisco seaport. All it takes is a roll across the street to find numerous vert and flatground opportunities lurking amongst the many piers. Skaters will find ramps and rails of all sizes and elevations around every bend, whether it be near the Slam Brothers warehouses at Pier 18 or down by the Fisherman's Wharf area.

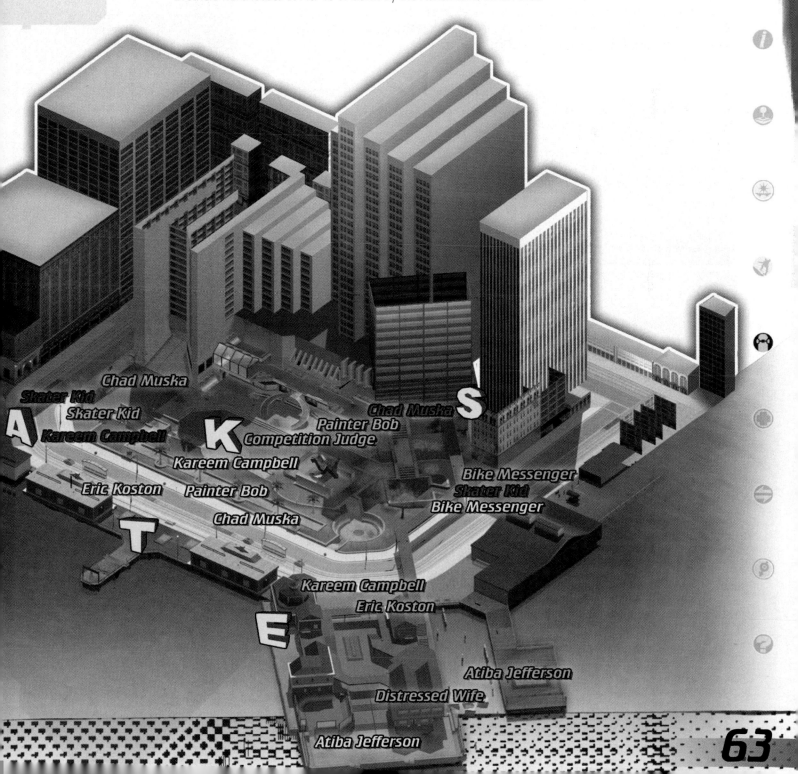

Chad Muska

Skater Kid

Skater Kid

A

Kareem Campbell

K

Competition Judge

Painter Bob

Chad Muska

S

Kareem Campbell

Eric Koston

Painter Bob

T

Chad Muska

Bike Messenger

Skater Kid

Bike Messenger

Kareem Campbell

Eric Koston

E

Atiba Jefferson

Distressed Wife

Atiba Jefferson

Amateur Challenges

GET A HIGH SCORE: 50,000 POINTS

Location	In front of the Pier Market
Time	2:00
Awards	$250 and a Stat Point
How unlocked	N/A
Unlocks	Get a Pro Score: 100,000 points

Charge the right-hand quarter pipe under the overhead walkway and launch into a 540 Pop Shove-It to the Japan, Revert the landing, and manual across the street towards the EMB ledge. Pop into a grind on the EMB, ollie over the stone block that breaks up the ledge for the **EMB Ledge Hop** gap and land in a Special Grind. Kickflip out of the grind and onto the street to end the line.

COLLECT THE S-K-A-T-E LETTERS

Location	Above the film store in the plaza
Time	2:00
Awards	$250 and a Stat Point
How unlocked	N/A
Unlocks	Nothing

Painter Bob
"Oh man! I'm supposed to set up a contest billboard, but my partner lost all the letters that spell S-K-A-T-E. Could you help me find 'em?"

 Skate past Painter Bob and launch off the vert ramp in the corner to grab the "S" while transferring to ground level.

 Head across the plaza towards the circular stairs in the center and Beanplant up the steps to grab the "K".

 Spine Transfer off the ramp left of the garage doors on Pier 18 to grab the "A" on the roof.

 Skate across the roof of the warehouses towards the main fishing wharf and leap into a grind on the cable running between the two lampposts.

 From the "T", continue grinding the edge of the buildings near the water towards Pier 39. The "E" is off the corner of the brown building.

COLLECT THE C-O-M-B-O LETTERS

Location	Across the street from Pier 18
Time	2:00
Awards	$250 and a Stat Point
How unlocked	N/A
Unlocks	Nothing

Skater Kid
"All right, it's like this: Collect the C-O-M-B-O letters, but y'all got to do it in one single-trick combo."

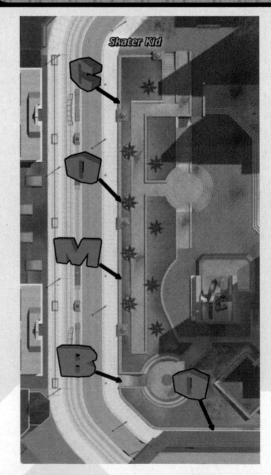

All five letters are positioned on the curbside ledge in Embarcadero Plaza; getting them is just a matter of linking enough grinds together without bailing. Ollie into a grind on the EMB ledge and jump over the blocks of stone that interrupt the ledge for the **EMB Ledge Hop** gap. Keep the grind alive for the first four letters, then carefully ollie over the sidewalk to the ledge on the corner and grind to the left to find the "O".

FIND THE MESSENGER'S 5 MISSING PACKAGES

Location	Under the overhead walkway
Time	2:00
Awards	$250 and a Stat Point
How unlocked	N/A
Unlocks	Race the Bike Messenger

Bike Messenger
"Man... I took a header and lost all my packages. Can you help me find them? There's 5 of them missing. Thanks!"

All five packages are near the sidewalk on the side of the street near the piers. Cross the street towards the first warehouse and transfer the ramps near the garage door to get the first package and to snag the **Ramp to Ramp** gap.

Skate over to the main fishing wharf and transfer the red and white quarter pipes that flank the central rampway. The second package floats above the handrail.

Follow the street to the beige building near the bus stop and ollie into a grind on the ledge and leap across the gap near the garage door to pick up the next package and the **Ledge Hop** gap.

The fourth package is obtained the same way as the third, but on the building further down the street, near Pier 18.

Transfer the ramps near the garage door of the warehouse at Pier 18 to grab the final package.

LIP TRICK THE 3 PIER SIGNS

Location	On the stage at the edge of the fishing pier.
Time	2:00
Awards	$250 and a Stat point
How unlocked	N/A
Unlocks	ProSet2 and 'Race to get the camera'

Atiba Jefferson
"Yo! Try this one. Put down a lip trick on each of the three pier signs. The trick? Check it!"

The three pier signs are each near the water's edge on the edge of the fishing wharf. To complete this objective, leap off the quarter pipe under each of the signs and perform the lip trick indicated (Axle Stall by default) by pressing Right + Grind. Approach the ramps straight on and let go of the Jump Button while in the air to avoid accidentally grinding the top of the sign.

Leap into the trick on the pier sign behind Atiba and hold it for the **Pier Perch** gap. Hold the stall for the gap to trigger and jump down to safety to receive credit for the stunt. Although there's plenty of time to follow the walkway back towards the street and around the area with the sea lions, advanced players may wish to ollie

the guardrail and grind the ropes across to the other pier. Either way, perform the lip trick on each of the two pier signs on the neighboring pier to complete Atiba's challenge.

FEED THE 4 ANGRY SEA LIONS

Location	On the Bay Walk near the sea lions
Time	2:00
Awards	$250 and a Stat point
How unlocked	N/A
Unlocks	Nothing

Distressed Wife

"Please! Help my husband! He tried to get a picture, but he fell over the rail, and the sea lions aren't very happy about it! Distract them so that he can climb back up here!"

There's only one way to distract an angry sea lion and that's with food! But where can a skater find enough food to lure four sea lions off their platforms? There just so happens to be four fisherman in the area who have left their catch dangling off the edge of the pier. In order to distract the sea lions, you must first distract the fishermen.

Skate up to each of the fishermen and grind across the bench behind them to knock their tackle boxes onto the floor. Quickly turn around and grind the railing near the water while the fisherman is picking up his gear. The board's trucks will cut the line holding his catch, dropping it into the water. Circle around the pier doing this to each of the four fishermen. Each time their fish hits the water, one of the sea lions swims over to feast. Once all four sea lions have been distracted, the stranded husband is free to rejoin his lady on dry land. Only one of the fishermen is on the same side of the pier as the Distressed Wife, the other three are on the other side.

MANUAL THE OVERHEAD WALKWAY

Location	On the overhead walkway near the fishing wharf
Time	0:10
Awards	$250 and a Stat point
How unlocked	N/A
Unlocks	Manual, Gap and Manual the setup

Eric Koston

"Hey, you see these cones I put down here? I want to see if you can do a manual all the way from the first set to the second set!"

Although this objective is easier with someone with great Manual Balance, such as Rodney Mullen, it can be accomplished with any of the skaters provided one or two Stat Points have been used to bolster their Manual Balance. Either way, the key to this challenge is to trick out the Special Meter for increased speed and even better balance.

Since the cones are all the way down the walkway near the street, there's plenty of room to trick in and out of a grind on the railing. Ollie into a Tailslide on the railing, Pop Shove-It into a 50-50 grind to further boost the Special Meter and leap into a manual on the walkway before the first set of cones for the **Manualin** gap. Keep the Jump Button depressed for speed and balance all the way to the second set of cones to complete the objective and to complete the **Manual Pleasure** gap.

BEAT MUSKA'S 3 BEST COMBOS

Location	Near the left-hand staircase in Embarcadero Plaza
Time	0:30
Awards	$250
How unlocked	N/A
Unlocks	Nail the tricks they yell out

Chad Muska

"Yo, you think you can beat my best 3 combos in a row? Man, you can't even front on that one, kid. You best go home to pre-school."

Chad Muska has laid down three different combos that he thinks can't be beat. It's time to prove him wrong by exceeding his scores of 4,000 points, 5,000 points, and 6,000 points at the three spots he has picked out.

Muska's first spot is at the top of the staircase where you found him. Ollie into a Noseslide on the railing and Shove-It into a manual at the bottom. Balance the wheelie up the ramp to the right and pull off an Invert. This boosts the multiplier to 4, which is more than enough to beat the goal score of 4,000 points.

The second combo begins on the roof of the warehouses near the water. Tailslide the pipe towards the beige building to the left and Pop Shove-It across the gap to continue the grind on the pipe on the other building. Flip trick across to the next pipe and continue the grind. Trick off the end of the building and land on the pavement below.

The final combo begins on the concrete walkway near the ledge with the metal bars on it, they're *supposed* to prevent skaters and bikers from grinding them. Ha! Boneless into a Boardslide on the right-hand ledge and carry the grind down the stairs for the **Hubba Ledge** gap. Ollie into a different grind at the flat section to boost the multiplier and trick into a grind on one of the curbs at the base of the stairs to finish the combo.

DARKSLIDE THE WATERSIDE RAILING

Location	Behind the Slam Brothers warehouses
Time	0:30
Awards	$250 and a Special Trick Slot
How unlocked	N/A
Unlocks	Nothing

Tourist
"Um, excuse me... it's our first visit and we really want to remember it! Could I get a photo of you with my hubby? Fill your Special Meter, then do a Darkslide on the waterside railing!"

One Darkslide coming up! Transfer a grind across the series of curvy pipes for the **3rd n Army Hop n Grind** gap to max out the Special Meter and use the quarter pipe at the end of the pier to turn around. Jump into a grind on the handrail near the water and ollie into a Darkslide by tapping Down, Left + Grind before reaching the couple. Hold the grind the length of the handrail to score the **3rd Army Grind** gap while you're at it!

MEDAL THE COMPETITION

Location	Embarcadero Plaza
Time	1:00
Awards	$250
How unlocked	N/A
Unlocks	Nothing

Competition Judge
"You, uh, want to compete? First place goes to the skater with the best two out of three runs!"

Unlike the competition at the College level, this one features full one-minute heats and is not restricted to combos. Not only that, but the area used for competition is much larger. Dozens of ramps and ledges have been set up throughout the plaza, creating one outstanding street course. Although a pair of scores over 80,000 points is enough to bring home the bronze, those looking for gold need to score at least 100,000 points in two of the three runs.

The design of the course allows for several potent scoring lines to be laid down back-to-back. For starters, drop in and angle towards the funbox on the left. Pop into a grind on the riser and carry it directly onto the ledge below. Hop into a grind on the upper ledge beyond the mini vert ramp for the **EMB Ledge Hop** and manual off the end towards the ramps near the street. Launch into an aerial Special Trick, Revert into a manual upon landing the trick into one more grind to finish it off.

Another option is to transfer the rollin with a quick combination of tricks and Revert the landing. Manual across the course to the large funbox on the right and hop into a Special Grind on the wooden railing. Trick off the end and into a manual towards the lone quarter pipe nearest the street and launch into an aerial Special Trick.

One more potent scoring line can be initiated on the lone vert ramp off towards the street. Launch into a Special Trick, Revert the landing and manual towards the tiny kicker near the ledge. Leap across the gap and land in a Special Grind on the wooden railing. It's easy to overshoot the railing, so try to Boneless across the

gap instead of relying on the kicker. From there, grind the steps of the plaza back towards the starting point and go big off the vert ramp near the rollin.

GET A PRO SCORE: 100,000 POINTS

Location	In the center of Embarcadero Plaza
Time	2:00
Awards	$250
How unlocked	Complete 'Get a High Score: 50,000 points'
Unlocks	Nothing

Kareem Campbell
"See you handled a little business. Let me see you step it up though. You got two minutes to get this Pro Score. Let's get it popping now."

Skate past Kareem and turn around. Kickflip into a Bluntslide on the lengthy curb leading down the ramp to the left towards the bowl. Press the Grab Button to switch up the grind to a Smith Grind then to a Crooked Grind to boost the multiplier. Double Heelflip off the ledge near the gray tree to land in a manual in the bowl. Leap out of the bowl and into a Special Trick, Revert the landing, and throw down a combination of grab and flip tricks with rotation to finish the string and to score over 100,000 points.

SAVE PAINTER NEAL

Location	Whale watching pier
Time	0:30
Awards	$250
How unlocked	N/A
Unlocks	Nothing

Painter Neal
"Look—if you really wanna help me—clean the bird turd off of the railing in one shot pole-to-pole-I'm paintin' that next..."

Hop into a grind on the railing near the lamppost and grind around the curve at the end of the pier and back towards the lamppost on the other side. The extra weight of the skater on the railing is enough to cause the old pier to crumble into the sea. And before you know it, Painter Neal is dangling from the sign just feet over the gaping maw of a hungry shark!

Painter Bob
"What!? My partner's in trouble? Somebody's got to help him!! Don't just stand there, do something!!"

Painter Bob is right, something has to be done to get rid of that shark! Right where Painter Bob was working is a large stone ball that is roped to the ledge. Leap into a grind on the ropes and balance a lap around the stone to completely shred the rope. This allows the stone ball to roll off its

pedestal and go crashing down the slope towards the shark. Painter Neal has been saved!

RACE THE BIKE MESSENGER

Location	Near the public parking lot
Time	0:30
Awards	$250
How unlocked	Complete 'Find the Messenger's 5 Missing Packages'
Unlocks	Nothing

Bike Messenger
"Let's see if you can match my blinding speed! We'll race down to the Slam Brothers warehouse and back. You better skitch cars, or you'll never keep up!"

The race against the Bike Messenger is from the warehouse near the public parking lot at the edge of town to the Slam Brothers warehouse at Pier 18. Although the Bike Messenger gets off to a quick start and will likely make it to the turnaround point first, a little Skitchin' helps you pull into the lead on the way back.

PROPER SKITCHIN'

Be sure to grab a hold of the bumper at the corner of the car instead of in the middle when going for the Skitch. It's much easier to get the speed boost when letting go of the car's bumper if you don't have to swerve to avoid the car.

Once the race starts, roll out into the street and grab a hold of a car's bumper to start Skitchin'. Round the bend in the road and tap Down to let go of the car for a speed boost. Turn around at the orange marker near the warehouse and quickly latch onto another car. Let go once the road is clear and drift to the left of the road to cut the bend in the road by the fishing wharf—the Bike Messenger sticks to the sidewalk and has a longer distance to travel. Cut back across the street towards the finish line on the right after the bend in the road to win the race.

Race back down the road to the second bus stop near the rails on the right. If possible, skitch a ride for some extra speed, but the Special Meter should still be fully lit from the trip across town. Skate past the dude at the bus stop to take the camera back..

Bringing an empty camera back to Atiba isn't going to help that cover shot—you've got to get film for it first! Cut across the street and ollie over the walkways and ledges by the plaza towards the stores. Skate past the electronics store to grab some film for the camera.

Boneless over the ledges in the plaza to get back to the street and continue towards the pier where Atiba was last seen. Return the camera to Atiba before time runs out to complete the task.

RACE TO GET THE CAMERA

Location	Beside the glass-enclosed pool on the wharf
Time	0:25
Awards	$250
How unlocked	Complete 'Axle Stall the 3 pier signs'
Unlocks	Nothing

Atiba Jefferson
"Yo, the guy who has my camera is missing. Can you find him and bring me my camera? Hey Yo, hurry up, these guys are going to break out if I don't get a cover shot."

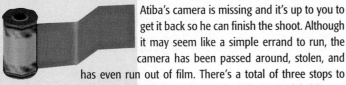 Atiba's camera is missing and it's up to you to get it back so he can finish the shoot. Although it may seem like a simple errand to run, the camera has been passed around, stolen, and has even run out of film. There's a total of three stops to make and 12 seconds are added to the clock with each successful visit.

The guy Atiba lent the camera to is standing on the corner near Pier 18. Head out onto the street and either Skitch a ride down the road or, if no cars are

 passing by, grind the EMB ledge to gain speed. Add enough tricks to max out the Special Meter now and the skater will have enough speed for the entire objective. The guy standing near the stone building doesn't have the camera anymore—it's been stolen by the guy at the bus stop!

MANUAL, GAP AND MANUAL THE SETUP

Location	Between the beige warehouses
Time	0:10
Awards	$250
How unlocked	Complete 'Manual the Overhead Walkway'
Unlocks	ProSet3

Eric Koston
"See this plywood rollercoaster I set up? Okay—I want to see you manual, clear the gap, back to manual, all in one combo."

CHOOSE YOUR PRO

This challenge is much easier with a skater who excels in Manual Balance. Select either Rodney Mullen or Eric Koston for best results.

Eric has set up a series of plywood tabletops and he wants to see if anyone can manual across the first set, ollie the gap, and continue the manual to the far end. Approach the first set of boards and ollie into a manual. Hold the Jump Button down for speed and balance across the rollercoaster for the **On the Way** and **Halfway There!** gaps. Jump the gap in the and land continue the manual on the far side for the **Cleared the Gap**, **Almost**, and **Made It!** gaps.

If the skater is having trouble clearing the gap between the rollercoasters, consider tricking in and out of a grind on the ledge of the nearby building before starting the manual. Take advantage of the 10 seconds at the start of the goal by turning around and Kickflipping into a grind on the ledge and performing a Double Heelflip out of the grind. This lights the Special Meter which gives the skater better overall speed, jumping ability, and balance!

NAIL THE TRICKS THEY YELL OUT

Location	By the EMB ledge
Time	1:00
Awards	$250
How unlocked	Complete 'Beat Muska's 3 Best Combos'
Unlocks	Nothing

Chad Muska
"Hey what's up? You think you got mad flip tricks? Well let's see if you can flip in and flip out on this ledge right here at EMB, man – classic skate spot."

Here in San Francisco skaters have 60 seconds to perform 16 flip tricks while ollieing in and out of grinds on the EMB ledge. Although the tricks can be performed while ollieing in and out of a continuous grind (when hitting the **EMB Ledge Hop** gap for example) the grind must be performed on the edge nearest the street for the tricks to count.

Despite having fewer tricks to perform than the challenge back at the College, this goal is much harder to complete. Not only do many of the tricks required diagonal button presses on the controller, but time is eaten up by grinding and turning around. For this reason it's important to start from one end of the ledge and trick and grind all the way to the far end before returning to the street. This increases the chance of a costly bail, but it allows the skater to clear multiple tricks off the list at once... possibly even those that appear after the trick has been performed!

This objective is best done with a skater who has at least moderate Grind Balance and Flip Speed ratings. Make adjustments to the Stat Points as necessary.

Pro Challenges

GET A SICK SCORE: 300,000 POINTS

Location	Near the Slam Brothers Warehouse
Time	2:00
Awards	$500
How unlocked	Complete a Pro-Specific Challenge
Unlocks	Nothing

Kareem Campbell
"So you back again? Oh, so you taking care of biz. I like that, I like that. This time let me see you get a Sick Score. You got 2 minutes to do it. Now show and prove it."

Use the concrete kicker near Kareem to trick into a grind on the wire directly overhead. Grind the wire to max out the Special Meter and Kickflip into a Special Grind on the wire to the left for the **Wire Hop** gap. Trick off the end of the wire into a manual and aim for the left-hand quarter pipe under the walkway. Bust out a Special Trick while transferring over the blue handrail to the other ramp to snag the **Ramp to Ramp** gap. Revert the landing and manual across the street towards the EMB ledge. Hop into a grind and mix in a couple of **EMB Ledge Hop** gaps to boost the multiplier some more. Trick back onto the street to cash in those points.

COLLECT PRO C-O-M-B-O

Location	Near the Slam Brothers Warehouse
Time	2:00
Awards	$500
How unlocked	Complete a Pro-Specific Challenge
Unlocks	Nothing

Skater Kid
"That last line was tight, but I bet you can't lay down this C-O-M-B-O. Remember: all the letters, one combo!"

Use the concrete planter to pop into a grind on the right-hand edge of the bus stop to snag the "C" and quickly hop into a grind on the adjacent wire. Jump across to a grind on the other wire to grab the first "O" then immediately hop back to the wire on the left to collect the "M". Hop down off the wire and into a manual and air off the right-hand ramp to get the "B" from near the walkway. Revert the landing and manual towards the warehouse in the corner by the water. Grind the banked wall to pick up the final "O".

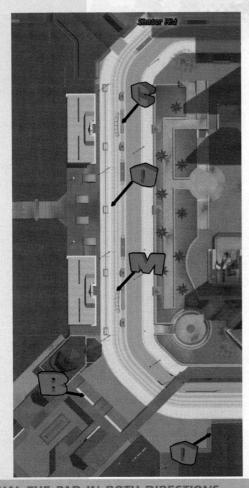

Skater Kid

DO THE SPINE TRANSFER-TRANSFER

Location	On the upper walkway in the Plaza
Time	0:06
Awards	$500
How unlocked	Complete a Pro-Specific Challenge
Unlocks	ProSet1

Chad Muska

"Yo Yo Check Yo! I got the crazy transfer for ya, kid! You're gonna have to go between these two quarter pipes and clear the grass channel while transferring the spine at the same time. Bust that!"

With only 6 seconds on the clock, there's no time to waste! Charge the quarter pipe behind Chad and trick down to the one below to gain momentum. Hit the wooden spine he set up on an angle towards the grass channel and Spine Transfer as soon as the skater lifts above the coping on the ramp. If done correctly the skater airs over to the second spine, but leans forward in order to Spine Transfer.

GRIND THE BLOCKERS OFF THE LEDGES

Location	On the upper walkway in the Plaza
Time	0:30
Awards	$500
How unlocked	Complete a Pro-Specific Challenge
Unlocks	Nothing

Skater Kid

"Yo! Cop-and-a-half up there killed the Hubba ledge with his dumb blockers. Think you can grind 'em off dog? You're gonna have to distract him first, because he's pretty agro. Good luck yo."

MANUAL THE PAD IN BOTH DIRECTIONS

Location	Near the pipes behind Pier 18
Time	2:00
Awards	$500
How unlocked	Complete a Pro-Specific Challenge
Unlocks	Nothing

Eric Koston

"All right, you see this manny right here? I want to see a manual down and back in one combo. That's it!"

Ollie into a manual on the pad near the stones and balance it all the way to the far end for the **Pad Manual West** gap. Ollie into a manual on the ground, use the quarter pipe to Revert back around towards the pad, and hop into another manual on it for the **Heading Back** gap. Balance all the way to the far end to grab the **Pad Manual East** gap and to complete the objective.

PROSET SETUP

Be sure to turn off ProSet1 if it's on, as Chad's spines get in the way of the route to the fire alarm.

The normal path up to the Hubba ledge is being guarded by some crazy copper—one who won't hesitate to take a swing at a skater. He's going to have to be distracted if those blockers are to come down. Luckily, there's a fire alarm on the wall just below the Hubba ledge. The blockers are on both sides of the ledge and with only 30 ticks on the clock, it's going to be tight! Get to it.

Follow the path around to the left towards the fountain and ollie up the three steps towards the fire alarm. Wallride across the fire alarm in a left-to-right direction to not only set it off, but to be lined up to make the **Rampin' Up** transfer to the walkway above.

The copper won't stray from his post for more than 10 seconds. Quickly leap into a grind on the ledge above the uppermost blocker; there are 6 blockers on each side of the ledge. Once at the bottom, double back towards the fire alarm and wallride it one more time. Make the leap back to the upper walkway and hop into a grind on the other side of the ledge before time runs out.

Although it may seem that the skater would be able to grind the second set of blockers off the ledge while the cop is standing guard, it's not possible. The cop will rush in and clean the skater's clock before the lowest blocker is off the ledge. The cop must be lured away from his post before each grind down the Hubba ledge.

CASH ICONS / PRO SETS / GAPS

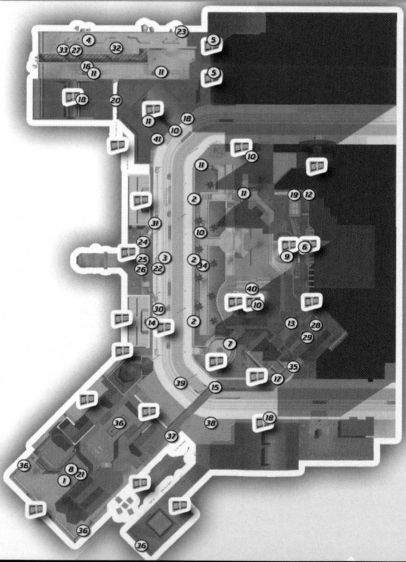

GAP CHECKLIST

[1] DOWN THE STAIRS   **25 POINTS**
Ollie down the stairs on the main fishing wharf.

[2] EMB LEDGE HOP   **25 POINTS**
Transfer a grind between any two ledges in Embarcadero Plaza.

[3] WIRE HOP   **25 POINTS**
Grind one of the wires for the electric busses and hop across to the wire paralleling it.

[4] 3RD N ARMY HOP N GRIND   **50 POINTS**
Transfer a grind across all four pipes sticking out of the ground behind the Slam Brothers warehouses near Pier 18.

[5] 3RD N ARMY LIP   **50 POINTS**

Lip trick on either of the rails above the quarter pipes behind Pier 18.

[6] BENCH GRIND   **50 POINTS**

Grind the series of park benches in front of the Nokia store.

[7] BOWL TRANSFER   **50 POINTS**

Get in the bowl and sky up and over either of the walkways.

[8] CLEARED THE STAIR SET   **50 POINTS**

Ollie down the both small sets of stairs on the main fishing wharf.

[9] DOWN THE SPIRAL   **50 POINTS**

Grind down any of the white curvy railings in the plaza.

[10] FOUNTAIN RAMP TO RAMP   **50 POINTS**

Transfer between the two halfpipes built into the fountain in the plaza.

[11] GAP THE BUS   **50 POINTS**

Skate over to the broken down busses behind Pier 18 and use the ramps on either end to launch up and over one of them.

[12] GONE HIGH   **50 POINTS**

Skate up the curvy ramp in the plaza to the walkway above the stores and transfer from the vert ramp in the glass-covered area up to the 3rd floor ledge.

[13] HUBBA LEDGE   **50 POINTS**

Grind down or up the lengthy concrete ledge with the bars across it. This ledge leads down from the office building to the right when facing Embarcadero Plaza from the street.

[14] LEDGE HOP   **50 POINTS**

Transfer a grind between two different stone ledges near the piers.

[15] MANUALIN   **50 POINTS**

Only possible in the 'Manual the Overhead Walkway' objective. Manual through the first set of cones on the walkway.

[16] MECHANIC POP 50 POINTS

Ollie over a mechanic as he slides out from under a bus near Pier 18.

[17] OVERHEAD GRIND HOP   **50 POINTS**

Grind one of the railings on the overhead walkway and ollie into a grind on the other railing.

[18] RAMP TO RAMP   **50 POINTS**

Transfer most any two vert ramps that are near one another. This includes the ramps on top of the warehouses as well as those near the street.

[19] RAMPIN UP   **50 POINTS**

Transfer from the vert ramp in either corner of the plaza to the one on the second floor walkway.

[20] TC'S ROOF GAP TOO   **50 POINTS**

Gap between the roofs of the Slam Brothers warehouses on Pier 18.

[21] UP THE STAIRS   **50 POINTS**

Ollie up the stairs on the main fishing wharf.

[22] UP TO THE WIRES   **50 POINTS**

Ollie off the concrete kickers near the rails and land in a grind on the wires for the electric busses.

[23] 3RD ARMY GRIND   **100 POINTS**

In 'Darkslide the Waterside Railing' only. Grind the length of the rail near the water.

[24] ALMOST   **100 POINTS**

In 'Manual, Gap and Manual the Setup' only. Continue manualing along the rollercoaster towards the gap.

[25] CLEARED THE GAP   **100 POINTS**

In 'Manual, Gap and Manual the Setup' only. Ollie across the gap in the rollercoaster.

[26] HALFWAY THERE!   **100 POINTS**

In 'Manual, Gap and Manual the Setup' only. Clear the gap and land in a manual on the second part of the rollercoaster.

[27] HEADING BACK   **100 POINTS**

In 'Manual the Pad in Both Directions' only. Manual across the pad and start the manual back in the other direction.

[28] HUBBA SPINE!   **100 POINTS**

Spine Transfer over either of the spine ramps in ProSet1. Must complete 'Do the Spine Transfer-Transfer' to unlock ProSet1.

[29] HUBBA TRANSFER!   **100 POINTS**

Transfer between the spine ramps in ProSet1. Must complete 'Do the Spine Transfer-Transfer' to unlock ProSet1.

[30] MADE IT!   **100 POINTS**

In 'Manual, Gap and Manual the Setup' only. Manual all the way to the end of the second portion of the rollercoaster.

[31] ON THE WAY   **100 POINTS**

In 'Manual, Gap and Manual the Setup' only. Start manualing along the rollercoaster.

[32] PAD MANUAL EAST   **100 POINTS**

In 'Manual the Pad in Both Directions' only. Complete the second leg of the manual.

[33] PAD MANUAL WEST   **100 POINTS**

In 'Manual the Pad in Both Directions' only. Manual the first leg of the pad.

[34] WIRE BREAKIN!!!   **200 POINTS**

In 'Save Painter Neal' only. Grind the cable that is wrapped around the large stone ball.

[35] MANUAL PLEASURE   **250 POINTS**

Only possible in the 'Manual the Overhead Walkway' objective. Hold the manual from the first set of cones to the second set at the end of the walkway.

[36] PIER PERCH   **250 POINTS**

Leap into a stall on any of the large wooden signs on the fishing piers.

[37] ANDREW'S PRO CHALLENGE PIER   **300 POINTS**

Gap the pier in Andrew's Pro Challenge.

[38] ANDREW'S PRO CHALLENGE WALKWAY   **600 POINTS**

Gap the overhead walkway in Andrew's Pro Challenge.

[39] ANDREW'S PRO CHALLENGE BOWL   **1000 POINTS**

Gap into the EMB bowl in Andrew's Pro Challenge.

[40] ANDREW'S PRO CHALLENGE FOUNTAIN   **1000 POINTS**

Gap the fountain in Andrew's Pro Challenge.

[41] ANDREW'S PRO CHALLENGE STREET   **1000 POINTS**

Gap the street in Andrew's Pro Challenge.

Alcatraz

Unlocked with 16 Pro Points

No trip to the Bay Area is complete without a stop at Alcatraz. This maximum security prison-turned-tourist attraction is one of the largest courses in the game and features several levels of skating action, both inside and out! All the parts of Alcatraz are featured here: the docks, the switchbacking path leading up the hill, the parade grounds, exercise yard, and even the cell block!

Alcatraz marks a ramping up of the learning curve and features a couple of the hardest objectives in the game, both on the amateur and pro level. Spend some time getting familiar with the course and be sure to study the maps to figure out where all of the many stairwells lead. Although it may seem from the many rails and ledges that Alcatraz is the private domain of the street skater, there are several opportunities for the vert skater, they're just well-hidden. While it's true that lengthy grinds can be initiated at every turn, there's a lot of air to be had inside the cell block, after draining the pools, and even inside the water tower!

LEVEL GOALS

Unlocked Objectives

Get a High Score: 55,000 points
Collect the C-O-M-B-O letters
Collect the S-K-A-T-E letters
Take the Alcatraz tour
Revert Madness
Dunk 30 tourists
Distract the guards
Semi Flip the bulldozer
Find the Guard's Keys
Medal in the competition

Locked Objectives

Get a Pro Score: 100,000 points
Pull off Mullen's tech trick
Ranger Ron's Skitch Launch
Escape from Alcatraz
Nail the tricks they yell out
Bullseye Launch

Pro Challenges

Get a Sick Score: 400,000 points
Collect Pro C-O-M-B-O
Pose for 6 Pictures
Manual the Switchbacks
Nail the Mega-Combos they yell out

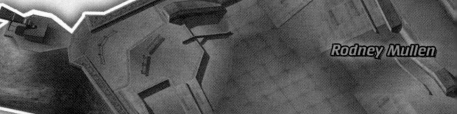

Rodney Mullen

The Warden

Bam Margera
Elissa Steamer

Prisoner

Elissa Steamer

Tourist

Security Guard
(inside)

S

Security Guard

Security Guard

K

A

Ranger Ron

Atiba Jefferson

Rodney Mullen

The Warden

Atiba Jefferson

Elissa Steamer

Prisoner

The Warden

T

E

Bam Margera

Rodney Mullen

Ranger Ron

GET A HIGH SCORE: 55,000 POINTS

Location	At the second switchback
Time	2:00
Awards	$250 and a Stat Point
How unlocked	N/A
Unlocks	Get a Pro Score: 100,000 points

Elissa Steamer
"You think you're good, cousin? Try to beat this High Score!"

Ride up the graffiti-covered concrete slope and let loose with a hidden combo such as the 540 Shove-It, Revert the landing, and Nose Manual towards the elevated railing across from the bathroom and ollie into a grind to the left. Trick down to the median on the switchback and Special Grind downhill towards the demolished building. Flip trick into a manual and leap from the banked wall into a stall on the ledge of the building straight ahead for the **Lip Extension** gap.

COLLECT THE C-O-M-B-O LETTERS

Location	Near the demolished building
Time	2:00
Awards	$250 and a Stat Point
How unlocked	N/A
Unlocks	Nothing

The Warden
"Look kid, if you're going to skate, at least help out. OK? Pick up the letters lying around here, would ya? See if you can get 'em all in one combo too."

Jump into a grind on the left-hand edge of the half pipe behind the Warden to grab the "C" and ollie off the end onto the pipe on the next building for the first "O". Ollie from the end of the pipe to the edge of the tin roof near the "M" and grind towards the docks for the "B". Leap down onto the docks and manual towards the ramp in the distance to snag the final "O" from the air above.

COLLECT THE S-K-A-T-E LETTERS

Location	On the roof of the cell block
Time	2:00
Awards	$250 and a Stat Point
How unlocked	N/A
Unlocks	Nothing

Tourist
"Hey, can you collect S-K-A-T-E in 2 minutes?"

The "S" is visible over Your Buddy's shoulder. Gather up some speed and ollie off the kicker on the side of the roof to grab it out of mid-air. Don't jump too far, or you'll have to backtrack to get the next letter.

Descend the hill to the first switchback. The "K" is directly in front of the dirt path leading down the side of the hill towards the demolished buildings.

Skate down the dirt trail beyond the "K" and launch from the kicker at the end to a grind on the dilapidated tower to the right of the one still standing for the **Bomb Drop Professional** gap. Aim for the "A" and grind down the spiraling relic.

Grind the railing on the edge of the island that leads from the demolished building down towards the tour boat.

Continue the grind after grabbing the "T". Ollie into a grind on the gutter of the building to the right when the railing angles inward for the **Gutter Punk** gap. Leap off the kinked end of the gutter into the air to grab the "E"

TAKE THE ALCATRAZ TOUR

Location	Near the dock
Time	1:00
Awards	$250 and a Stat Point
How unlocked	N/A
Unlocks	Ranger Ron's Skitch Launch

Ranger Ron
"Well, you ready to take the tour? Ranger Bob thinks he's faster than me. Since you have your own wheels, you can skitch on my cart, and we'll do the one minute tour. That'll show him."

SOUND ADVICE

Since you're likely to be focusing on the Balance Meter during this challenge, the white text messages detailing what needs to be done may get missed. Enter the 'Sound Options' screen from the Options Menu and lower the volume of the music and raise that of the sound effects. This makes it easier to hear what Ranger Ron is asking you to do. Not only that, but his entire rant is pretty funny too!

Ranger Ron is not only looking to shatter Ranger Bob's record for the fastest tour ever, but he's in the mood to talk some trash while doing it. Ride up to the rear of the cart and press Up to skitch a ride around the island. Be warned, however, that Ranger Ron is going to ask you to help out with a few chores along the way.

There are three birds on a ledge near the demolished buildings that need to be scared away. Press Down to let go of the tram and use the ramp below the birds to air up and scare them away. Grab back on to the cart's bumper and continue with the tour.

The next stop is at the parade grounds (the area under construction). Let go of the cart and grind the yellow ledge on the left to knock down the empty kegs that Ranger Bob left lying around. With the kegs knocked off the ledge there's only one stop left to make. Skitch the cart up to the cell block.

Ranger Ron had good reason to loathe Ranger Bob—the guy's hypnotizing tourists to aid in his evil plot of world domination! Once the cart comes to a stop outside the cell block let go and hop into a grind on the ledge near the lighthouse to take him out!

REVERT MADNESS

Location	Next to the demolished building
Time	1:00
Awards	$250 and a Stat point
How unlocked	N/A
Unlocks	Nothing

Atiba wants to get some shots of you incorporating the Revert into a scoring line. Use the banked walls inside the demolished building as a half pipe and perform the tricks he calls out.

Things start out simple enough—just launch off one of the ramps and perform a Revert while landing to prove you know how to link vert tricks. Next up is a Revert to a manual. Take to the air again, Revert the landing, and tap into either a Manual or Nose Manual while after the slide is over. Ollie out of the manual to end it cleanly.

Atiba Jefferson

"Hey, have you seen the pros? They revert to string their tricks together! Try a revert in this demolished building."

Atiba's final request is for a lip trick to a Revert to a manual. Use the ramps near the walls on the sides of the building to leap into a stall on the ledge above, hold it for a second, and Revert into a manual while landing.

DUNK 30 TOURISTS

Location	On ground level under the walkway
Time	0:30
Awards	$250 and a Stat point
How unlocked	N/A
Unlocks	Bullseye Launch

Bam is up to his old tricks; this time he wants to see 30 tourists get tossed into the frigid waters of San Francisco Bay. There's not a lot of time to satisfy Bam's hunger for mischief so don't hesitate before jumping into a grind on the brick ledge behind him. Take out the 8 tourists near the ledge and continue the grind across the rope and onto the boat. Keep grinding for an entire counter-clockwise lap around the boat to knock another 9 tourists into the drink. Ollie off the stern of the boat to regain solid ground.

Bam Margera

"All right listen you little worm! This'll be good. See how fast you can knock 30 of these random pathetic tourists into the water. Go!"

Take out the 3 tourists near the curved railing by the plywood ramp and go after the 7 on the dock by grinding the railing that wraps around its perimeter. By now, those near the brick ledge have had time to climb out of the water. Hurry over and toss them back in!

DISTRACT THE GUARDS

Location	Under the grates near the tunnel.
Time	0:20
Awards	$250 and a Stat point
How unlocked	N/A
Unlocks	Escape from Alcatraz

Prisoner

"Hey, listen! I escaped 40 years ago and they ain't caught me yet! Make a ruckus while I make a run for it! Knock over stuff and hit that foghorn!"

ELEVEN PLUS ONE

Although the in-game tally suggests that there are 12 garbage cans, the number actually represents the 11 garbage cans *and* the foghorn. There are only 11 garbage cans, not 12.

Although the security around Alcatraz these days is mostly there to prevent shoplifting in the visitor's center, white and black striped pajamas can still attract quite a crowd. Lend the decrepit escapee a helping hand by knocking down 11 garbage cans en route to the foghorn. The commotion distracts the security guards long enough for the Prisoner to make it to the roof of the cell block. The garbage cans must be toppled in order and the skater has 3 seconds added to the clock for each one hit.

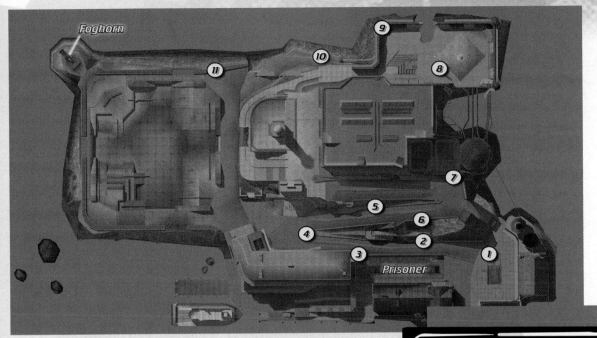

Foghorn

Prisoner

Knock over the garbage can directly in front of the starting point, then grind the right-hand curb to take out the next one. The third can is on the left just before the first switchback, take it out, ollie across to the ledge near the turn for the **Switchback Shuffle** gap and to topple another garbage can.

The next two cans are on the left and right-hand sides of the middle leg of the hill climb, respectively. Round the bend at the second switchback and carefully slide into a grind on the large pipe below the water tower. Grind through the 7th garbage can and around towards the exercise yard. Ollie into a grind on the benches to knock over the next garbage can. Only three garbage cans left to get, then it's on to the foghorn!

RELEASE THE GRIND

Press the Revert Button after grinding past the final garbage can to make the skater end the grind. It's a difficult transition from that particular ledge (especially the outer edge) to the railing near the foghorn. It was a long trip up to the parade grounds, it's best to not risk flying off the island!

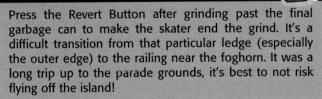

Cross the exercise yard to the pipe under the watchtower in the far corner. Grind this pipe cautiously as there are several sharp turns in it just beyond the next garbage can. Ollie off the end of the pipe and fly straight through towards the next can. Land in a grind on the railing near the edge and keep it going towards the hole. Hit the **Clear the Hole** gap and continue grinding towards the foghorn. Ollie to the next ledge for the **Ledge-2-Ledge** gap. Grind past the final garbage can and onto the railing that wraps around the red foghorn in the corner for the **Foghorn** gap.

SEMI FLIP THE BULLDOZER

Location	In the construction area
Time	0:45
Awards	$250 and a Special Trick slot
How unlocked	N/A
Unlocks	Pull off Mullen's tech trick

Rodney Mullen
"Hey let's try something different. Get SPECIAL, then try the Semi-Flip over the whole bulldozer!"

Use the vert ramps and/or the ledges in the construction area to max out the Special Meter and charge either of the blades on the bulldozer. Use the blade as a ramp and leap up and over the dozer. Input the default commands for the Semi Flip (Right, Down + Grab) while airborne and land it cleanly to complete Rodney's challenge and to gain the **Over the Dozer!** gap.

FIND THE GUARD'S KEYS

Location	Outside the cell block
Time	1:00
Awards	$250
How unlocked	N/A
Unlocks	Nail the tricks they yell out

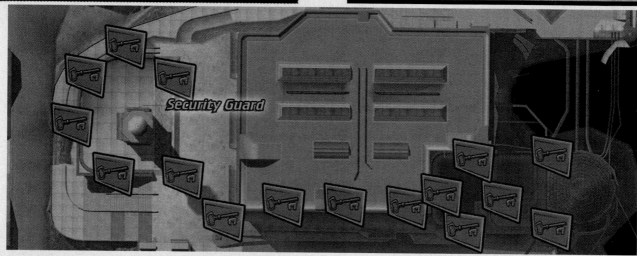

Security Guard
"Hey, it seems I've lost all my keys! And what's worse, I've locked myself out of the cell block! If you can find all my keys for me, I'll let you skate inside."

The Security Guard's keys have been scattered throughout the area and it's up to the skilled skater to find them all. Although it's not necessary, this goal is safer to complete when the pool near the water tower has been drained. Grind the ledge around the pools to hit the drain valve and return to the cell block to talk with the Security Guard.

Grab the first key next to the Security Guard and skate across the grass to the ledge that wraps around the lighthouse. Grind this ledge in a counter-clockwise direction to pick up another 5 keys, then start towards the walkway to the right of the cell block. Grab the key on the ground and Wallride into a grind on the ledge near the cell

block windows to gather up another 4 keys. Ollie off the ledge and into a grind on the upper lip above the pools to collect the final 5 keys.

GO DIRECTLY TO JAIL!
Complete this objective and the Security Guard unlocks the doors to the cell block. Skaters are sure to find the many vert ramps and spiraling rails inside quite enjoyable.

MEDAL IN THE COMPETITION

Location	Corner of the construction area
Time	0:30
Awards	$250
How unlocked	N/A
Unlocks	Nothing

The Warden
"You know, tourism's been a little low lately. Let's organize a competition to raise ticket sales!"

The Warden wants to cash in on the popularity of skateboarding; can you blame him? Help him boost ticket sales by competing in a contest in the parade grounds area of Alcatraz. One look at the numerous ledges, walls, and fences and it becomes clear that this course is much better-suited for the street skater. That's not to say that there is no vert, it's just a little out of the way. Take a moment to assign two or more Special Grinds to the available Special Trick slots.

Skaters first entering this contest may be somewhat shocked at the relatively short time limit, but thirty seconds is more than enough to link together a six-figure scoring string. Although countless grind-heavy lines can be assembled in this area utilizing many of the different "ledge and rail" gaps, few offer higher reward with less complexity than the line detailed here.

Hop into a grind on the yellow ledge to the left of the Warden and flip trick across the gap to continue the grind towards the foghorn for the **Ledge-2-Ledge** gap. Grind to the end and trick into a counter-clockwise grind around the foghorn for the **Ledge-2-Rail** and **Foghorn** gaps. Trick back onto the very same yellow ledge used before, but this time Special Grind it back towards the Warden for the **Rail-2-Ledge** gap. Hit the **Ledge-2-Ledge** gap once again, this time landing in a different Special Grind. Ollie out of the grind and onto the chainlink fence in the corner to snag another **Ledge-2-Rail** gap. Although this line can easily be extended for hundreds of thousands of points by tricking on and off the many ledges in the area, those with less experience at lengthy scoring lines may wish to simply trick out of the grind and claim the five perfect scores the judges are waiting to award.

Although the above scoring line can be used over and over to continuously earn perfect marks from the judges, those looking to add some air to their run need not go away empty-handed. For starters, at any time during the run, mix in an air-based Special Trick by manualing towards one of the quarter pipes along the base of each wall. Unfortunately, these ramps may prove to be too far apart for linking together back-to-back air tricks.

Another option for those seeking some aerial acrobatics, albeit a riskier one, is to grind the yellow ledge towards the bathroom near the switchback and manual towards the ramps against the bathroom. Although these ramps are outside the competition area, a savvy skater can alley-oop up and over the bathroom doorway for the **Bathroom Break** gap, Revert the landing, and manual back into the competition area before touching down. Of course, if the skater touches down outside the competition area, the entire trick string is squandered.

GET A PRO SCORE: 100,000 POINTS

Location	In the exercise yard
Time	2:00
Awards	$250
How unlocked	Complete 'Get a High Score: 55,000 points'
Unlocks	Nothing

Elissa Steamer
"See you handled a little business. Let me see you step it up though. You got two minutes to get this Pro Score. Let's get it popping now."

Zip past Elissa and trick between the two concrete ramps flanking the bleachers. Revert the landing and manual across the baseball diamond and hop into a Special Grind on the middle pipe. Flip trick off the end of the pipe and land in a grind on the ledge beside the staircase. Transfer the gap to the next ledge for the **Switchback Shuffle** gap and grind all the way towards the bathroom at the next turn. Kickflip out of the grind to finish the run.

PULL OFF MULLEN'S TECH TRICK

Location	Under the elevated walkway
Time	2:00
Awards	$250
How unlocked	Complete 'Semi Flip the bulldozer'
Unlocks	ProSet1

Rodney Mullen
"Hey, let's try some flip in and flip out stuff! Let's hit this ramp and let's give it a shot. Keep your head up and stay light."

Rodney has set up a couple of ramps near the tin roof by the tunnel and wants to see a skater demonstrate their technical prowess. Keep the Jump Button depressed while cruising downhill towards the ramp and perform the required flip trick off the ramp. Land in a manual on the tin roof and balance across to the far

edge for the **Tin Roof Manual** gap. Flip out of the manual and down onto the ground to complete this objective.

RANGER RON'S SKITCH LAUNCH

Location	Near the lighthouse
Time	1:00
Awards	$250
How unlocked	Complete 'Take the Alcatraz tour'
Unlocks	ProSet3

Ranger Ron
"Ok—Here's the idea: I could set up a ramp over there and if you skitched on my tram, I bet you could clear both those restrooms, all the way to that parade ground bank."

This isn't just about Skitchin' a ride on the tram and clearing some restrooms. Heck no, Ranger Ron has set up a pair of ramps designed to send the skater hurtling out over the water (350 ft) or straight into the sky (150 ft). Talk about a *Professional Bomb Drop*... YIKES!

Grab a hold of the right-hand corner of the tram and Skitch up the hill. Ranger Ron brings his buggy to a screeching halt just before the

ramp he set up. Don't wait that long to let go. Instead, press Down to release from the Skitch before the ground surface changes so as to get a speed boost going into the ramp. Perform a few tricks while airborne to max out the Special Meter and land as cleanly as possible. Charge the right-hand ramp and let loose out over the open water. Reaching 350 ft is easier if the transition from the Skitch to the parade grounds was done cleanly. Just be sure to hit the ramp straight on so as to not go out of bounds.

Now it's time for the high-jumping test. Grab onto the left-hand corner of the tram and repeat everything done moments ago. The only difference is this time the skater needs to aim straight for the vert ramp on the left. Gain enough speed during the Skitch and boost the Special Meter during the initial jump to reach and exceed 150 ft.

SPEED BUMPS

Having trouble reaching the required distances? Try redistributing some of the earned Stat Points to increase Speed, Air, and Hangtime. That ought to do the trick!

ESCAPE FROM ALCATRAZ

Location	On the roof of the cellblock
Time	1:00
Awards	$250
How unlocked	Complete 'Distract the guards'
Unlocks	Nothing

Prisoner
"Great work on running interference! Now we just need to make it to the docks! I can get there, but I need your help. Collect all those supplies and meet me down at the ferry!"

Those who had a tough time collecting the Security Guard's keys may want to continue practicing that challenge before attempting this one. There are 33 supply items that must be gathered up en route from the top of the lighthouse to the docks. This is arguably the most difficult amateur challenge at Alcatraz and is actually more complex than some Pro Challenges.

Jump into a grind on the rope leading down to the flagpoles and hold it to the first skylight. Grab the item near the pipe between the skylights and approach the lip of the roof just to the left of the stairwell in the corner. The next three supply items all hover over this stairwell and are only reachable by launching off the lip of the roof and transferring over the stairwell and into the pool far below for the **Sludge Bomb** gap.

MAKE OR BREAK

The dive off the roof into the pool below is essentially an all or nothing moment in this objective. If the skater doesn't grab all three supply items hovering above the stairwell, immediately select "Retry Last Goal" in the Pause Menu. The in-game tally of supplies should be at 6 before the **Sludge Bomb** gap triggers.

Once in the pools, ride up the side and into a grind on the stone ledge above the yellow stripe. Once all 4 supply items near the pools have been collected, head off down the walkway beside the cell block. Grab the item on the cell block and wallride up to the 12th item on the ledge above.

Jump off the ledge, grab the item on the left, and hop into a grind on the handrail. Grab the items on the rail and over the **Broken Walk** gap and continue on towards the exercise yard. Grind the rail down towards the gap in the wall, transfer the ramps for the **Don't Look Down!!** gap and roll out the landing over the pitcher's mound. The in-game tally at this point should read 21 of 33 supply items found.

Ollie into a grind on the left-hand pipe leading out towards the water tower and grind towards the items in the distance. Ollie off the pipe as soon as it begins to slope upwards to pluck the 3 items out of the air. Land in a grind on the pipes down by the demolished building to snag the **Pipe Smoker** gap and another item, thereby bringing the total to 26.

MAKE OR BREAK REVISITED

It is imperative to leap off the pipe at just the right moment in order to grab all of the supplies out of the air. Wait until the pipe goes under the water tower and ollie straight ahead for the items just as the pipe curls to the right. If the tally doesn't say 26 of 33 after grabbing the one on the pipe below, hit start to pause and retry.

Grind the lip of the banked wall straight ahead and jump through the window in the demolished building to continue the grind. Grab the 29th item near the railing and hop into a grind to grab the next item around the corner.

The final three supply items are all near the tourists and the boat. Grind the ledge near the tourists and continue across the rope to the boat. The last supply item is on the upper deck of the boat; ride up either of the walkways at the rear to get it.

NAIL THE TRICKS THEY YELL OUT

Location	Inside the cell block
Time	1:00
Awards	$250
How unlocked	Complete 'Find the Guard's keys'
Unlocks	Nothing

Security Guard
"Man, I hear voices from the cells sometimes. They call out the strangest things. I can't get 'em to shut up. Won't nothing appease them?"

It's time for another game of falling tricks! The guard inside the cell block needs you to perform 17 tricks of the ghosts' choosing. Use the vert ramps as a halfpipe and go back and forth performing each of the tricks as they appear in the lower-right corner of the screen.

It's a good idea to session the pipe for a while before initiating the challenge so as to know how much speed and height to expect. Also, this is a good time to bust out the skylights above as they can block the player's view of the action if the skater gets too high.

BULLSEYE LAUNCH

Location	In the exercise yard
Time	Infinite
Awards	$250
How unlocked	Complete 'Dunk 30 tourists'
Unlocks	ProSet2

Bam Margera
"All right, this idea is really stupid, but I don't care. I set up this haggard ramp and inflated a target out in the water. See how many points you can rack up."

Bam has constructed a large roll-in that feeds into a loop-de-loop right near the edge of the exercise yard. That's not all—there's a large floating target in the water with a bull's-eye painted on it. The green, blue, yellow, and red areas of the target are worth 10, 20, 50, and 100 points, respectively.

There are 10 jumps to rack up at least 400 points, an average 40 points per jump. The key to racking up a high score is to stay to the center of the ramp when going through the loop and to have the board lined up perfectly with the end of the ramp when jumping. This way, even if the speed isn't perfect, the skater is likely to hit the 50-point ring.

Since the skater's individual Air, Speed, Ollie, and Hangtime attributes affect the length of his or her jump, some experimenting is needed to fine tune how much speed is required. See how far the skater jumps when the Jump Button is pressed at the very start of the attempt versus when it is pressed while going through the loop. Keep in mind that even at a Speed rating of 4, the skaters have enough speed to get through the loop without pressing the Jump Button.

Pro Challenges

GET A SICK SCORE: 400,000 POINTS

Location	On the roof of the cell block
Time	2:00
Awards	$500
How unlocked	Complete a Pro-Specific Challenge
Unlocks	Nothing

Elissa Steamer
"Cuz—from up here you should be able to rack up some killer points. Try to get this Sick Score."

Remember the path to all of the supplies in the 'Escape From Alcatraz' objective? Well, in case you didn't pick up on it then, it was a very potent scoring line!

Flip into a grind on the skylight behind Elissa and transfer it to the next skylight for the **Skylight-2-Skylight** gap. Manual towards the lip of the rooftop to the left of the stairwell and Special Trick off the side of the building and into the pool below for the **Sludge Bomb** gap. Revert the landing and quickly tap into a Special Grind on the upper ledge of the pool to take a clockwise trip around both pools. Manual the sidewalk leading towards the lighthouse and Wallie up into a grind on the ledge below the cell block windows. Trick off the end of the ledge and into another Special Grind on the railing straight ahead. Transfer the grind across the **Broken Walk** gap and around towards the exercise yard. Boost the multiplier with a couple of last quick flip tricks down the stairs towards the baseball diamond to ensure the 400k!

COLLECT PRO C-O-M-B-O

Location	Near the parade grounds
Time	2:00
Awards	$500
How unlocked	Complete a Pro-Specific Challenge
Unlocks	Nothing

The Warden
"Okay, I've got more letters to clean up, but I don't think ANYONE can do this! See if you can hit all of the letters in a single massive line!"

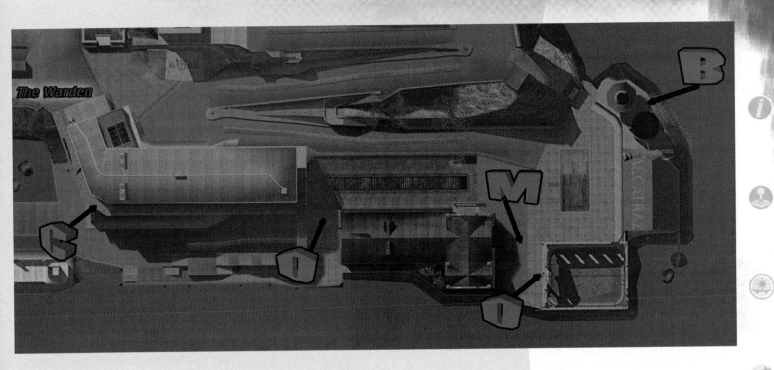

The Warden

Roll down the walkway on the left side of the building and ollie the part that has collapsed and land in a manual. Grab the "C" and Wallie into a grind on the ledge of the building. Grind out over the lamp and ollie to the peak of the building with the tunnel for the "O" and the **Rooftop Hero** gap. Grind the peak to the left, ollie the other roofline and continue grinding to the very edge. Ollie off the roof to grab the "M" and land in a grind on the side of the demolished building. Hold the grind onto the powerhouse and ollie off the edge and into a grind on the railing that wraps around the smokestack for the **Rail-2-Rail** gap. Grind a quick lap around the smokestack and ollie off the end to grab the "B" and to land in a grind on the backside of the powerhouse. Hold this grind as it curves back towards the demolished building and transfer the grind onto the rail that runs along the center of the structure to snag the final "O". Ollie through the glass window and land in a grind to pick up some cash and the **Skate Attic** gap as well.

POSE FOR 6 PICTURES

Location	Near the powerhouse
Time	0:40
Awards	$500
How unlocked	Complete a Pro-Specific Challenge
Unlocks	Nothing

Atiba Jefferson
"Yo! You ready to snap some shots? Then start out with a transfer over that busted-ass wall."

Atiba still has 6 shots left on his roll of film and wants to get some action shots from all over Alcatraz. He's got very specific instructions for each shot, so make sure to perform the right trick at the right spot—he's set up some orange arrows to mark the spots that he wants to shoot. Atiba adds 20 seconds to the clock for each successful photograph.

For the first trick, perform the specified grab trick (Up + Grab Button) while transferring from the wall of the powerhouse to the interior of the demolished building. Hit the ramp just below the last window on the powerhouse and transfer up and over the wall and gutter for the **Over the Crumbled Wall** gap.

Exit the demolished building and head up the road towards the parade grounds. Atiba wants to see a lip trick on the Red Power Railing, so launch off the "Red Power" graffiti and perform the lip trick (Up + Grind Button) to trick on the yellow railing high above. Release the trick once the **Red Power Railing** gap triggers.

The next stop is at the hole in the parade ground walkway leading over to the exercise yard. Circle around the parade grounds and perform the requested flip trick (Down + Flip Button) while ollieing the gap in the walkway next to the lengthy staircase. Land it cleanly to snag the **Clear the Hole** gap and to move on to the next location.

The fourth photo is to take place at a spot you've likely gapped across countless times already—the chasm in the exercise yard. Head down the stairs and transfer the pair of vert ramps while performing the required flip trick (Right + Flip Button). Grab the **Don't Look Down!** gap and move on.

The fifth photo is to take place on the roof of the cell block. Ollie the bench near the baseball diamond and enter the stairwell there to be teleported to the rooftop. Avoid the skylights and cross the roof towards the flagpoles. Atiba wants to get a shot of you lip tricking (Down + Grind Button) on top of either of the flagpoles.

The final photo is to tale place on a wire that may have gone undetected until now. Ride up and over the stairwell in the northern corner of the cell block rooftop and start grinding the pipe leading to the water tower. Ollie off the end of the pipe and onto the cable leading to the smokestack for the **Holy F@&#!** gap. Land on the cable in a Bluntslide (Down, Down + Grind Button), grab the cash, and ollie down to the ground.

THOSE AREN'T ON THE LIST!

If you've been scrolling through the gaps checklist looking for **Salute!** and **Holy F@&#!**, don't. A handful of gaps such as these have been hidden throughout *Tony Hawk's Pro Skater 4* and only the guys at Neversoft know their whereabouts. Consider it a challenge from Neversoft. How many can you find?

MANUAL THE SWITCHBACKS

Location	At the top of the switchbacks
Time	0:10
Awards	$500
How unlocked	Complete a Pro-Specific Challenge
Unlocks	Nothing

Rodney Mullen

"Hey this one's super tough, only for the pros! Start a manual here, go down both sets of switchbacks, all the way to the bottom! Think you got the balance?"

Think you got balance? Here's a chance to prove it! Rodney wants to see you start a manual at the top of the road and hold it, without interruption, all the way down the switchbacks to the powerhouse. This is definitely one of the hardest challenges and demands a lot of patience from those who attempt it.

Successfully manualing the switchbacks boils down to how well you use the Up and Down buttons to keep the manual balanced, but there are a couple of ways to better the odds. For starters, this objective is the sole domain of those with a maximum Manual Balance rating—adjust the Stat Points accordingly. Second, the skater should use the allotted 10 seconds to trick off the banked wall of the bathroom to light the Special Meter. When fully lit, the Special Meter improves the skater's abilities in all areas, especially in mile-long manuals! Just be sure to ollie into the manual uphill from Rodney before the clock stops.

It is much easier to navigate the hairpin turns when manualing slower. For this reason, it's important to refrain from pressing the Jump Button until just before the second turn. Let the skater inch around the first turn for the **Switchback 1st Leg** gap and roll over to the right-hand side of the road. Once near the second turn, press and hold the Jump Button to gain speed and swing into the turn sharply so as to avoid the banked wall near the building on the outside. Once the **Switchback 2nd Leg!!** gap is triggered, you're in the home stretch. Manual down the hill towards the powerhouse and touch down safely after the **MANUALED THE WHOLE THING!!!** gap is awarded. Phew!

NAIL THE MEGA-COMBOS THEY YELL OUT

Location	Near the pools
Time	1:00
Awards	$500
How unlocked	Complete a Pro-Specific Challenge
Unlocks	Nothing

Security Guard

"You youngins are all SLACKERS! You need to learn how to work for your living! Now drop and give me all these tricks all in one combo!"

The entire list of tricks that appear on the side of the screen need to be performed in one combination. However, since it would be impossible to leap from the pool and perform 8 tricks all at once, the combo must include some fancy Reverts and manuals too! Since the trick list can be somewhat overwhelming at first, try breaking it up into four pairs and perform a pair of the tricks during each jump. Revert the landing and immediately tap into a manual. Although the skater will likely lift off the far side of the pool before the manual appears in the scoring string at the bottom of the screen, failure to manual causes the combo to be dropped.

There is a way to make this challenge much easier. Continue selecting the 'Retry Last Goal' option in the Pause Menu until a set of tricks appears that has minimal diagonal button presses and several duplicated tricks. Although this may seem like cheating, all but the best skaters are going to require several attempts before success is reached anyway. The randomly-generated list of tricks is bound to produce an easier "Mega-Combo" eventually. Just be ready for it when it does!

SIDE MONEY

HITTING THE LONG BALL

Time	Infinite
Awards	$25 per home run

Mysterious Voices

"Would you care to hit a few?!?!"

Although the skater can rotate towards first or third base, it's best to keep square with home plate and work out the timing. The most common mistake is a late swing, which either misses the ball completely or causes it to fly off over first base (to the right). This can be corrected by swinging slightly earlier. On the other hand, if the ball keeps flying off to the left of the screen, it means the skater is swinging too early—wait a moment longer before swinging.

Skate over the pitcher's mound of the baseball diamond in the old exercise yard and press the Grab Button to see what the Mysterious Voices have to say. Agree to their offer to hit a few baseballs and the skater digs in next to home plate and prepares for batting practice. The ghosts rise up and pitch 10 balls right down the pipe. Wait for the ball to approach home plate and press the Jump Button to swing the skateboard. The skater earns $25 for every ball hit over the rear wall of the exercise yard, between the two watch towers.

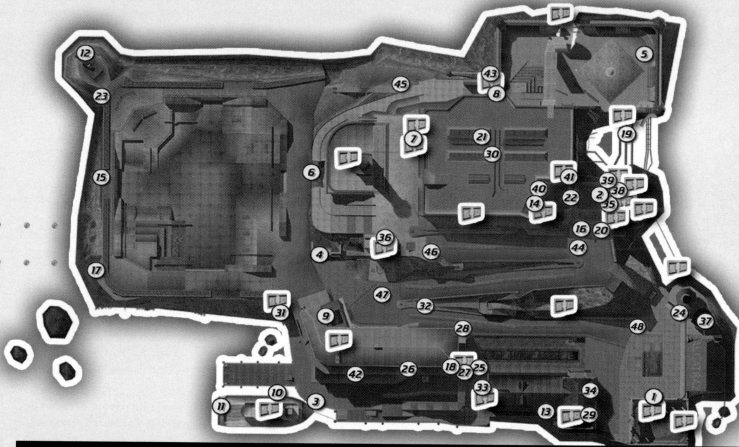

GAP CHECKLIST

[1] LIP EXTENSION   **25 POINTS**

Perform a stall on nearly any ledge or lip that overhangs a quarter pipe. Everything from the demolished building to the lighthouse is fair game.

[2] WATERTOWER LIP   **25 POINTS**

Drain the pool and air up to a stall on the railing around the water tower.

[3] WIRED   **25 POINTS**

Leap into a grind on the wire connecting the lampposts down near the dock.

[4] BATHROOM BREAK   **50 POINTS**

Transfer the ramps flanking the bathroom doorway. The bathroom is between the parade grounds and the second switchback.

[5] BLEACHER HOP   **50 POINTS**

Transfer a grind across two of the sets of bleachers near the baseball diamond.

[6] BROKEN WALK   **50 POINTS**

Transfer a grind across the gap between the handrails on the walkway just below the lighthouse.

[7] CELLBLOCK TRANSFER   **50 POINTS**

Transfer the quarter pipes against the outside of the cellblock entrance. Air over the entrance to the cell block interior or the stairwell leading to the roof.

[8] CELLBLOCK ROOF 2 EXERCISE YARD WALL TRANSFER   **50 POINTS**

Go straight off the wooden ramp on top of the cellblocks into a grind on the exercise yard wall below.

[9] DOWN THE HATCH   **50 POINTS**

The building directly across from the bathroom at the middle switchback has two glass skylights on its roof. Break through the one closer to the parade grounds to break through a boarded up wall near the dock.

[10] FERRY PRINCESS   **50 POINTS**

Grind the curving handrail beside the ferry and ollie into a grind on the edge of the boat.

[11] FERRY TRANSFER   **50 POINTS**

Transfer between the quarter pipe at the end of the dock and the one on the stern of the ferry.

[12] FOGHORN   **50 POINTS**

Grind the railing around the foghorn in the corner of the parade grounds.

[13] GUTTER PUNK   **50 POINTS**

Grind the railing beside the building with the tunnel (near the edge of the island) and transfer to the gutter on the building with the tunnel.

[14] HOW'D YOU GET UP THERE?   **50 POINTS**

Hop out of the pool and lip trick on the roof of the cell block.

[15] LEDGE-2-LEDGE   **50 POINTS**

Transfer a grind between any two ledges.

[16] LEDGE-2-PIPE   **50 POINTS**

Transfer a grind between a stone ledge and one of the large pipes near the water tower.

[17] LEDGE-2-RAIL   **50 POINTS**

Transfer a grind from a ledge to a rail. Best done in the parade grounds area.

[18] OVER DOCK STAIRS   **50 POINTS**

Grind the upper wooden rail around the backside of the building near the parade grounds and ollie off the railing and over the walkway and stairs that lead down towards the docks.

[19] PIPE SMOKER   **50 POINTS**

Transfer a grind between two of the pipes running between the exercise yard the powerhouse.

[20] PIPE-2-LEDGE   **50 POINTS**

Grind one of the large pipes near the water tower and transfer directly to a stone ledge. Grind the middle large pipe from the baseball diamond towards the upper switchback and ollie straight across to the ledge near steps.

[21] PIPE-2-PIPE   **50 POINTS**

Transfer a grind between two pipes on the roof of the cell block.

[22] POOL CHANGE   **50 POINTS**

Spine Transfer between the two pools.

[23] RAIL-2-LEDGE   **50 POINTS**

Transfer a grind from a rail to a ledge. Best done in the parade grounds area.

[24] RAIL-2-RAIL   **50 POINTS**

Transfer a grind between any two rails.

[25] RISING FROM THE GUTTER   **50 POINTS**

Grind the gutter of the building with the tunnel towards the docks and transfer the grind to the upper walkway of the neighboring building.

[26] ROOF-2-RAIL   **50 POINTS**

Grind from the tin roof beside the tunnel onto the rail nearby.

[27] ROOFTOP HERO   **50 POINTS**

Grind the pipe atop the large building uphill from the powerhouse and ollie over the ductwork and continue the grind.

[28] SIK SEWER LEDGE MANUAL   **50 POINTS**

Manual down the ledge of the switchback that is above the large sewer near the tunnel building. Start at the top near the walkway and manual all the way to the powerhouse.

[29] SKATE ATTIC   **50 POINTS**

Hit the ramp beside the tunnel and Spine Transfer through the large glass window at the top of the building. Land in a grind on the rail inside and grind out the other side of the room.

[30] SKYLIGHT-2-SKYLIGHT   **50 POINTS**

Transfer a grind between any two skylights on the roof of the cell block.

[31] SWAMP GAP   **50 POINTS**

Grind the wire between the lampposts from the dock steps, past the ferry and across the dock. Ollie off the end of the lights and land on top of the teleporter that leads to the parade grounds.

[32] SWITCHBACK SHUFFLE   **50 POINTS**

Transfer a grind between any of the ledges on the switchbacks, including the median running down the center of the path.

[33] TUNNEL CLEARANCE   **50 POINTS**

Hit the ramps beside the tunnel and transfer up and over the entrance to the other ramp.

[34] TUNNEL MANUAL   **50 POINTS**

Manual the short median inside the tunnel. This is best done going downhill, although it's not necessary.

[35] WATERTOWER ROOF LIP   **50 POINTS**

Jump out of the pool near the water tower and stall on the top edge of the tower.

[36] WHO BOMBED THE BATHROOM? SPINE   **50 POINTS**

Spine Transfer from the banked wall of the bathroom near the lighthouse all the way down to the Red Power graffiti below.

[37] BOMB DROP PROFESSIONAL   **100 POINTS**

Skate down the dirt path towards the powerhouse and leap off the kicker ramp at the bottom of the slope and land in a grind on what remains of the second tower.

[38] SUPER-HIGH WATERTOWER SPINE   **100 POINTS**

Spine Transfer between the bowl inside the water tower and the pool below. The Spine Transfer must go through the roof of the water tower.

[39] RUNE'S GROMMET GAP   **200 POINTS**

Air up from the bowl and lip trick on the Grommet's skateboard while he hold it over his head on the water tower roof.

[40] RUNE'S PLANK GAP   **200 POINTS**

Transfer over the plank on the cell block during Rune's Pro Challenge.

[41] SLUDGE BOMB   **200 POINTS**

Transfer from the roof of the cell block to the pools below. Air off the lip of the roof and up and over the stairwell in the north corner of the roof.

[42] TIN ROOF MANUAL   **250 POINTS**

Leap onto the tin roof beside the tunnel and manual from one end to the other.

[43] GUARDS WALK 2 STEP PLANKS   **300 POINTS**

Ollie from the ramped part of the guard's walk over the wall and onto the plywood lying on the steps near the baseball diamond.

[44] SWITCHBACK 1ST LEG   **500 POINTS**

Start the manual at the top of the path, near the lighthouse, and balance all the way around the first turn.

[45] MASSIVE CRUMBLING STAIRSET   **600 POINTS**

Ollie the entire set of dilapidated stairs leading down from the lighthouse to the parade grounds. This requires a fully lit Special Meter and very high Speed and Ollie ratings.

[46] ELLISA'S SWITCHBACK 2 SEWER PIPE   **1000 POINTS**

Gap from the top of the switchbacks into the sewer in Elissa's Pro Challenge.

[47] SWITCHBACK 2ND LEG!!   **1000 POINTS**

Carry the manual through the first turn and down the hill and around the second bend near the parade grounds.

[48] MANUALED THE WHOLE THING!!!   **5000 POINTS**

Manual all the way down the switchbacks from the lighthouse all the way to the powerhouse.

Kona

Welcome to the Kona Skatepark, the oldest privately owned skatepark in the country! Built in Jacksonville, Florida in 1977, Kona has become one of the largest and most revered skateparks ever. This, of course, is due in no small part to the efforts of the Ramos family.

If there's one thing Kona has it's variety! Having been open for 25 years now, the park has survived the rise and fall of many different skating styles and levels of popularity. And this is what makes the park so great. Whether it's barreling down old-school snake runs, dropping into concrete pools, or laying down sick lines in a state-of-the-art street park, Kona has something for everyone. And one mustn't forget the monstrous halfpipe! This is surely to become one of the favorite courses for both offline and online Pro Skaters!

LEVEL GOALS

Unlocked Objectives

Get a High Score: 60,000 points
Collect the S-K-A-T-E letters
Collect the C-O-M-B-O letters
Place 3rd or better—Street Competition
Find the 4 missing rental gear items
Show off for the locals at the mini spine
Snake Run Slalom
Save the birds on the power lines
Misty Flip over the Big Hut gap
Impress Ollie and the bums with combos

Locked Objectives

Get a Pro Score: 125,000 points
Collect the skate camp waivers
Place 3rd or better—Vert Competition
Ollie the Magic Bum 5x...again
Show off your tech on the manual box
50k combo the bowl—No hitting bottles

Pro Challenges

Get a Sick Score: 500,000 points
Collect Pro C-O-M-B-O
Become the King of Kona
Show off for the locals at the tombstone
Find and Get all 7 Channel Gaps

Mrs. Ramos

Bucky Lasek

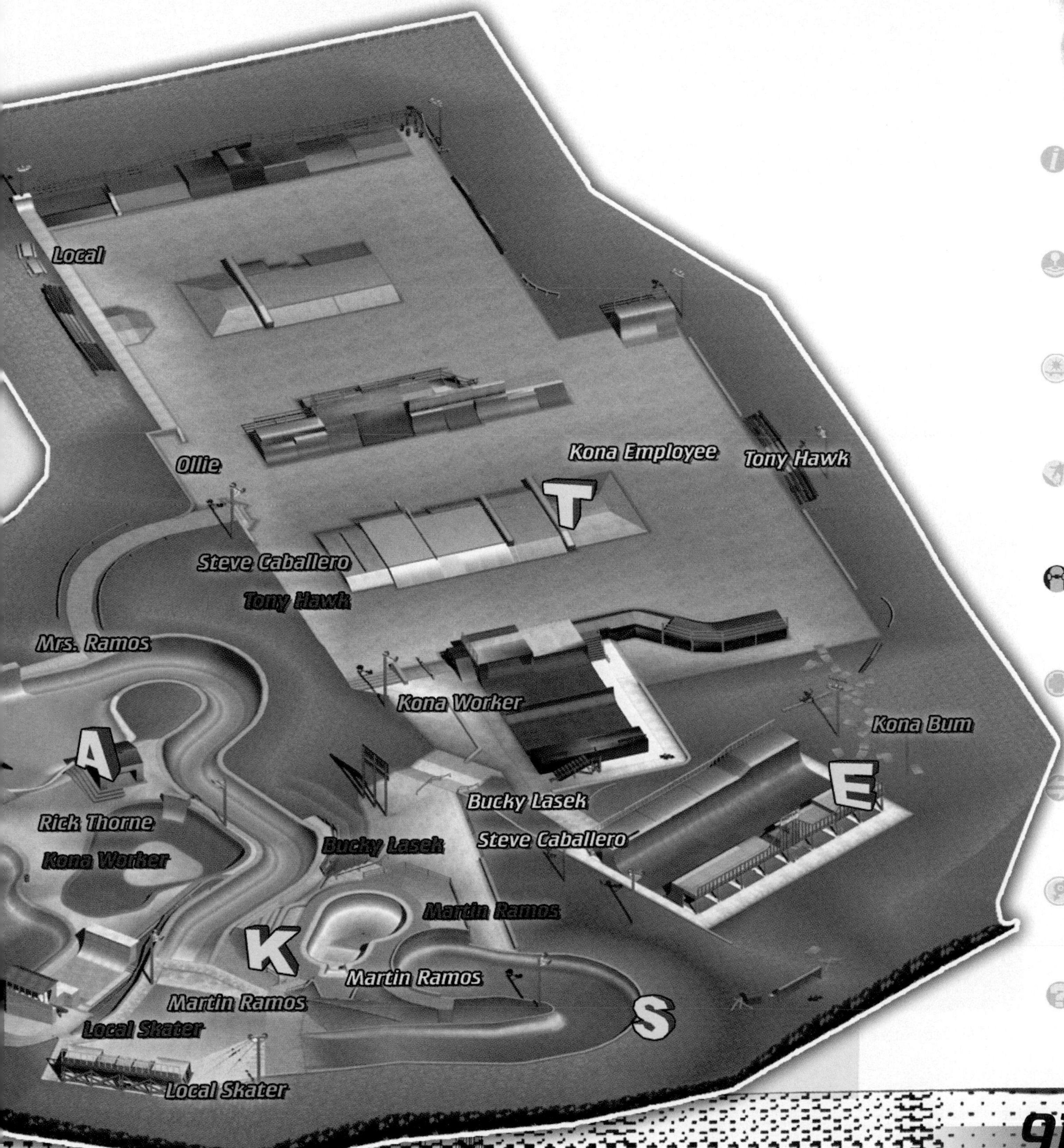

Local

Ollie

Kona Employee

Tony Hawk

T

Steve Caballero

Tony Hawk

Mrs. Ramos

Kona Worker

Kona Bum

A

E

Rick Thorne

Bucky Lasek

Kona Worker

Bucky Lasek

Steve Caballero

Martin Ramos

K

Martin Ramos

S

Martin Ramos

Local Skater

Local Skater

Amateur Challenges

GET A HIGH SCORE: 60,000 POINTS

Location	Near the shallow pool and concrete halfpipe
Time	2:00
Awards	$250 and a Stat Point
How unlocked	N/A
Unlocks	Get a Pro Score: 125,000 points

Bucky Lasek

"Yo, what up slim? You want to prove yourself? See if you can get a High Score in the next two minutes."

Drop into the shallow concrete pool and charge the little vert section near the US flag graffiti. Perform a double-tap flip trick such as the Ollie North Back Foot Flip, Revert the landing, and manual back towards the observation deck. Leap into a Special Lip Trick on the cable overhead and hold it for as long as possible. Heelflip back down into the pool, Revert the landing, and manual across the pool. Depending on how long the Special Lip Trick was held, this may be enough. Nevertheless, take to the air one last time and link up a couple of quick air tricks to guarantee success.

COLLECT THE S-K-A-T-E LETTERS

Location	To the right of the snake run start
Time	2:00
Awards	$250 and a Stat Point
How unlocked	N/A
Unlocks	Ollie the Magic Bum 5x... again

Local Skater

"Guess what! The S-K-A-T-E letters are on the loose again! Guess what else! I want you to collect them all again! You've got 2 minutes!"

S Start down the concrete chute near the Local Skater and launch off the wall to grab the "S" floating above the outside wall of the first turn.

K Spine Transfer out of the bowl at the end of the chute to cross over to the kidney bowl area. The "K" is on the bleachers near the roll-in.

A Leap out of the pink pool and onto (or over) the big hut towards the blue pool to grab the "A". Don't Spine Transfer out of the pool, just hold Up and ollie out like normal.

T Leave the pools and head down to the street course. The "T" is on a grind box set up on the right-hand side of the street course (the half nearer the mini pipes).

E Exit the street park and head over to the park's enormous halfpipe. The "E" is hovering above the coping to the left of the roll-in.

COLLECT THE C-O-M-B-O LETTERS

Location	By the bleachers in the corner of the street park
Time	2:00
Awards	$250 and a Stat Point
How unlocked	N/A
Unlocks	Nothing

Local

"5 little C-O-M-B-O letters... You have to get 'em all during the same combo. No whiners!'"

This COMBO challenge is a bit more difficult than the earlier ones as it requires lengthy manuals, grinds, and even a Spine Transfer and Revert!

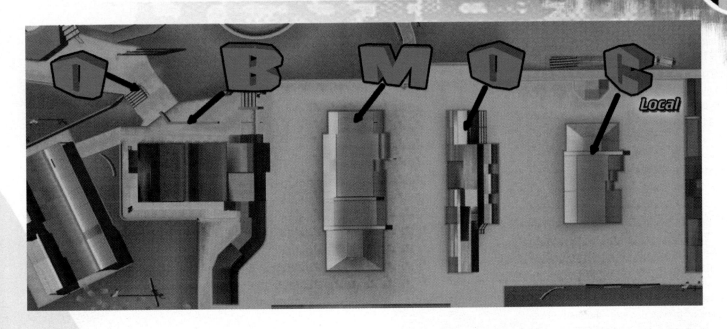

Hop into a grind on the box straight ahead to grab the "C" and manual towards the quarter pipe on the right side of the row of the ramps in the distance. Spine Transfer over the rail atop the ramp to get the "O" and quickly Revert into another manual. Grind the rail on the box directly ahead for the "M", then carry the trick string into a grind on the blue ledge beyond it for the **Rail 2 Ledge** gap. Grind past the "B" and ollie onto the red handrail near the stairs to gain the final "O" and the **Ledge 2 Rail** gap.

PLACE 3RD OR BETTER—STREET COMPETITION

Location	At the path leading to the street course
Time	1:00
Awards	$250 and a Stat Point
How unlocked	N/A
Unlocks	Place 3rd or Better—Vert Competition

Steve Caballero

"Hey, there's an all-around contest being set up! The first part's in the street course. Are you in? Hey—if you place in the top three, I'll get you a spot in the vert comp."

It's only fitting that Steve, arguably one of the best all-around skaters to ever take to four wheels, has arranged for a two-part contest. The street competition takes place between the roll-in and the back edge of the street course, the mini pipes behind the starting point are off-limits for now.

The street course offers numerous opportunities to link grinds, manuals, and big air together for a plenitude of points. With a full minute on the clock, there's plenty of time to use many different ramps and funboxes. Use the following scoring lines as an example of what's not only possible, but also proven to impress the judges. Although it's possible to combine these lines together for one massive scoring line, it's best to touch down after each of these 10-15 second strings so as to not risk blowing the run. It takes roughly 150,000 points for perfect marks from the judges at this competition.

From the starting point, trick into a grind on the rail directly ahead and switch up the grind with some Hidden Combos. Trick into a manual and roll it towards the ramps in the distance. Let loose with a Special Trick, Revert the landing, and manual into a Special Grind on the white rail atop the center funbox. Trick out of the grind to end the line.

This line also begins at the starting point. Drop in and pop into a grind on the rail and manual towards the second ramp from the left. Spine Transfer and Special Trick over to the other side, Revert the landing, and manual into a Special Grind on the grind box. Manual towards the ramps and transfer the two roll-ins for the **Channel - Double Roll-In!** gap. Tack on an extra Revert and flip trick for good measure.

Head across the course to the rails near the grass behind the vert ramp. Trick into a grind on the curving rail and transfer the grind to the lengthy wooden ledge for the **Robot Line Gaps!** bonus. Leap into a Special Grind on the wooden fence that leads up and around the ramps at the edge of the park for another **Robot Line Gaps!** grab and balance the grind counter-clockwise towards the bleachers. Trick down into a grind on the picnic table and trick across to the bleachers for one more grind before touching down.

FIND THE 4 MISSING RENTAL GEAR ITEMS

Location	On the grass near the blue pool
Time	2:00
Awards	$250 and a Stat point
How unlocked	N/A
Unlocks	Collect the skate camp waivers

Mrs. Ramos
"People are always leaving their rental gear out in the park. Would you gather up the missing stuff for me? We're missing a set of knee pads, a set of elbow pads and two helmets. Four items total. Thanks!"

You heard the lady, go find those missing items! Head down the sidewalk towards the street course and cut across the middle of it towards the lone vert ramp on the far side. Ride up the ramp to grab the first helmet.

Leave the street course and loop around the grassy area in a clockwise direction. The missing elbow pads are on the sidewalk behind the gigantic halfpipe.

Head up the hill from the halfpipe and jump into the concrete chute. The other helmet is at the circular bowl-like area adjacent the kidney bowl.

The knee pads are near the bleachers at the park's entrance. Look behind the building with the observation deck to find them.

SHOW OFF FOR THE LOCALS AT THE MINI SPINE

Location	Next to the mini halfpipe
Time	1:00
Awards	$250 and a Stat point
How unlocked	N/A
Unlocks	Show off your tech on the manual box

Kona Worker
"Uh, yeah. The locals want to see you bust over the spine on the mini. Hit the tricks they call out, but remember they have to be done OVER the spine."

Drop in on the mini halfpipe and perform the tricks the locals call out while spine transferring over the spine in the center. This is the latest version of falling tricks and is the most conducive of all for linking together multiple grab and flip tricks. Enormous amounts of speed and air can be had in the mini pipe. In fact, skaters get so much hangtime that they should avoid using the Jump Button when not at the spine, just to limit the amount of time wasted.

Release the Jump Button at the lip of the spine and quickly perform the Spine Transfer. The skater makes the transition to the other pipe but still launches high over the spine. Perform the required tricks during the Spine Transfer to get credit for them. Complete all 18 tricks in the time limit to complete the objective.

ROLLING REVERTS

After a few leaps in the mini halfpipe the skater will have so much speed that vert tricks can be linked together with just a simple Revert—no manual is necessary! Although this makes for easy combinations and high scores, none of the tricks performed during the Spine Transfer will be cleared from the list until the string ends. In other words, one wrong move can wipeout that enormous multiplier *and* leave the stack of tricks incomplete!

GROOVE ON THIS!

KONA

JACKSONVILLE, FL

SNAKE RUN SLALOM

Location	At the top of the snake run
Time	1:30
Awards	$250 and a Stat point
How unlocked	N/A
Unlocks	50k combo the bowl—No hitting bottles

Martin Ramos
"The Snake Run Slalom has humbled the best of 'em. You've got 3 runs. Each one is harder than the last. You've gotta pass every gate! Good luck. Hold on to your skin!"

The Snake Run Slalom puts skaters in an old school downhilling stance and tests their ability to pilot through a series of gates. There's no way to stop, sharp turns are a no-no, and the only "trick" that can be performed is the Old School Ollie which is of virtually no help. Although skaters can try to double-back for any missed gates, the incredible speed gained in the snake run makes this very difficult. It's more efficient to crash and take another run. All three courses must be completed in the 1:30 time limit.

Martin has three different slalom courses for the snake run, each one more difficult than the last. The first course has just 5 gates: one at the start, one in each of the three turns, and a final one marking the finish. Take some time to get used to the speed and how to turn during this course.

The second slalom course has a total of 7 gates—an extra one has been added between the 1st and 2nd gates and the 4th and 5th gates. Although some room to maneuver remains, this run forces skaters to take tighter turns and to look ahead to the next gate. While successfully navigating the first course at top speed was possible, holding down the Jump Button is a bad idea this time.

Finish

Start

1st & 2nd run
2nd run only
3rd run

The third and final course contains 10 gates and requires precision steering and the ability to manage the speed that comes with this excessive amount of carving. It's not enough to look ahead to the next gate, the skater must take a line that connects the inside cone of each gate with that of the next. Also, since adjacent gates are on opposite sides of the run, the skater must begin to break for the next gate before fully passing through the one that precedes it. Finally, be sure to press Down/Left and Down/Right when turning so as to incorporate some braking into the turn and to also make the board "snap" towards the next gate.

SAVE THE BIRDS ON THE POWER LINES

Location	In the grass near the main halfpipe
Time	2:00
Awards	$250
How unlocked	N/A
Unlocks	Nothing

Kona Bum
"I'm a little bit worried about my bird friends getting zapped up on those old power lines. Can you get up there and just shoo 'em away? You should hold a lip trick near 'em, otherwise they just keep coming on back!"

There are a total of 7 birds perched on the power lines running above the park's big half pipe. Four of the birds are spaced out across the wire on the far side and the other three are on the cable above the roll-in. In order to scare them enough so that they don't return, hold a stall near each bird long enough for it fly away. The bird flutters above the cable for three seconds before finally flying away.

It can be pretty tricky spotting the birds while cruising the pipe. Luckily, the birds have left some telltale proof of their presence. Look for the unmistakable white bird droppings on the sides of the halfpipe to know where the birds are and leap into a stall on the wire directly above. Since it can still be pretty tough finding birds to scare away when there's only one or two left, head up the roll-in and look around from there. Aim for the bird droppings head on so as to not accidentally grind past the birds. After the bird has successfully been scared away, and the **Highwire Act** gap has triggered, ollie back down to the ramp below and go after the next bird.

MISTY FLIP OVER THE BIG HUT GAP

Location	Next to the hut by the pink and blue bowls
Time	1:00
Awards	$250 and a Special Trick slot
How unlocked	N/A
Unlocks	Nothing

Rick Thorne
"Yo homie, you up for a challenge? Air from the pink bowl over the hut and land in the blue bowl. And just to up the ante a bit, I want to see you bust out a misty flip while you're doing it. Good luck and you better land on your feet. Have a nice day, baby!"

CHOOSE YOUR PRO
This challenge is best done with a skater who excels in Air and Hangtime. Select Tony Hawk, Rune Glifberg, or Bucky Lasek for best results.

Wanna know why Rick is so fired up when describing this objective? It's because he knows how difficult it is! Although it sounds simple enough, performing a Misty Flip over the hut and into the blue pool requires exceptional speed, height, and timing. Increase your chance of success by maxing out the skater Air and Hangtime stats and boost the Speed and Ollie ratings to 8 or more.

The first step is to max out the Special Meter. Work the pink bowl back and forth to accomplish this. Once the Special Meter is lit, slide into the skater's normal stance if not already in it and go big one last time (without rotation) off the wall to the right of the Kona graffiti.

When ready to make an attempt at the **Big Hut Gap**, hold the Jump Button down and steer straight for the hut. Press Up to automatically launch out of the bowl. Don't release the Jump Button until airborne and don't try to Spine Transfer, just hold Up. Once the skater is past the peak of the hut's roof, input the commands for the Misty Flip (Right, Down + Grab). If the Misty Flip is performed too early or too late, skaters will knock their heads on the roof of the hut, that's why it's important to perform the trick when sailing over the top of the hut. If the skater comes up short, it's most likely due to either not holding Up when exiting the pool, or a lack of speed. Perform more preliminary tricks to increase the amount of momentum the skater has going into the leap over the hut.

NO FRILLS GAPPING

If you're having trouble completing this challenge, try to make the leap from the pink bowl to the blue bowl without the Misty Flip. Once you can nail down the **Big Hut Gap**, then try it again with the Misty Flip.

IMPRESS OLLIE AND THE BUMS WITH COMBOS

Location	At bottom of path leading to street course
Time	0:30
Awards	$250
How unlocked	N/A
Unlocks	Nothing

Ollie the Magic Bum

"Hey hey hey! Me and my buddies wanna see you do some of your jumpy jumps and some spinny wizzers and some of those flippity-doos! So lemme see some magic, then go show off for my buddies!"

Ollie and his bum-buddies want to see some combos. First one worth 10,000 points, then one worth 11,000 points, and finally a 12,000 point combo. Those who have been keeping pace with the scoring lines provided for the High Score and Pro Score goals should have zero difficulty pleasing Ollie.

The first combo takes place in the street course. Heelflip into a grind on the railing in the center funbox, Double Kickflip into a manual on the ground and ride up one of the ramps on the other side to perform one final trick before touching down.

Ollie wants to see the 11,000 point combo be performed in the park's monster halfpipe. Since the Special Meter is lit from the previous combo, it's possible to start off this combo with a high-flying Special Trick. Select one worth over 5,500 points and all you'll have to do is Revert the landing to meet the 11,000 point requirement.

The final combo takes place in the chute to the right of the snake run. Once again, take advantage of the fully lit Special Meter and hop into a Special Grind on the ledge of the chute. Trick out of the grind once the score has reached 6,000 points to gain the multiplier and touch down to complete the objective.

GET A PRO SCORE: 125,000 POINTS

Location	Near the mini halfpipe
Time	2:00
Awards	$250
How unlocked	Complete 'Get a High Score: 60,000 points'
Unlocks	Nothing

Bucky Lasek

"All right dog, I'm impressed. But I'm gonna flip the switch! This Pro Score's gonna be way too much for you to handle. You've got two minutes. Prove me wrong!"

The mini halfpipe is a great place to link back-to-back vert tricks together, as the compact design minimizes the amount of speed loss. In fact, the skater goes so fast in this particular halfpipe that there's no need to manual between tricks!

Roll away from Bucky and make a u-turn into the pipe to start the run against the wall closest to Bucky. Start the insanity off with a 540 Indy, Revert the landing, and launch off the spine into a Special Trick. Perform another Revert and follow it up with another Special Trick. If the height is there, throw in a quick Pop Shove-It

before having to Revert again. Perform a Spine Transfer and mix in a couple of quick grabs and flips to boost the multiplier some more. Revert the landing and perform one more big aerial off the other side of the halfpipe—something on the order of a 540 Double Kickflip to Japan should be more than enough.

COLLECT THE SKATE CAMP WAIVERS

Location	Near the park's main entrance
Time	0:30
Awards	$250
How unlocked	Complete 'Find the 4 missing rental gear items'
Unlocks	Nothing

Mrs. Ramos
"Oh we've got a big problem! The kids from the skate camp are here, but all their waivers flew out of the bus when the door opened! Without those waivers, we can't let those kids skate! Can you find them all? There are 15 of them!"

The 15 waivers have blown all over the park and it's really important that they're found. The bus is going to take those kids back home if you don't hurry, so hop to it!

Grind the ledge of the shallow pool near Mrs. Ramos and hop out of the grind right after snagging the 3rd waiver. Grab the waiver near the entrance to the pink bowl and grind its ledge over the Kona graffiti to pick up two more. Hop into a grind on the near edge of the snake run and balance around the hairpin turn to bring the total to 9.

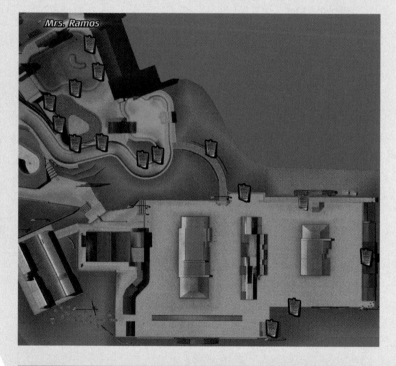

The final half-dozen waivers are near the street course. Grind the left-hand railing down the path to pick up the 10th waiver and transfer the grind to the edge of the sidewalk to score two more. Transfer the quarter pipes at the back of the park to pluck another waiver out of the air and to hit the **Channel - Double Roll-In!** gap. The final two waivers are near the grass on the far side of the street course. Angle off to the left after hitting the gap and grind the rail that curves off towards the grass to find the 14th waiver. The final waiver is floating above the quarter pipe set up in the grass behind the tall vert ramp. Air up and grab it before the final seconds run out!

PLACE 3RD OR BETTER—VERT COMPETITION

Location	Between the mini pipe and large pipe
Time	1:00
Awards	$250
How unlocked	Complete ' Place 3rd or Better—Street Competition'
Unlocks	Nothing

Steve Caballero
"You ripped it up in the street course. Now it's time to go over the vert ramp and see what you can do. They're warming up right now, so get over there dude. Top three guys get medals. Good luck."

There is a lot more room to improvise in the vert competition, as the specific tricks that are performed aren't as important as the sheer quantity of tricks. From the moment skaters drop into the pipe, their main focus should be on linking at least one Special Trick into every trick string and growing each multiplier to at least 10. It's going to take a score of 200,000 points to get perfect marks from the judges here, and one way to ensure it's done is by redistributing some of the Stat Points to maximize Air, Hangtime, and Speed. A Speed rating of 8 or higher will be enough to make manualing the flatbottom of the ramp unnecessary.

ROLL OUT!

The quickest way to ruin a run is to accidentally launch out of the pipe by rolling up the roll-in. Doing so may cause a spill, and the skater lands out in the grass—a spot out of bounds. Keep clear of the middle of the pipe and if the skater is about to launch off the roll-in, try to perform a quick stall or Footplant on the Nokia sign to save the points.

Start the run with something that gets the Special Meter glowing, such as a 540 Varial Kickflip to Japan. Revert the landing, and quickly leap into a Special Trick on the other side. Follow this up with another Revert and Special Trick and Revert the landing one more time for additional points.

A good mid-run trick string to use starts by leaping into a Special Lip Trick on the cable over the pipe for both big points and the **Highwire Act** gap. Pop Shove-It out of the stall, Revert the landing, and go big with an aerial Special Trick on the opposite wall. Follow this up with another Revert to Special Trick to wrap up first place.

The previous two combos are more than enough to impress the judges, but plenty of time remains for one more combo. Max out the Special Meter and charge the ramp beside the roll-in. Go big with a Special Trick while transferring the gully for the **Channel - Monster Pipe Roll-In!** gap, Revert the landing, and continue

the string with some quick flips and grabs off the other side of the pipe. Bring it all to an end by Reverting the landing and leaping into a short-lived grind on the cable for the **Highwire Act**, just be sure to avoid grinding out of the pipe!

OLLIE THE MAGIC BUM 5X...AGAIN

Location	On the far side of the street course
Time	2:00
Awards	$250
How unlocked	Complete 'Collect the S-K-A-T-E Letters'
Unlocks	Nothing

Tony Hawk
"Yo! The magic bum from Venice followed me all the way out here. It's just like last time. Try to find him and ollie over him 5 times. Each time you ollie over him he'll move to a new spot. Keep your eyes peeled, he's a stinky, uh—um sneaky guy."

Those who have played *Tony Hawk's Pro Skater 2* will no doubt pick up on Tony's reference, but those who are new to the series needn't feel as if they're missing out on an inside joke. Ollie the Magic Bum made his debut in the Venice Beach level of *Tony Hawk's Pro Skater 2* and at the time, Ollie wasn't so much his name as it was what you had to do to him while he slept! It's unclear how Ollie made it across the country, but he's followed the gang all the way to Jacksonville, Florida and, as usual, he's made his bed at 5 different spots around the park. Find out where he's sleeping, ollie over him, then track him down at his next cardboard mattress. Continue doing this until Ollie has been ollied 5 times.

SCOUTING REPORT

Take a trip around the skatepark looking for sheets of cardboard and trash. Find all five spots, and you've found Ollie's homes.

Ollie's first sleeping spot is between the mini halfpipe and the enormous one. Loop around the street course and cut across the grass to get to him fast.

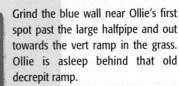

Grind the blue wall near Ollie's first spot past the large halfpipe and out towards the vert ramp in the grass. Ollie is asleep behind that old decrepit ramp.

Head up the hill towards the starting point. Ollie is asleep on the sidewalk that runs under the platform of the vert ramps.

Ollie's fourth spot is one of the hardest to find. He's asleep behind the concrete extension that rises up from the blue bowl.

Cut across the street course towards the vert ramp near the grass on the far side. Ollie can be found counting sheep behind the vert ramp, under the platform.

SHOW OFF YOUR TECH ON THE MANUAL BOX

Location	In the center of the street course
Time	2:00
Awards	$250
How unlocked	Complete 'Show off for the locals at the mini spine'
Unlocks	ProSet1

Kona Employee
"Hey—here's a tech challenge for ya! I put together a nice, long box. Manual or Nose Manual it first, then we'll go from there. Whatever you do, don't set that manual down, and keep it up on the box."

The Kona Employee wants to see some long-distance manualing on the box he built. He has three different lines he wants done. Maintain your balance and your pockets will be $250 fatter in no time.

First things first, skate up to the box and jump into a manual before the first set of cones. Balance all the way to the far end to prove you've got what it takes to continue. The second test is virtually the same, except this time he wants to see a Kickflip to Manual combo. Be sure to hold the Jump Button

down to maintain speed and tap Up and Down to stay upright. The final test follows up on the first two by adding a Heelflip at the end. So, to complete the objective, Kickflip into a Manual on the box, roll out the wheelie to the far end, and Heelflip down onto the tarmac.

50K COMBO THE BOWL—NO HITTING BOTTLES

Location	Near the bowls
Time	2:00
Awards	$250
How unlocked	Complete 'Snake Run Slalom'
Unlocks	Nothing

Martin Ramos
"Looks like the midnight pool crew has been here. I know when they've skated because they always leave a little something for me on the drain in the deep end. See if you can get a 50,000 point combo in the bowl, without touching my bottles!"

In this objective, it isn't the 50,000 point combo that's difficult, it's avoiding the bottles at the bottom of the bowl. Thankfully, the pool is kidney-shaped and the skater can get in one or two good leaps in the shallow end. Nevertheless, since it's only a matter of time before the skater is drawn across the center of the pool by gravity, try to build the multiplier up as fast as possible to reduce the number of leaps needed to score the 50,000.

Drop into the pool and go huge off the left-hand side of the shallow end by linking three or more tricks together. Revert the landing, and throw down a Special Trick on the next jump. Perform one more Revert and make the final jump really count by adding a lot of rotation to a pair of grab tricks.

Pro Challenges

GET A SICK SCORE: 500,000 POINTS

Location	Near the entrance to the street course
Time	2:00
Awards	$500
How unlocked	Complete a Pro-Specific Challenge
Unlocks	Nothing

Bucky Lasek
"All right dog, so you got some skiiill. Last ups, try to get a Sick Score in the next two minutes."

PROSET SETUP
Make sure ProSet1 has been turned on for this scoring line—the box offers a great edge to grind at the end of this scoring line. ProSet1 is unlocked by completing the 'Show Off Your Tech on the Manual Box' objective.

Trick into a grind on the red railing and hold the grind right onto the blue ledge for the **Rail 2 Ledge** gap. Trick onto the rail leading into the street park to follow it up with a **Ledge 2 Rail** gap and manual directly ahead to the funbox on the end. Grind the rail, manual towards the quarter pipe on the end of the next bank of ramps, and Special Trick while Spine Transferring to the other side. Revert the landing, manual towards the sidewalk on the left, and hop into a Special Grind. Ollie out of the grind and into another Special Grind on the wooden railing above the last row of ramps. Hold the grind around the turn near the garbage cans and transfer it to the wooden ledge for the **Robot Line Gaps!** bonus. Follow that line onto the rail that curves onto the grass for another gap and Spine Transfer over the vert ramp. Revert the landing and hop into another grind on the edge of the manual box to the right.

COLLECT PRO C-O-M-B-O

Location	At the start of the snake run
Time	2:00
Awards	$500
How unlocked	Complete a Pro-Specific Challenge
Unlocks	Nothing

Local Skater
"That last C-O-M-B-O was pretty tight! Try this line on for size! Same deal, get all the letters in a single combo. Get on it!"

All of the letters may be in the snake run, but that doesn't make this Pro C-O-M-B-O challenge any easier. Hop into a grind on the left edge of the snake run to grab the "C" and ollie down into a manual. Air up out of the run on the outside of the first turn to pluck the "O" out of the air, Revert the landing, and jump into a grind on the left edge again. Grind through the "M" and ollie down into another manual. Leap from the outside wall to get the "B" hovering above, and Revert into another manual upon landing. Two-wheel it across the blue pool at the end of the run and pop off the banked wall straight ahead to collect the final letter.

BECOME THE KING OF KONA

Location	In the street course
Time	0:30
Awards	$500
How unlocked	Complete a Pro-Specific Challenge
Unlocks	Nothing

Tony Hawk
"King of Kona!!! 5 spots to hit, 30 seconds in each one. Get as many points as you can in each spot, without leaving that area. If all your scores together meet the grand total, YOU'RE THE KING, BABY!!!"

Tony has laid down the gauntlet—score a combined 1,000,000 points while skating 5 different spots around the park. Do it, and become the new King of Kona! The five spots are as follows: the street park, the kidney bowl, the monster halfpipe, the snake run, and the crusty (aka concrete) halfpipe.

For many, the street park is the place to score the lion's share of the necessary 1,000,000 points. Drop in and roll directly into the same line that was used in the 'Get a Sick Score' objective—if it worked once, it'll work again! Grind the rail straight ahead, manual into a Special Trick while Spine Transferring the ramps in the center, and link it all up with a Special Grind on the sidewalk and the wooden railing at the back of the park. Keep it going on the wooden ledge for the **Robot Line Gaps!** bonus, but stay off the grass this time, you don't want to risk being disqualified.

OOPS... THERE IT IS

It might look a little funny, but a great way to earn a ton of extra points is to trick into the Ahhh Yeahhh! Special Manual just before the timer runs out. Since the skater is stationary, you're free to concentrate on the Balance Meter and not worry about the terrain. Throw in some quick flip tricks or flatland stunts to get the multiplier going. Ahhh Yeahhh! is unlocked when secret skater 4 is purchased.

The second stop is in the kidney bowl and although it can get a hairy at times, the tight confines and deep vert makes it ideal for linking together a lengthy string of aerial tricks. Drop in and set right to the task of chaining together multiple double-tap tricks, preferably while airing it out over the roll-in for the **Channel - Kidney Roll-In!** gap. Once the multiplier is good and primed, tack on a couple of aerial Special Tricks.

Next up is the monster halfpipe. Roll in and go big right off the bat with a 720 Varial Heelflip to Indy Nosebone, or something similar. Revert the landing into a manual and throw down a Special Trick while transferring the roll-in for the **Channel - Monster Pipe Roll-In!** gap. Revert into another manual and launch into a Special Lip Trick on the **Highwire Act** cable above. Spend the remainder of the time working the pipe, linking big aerials, lip tricks, and aerial Special Tricks together.

Now it's time to strut your stuff in the snake run. Although it may seem like a poor place to score points, there are actually several options for the well-balanced skater. For starters, it's possible to pop into a Special Grind and try to grind the edge of the run all the way to the pool below. Risky, but doable. Another option is to hop into a Special Manual on the blue line and try to balance on two wheels (or one) all the way to the pool to rack up the various manual gaps that are available. Finally, recreate the 'Collect Pro C-O-M-B-O' run, this time with a lot more flair.

Since there's a good chance most of the tricks in your repertoire have been used multiple times already, going into the final spot with less than 900,000 points is not recommended. Either way, the ultra-skinny crusty halfpipe is best used for stringing aerials together and the occasional lip trick, but avoid using a lot of rotation as one sloppy landing can send the skater careening out of the pipe. Also, because the ramp is so narrow, play it safe and cash in those trick strings every 10 seconds so as to not risk coming away with nothing because of a last-second faceplant.

SHOW OFF FOR THE LOCALS AT THE TOMBSTONE

Location	Near the pink bowl
Time	1:00
Awards	$500
How unlocked	Complete a Pro-Specific Challenge
Unlocks	Nothing

Kona Worker
"Yeah! The locals are impressed, but they're never satisfied... Now they wanna see you rip on the Tombstone. Hit the tricks they call out, but remember... they have to be on the Tombstone!"

Sure, the locals know you're the new King of Kona, but they want to see some tech on the Tombstone. The locals are going to yell out a total of 15 lip tricks that they want to see performed on the Tombstone. Ride up the big stone block, slide into the lip trick, and drop back into the bowl as soon as the **Tombstone Extension** gap triggers. There's absolutely no time to waste in this objective and just one incorrect lip trick could cause a do-over.

LIP FLAPPIN'

Depending on the assortment of tricks the locals call out, you may want to try ollieing out of one lip trick and landing in another. While this is a very good way to chain a couple of tricks together to save time, the skater cannot ollie out of an inverted trick such as the Invert or Eggplant and land in another lip trick.

It's very important to ride straight up the extension without holding down the Jump Button. Skaters may look too slow, but they'll reach the top all the same. Just as important is not wasting time after the trick, drop down into the bowl and immediately apply the brakes to stop. Once stopped, turn around, and roll right back up the extension for another lip trick. Continue in this manner until all 15 tricks have been completed.

DOUBLE UP

Got another lip trick on the list, but only 1 second on the clock? No problem, just Revert out of the second-to-last lip trick, manual a careful U-turn around the bowl and ride up the Tombstone and into that final lip trick after time expires.

FIND AND GET ALL 7 CHANNEL GAPS

Location	On the walkway uphill from the monster halfpipe
Time	3:00
Awards	$500
How unlocked	Complete a Pro-Specific Challenge
Unlocks	Nothing

Martin Ramos

"Here's a double challenge. Find AND hit all of the Channel Gaps in the park. Look for Ramp to Ramp and Roll-In channel stuff. Since ya gotta sniff 'em out, I'll give ya 3 minutes."

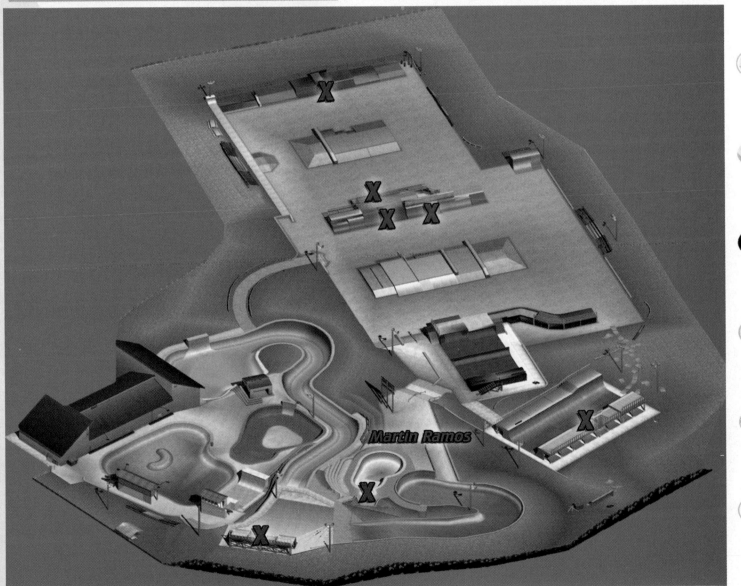

There are 7 channel gaps that have to be hit and only 3 minutes to do it! Refer to the above map along with the descriptions in the 'Gap Checklist' section below for the whereabouts of each of these channel gaps.

Four of the gaps, including the most difficult one to hit, are in the street park and should be "sniffed out" first. These include the **Channel - Double Roll-In!**, **Channel - Single Wedge!**, **Channel - Ramp 2 Ramp!**, and **Channel - Huge Bank n' Roll!!!** The latter of which is the most difficult gap to hit in this objective. Be sure to approach the ramps with maximum speed and on a hard angle. Aim for the corner of the ramp and rotate in the direction of travel while flying through the air.

The remaining three channel gaps are scattered throughout the rest of the park and include the self-explanatory **Channel - Monster Pipe Roll-In!** and **Channel - Kidney Roll-In!**, as well as the **Channel - Triple Roll-In!** which takes place on the vert ramps at the starting point.

CASH ICONS / PRO SETS / GAPS

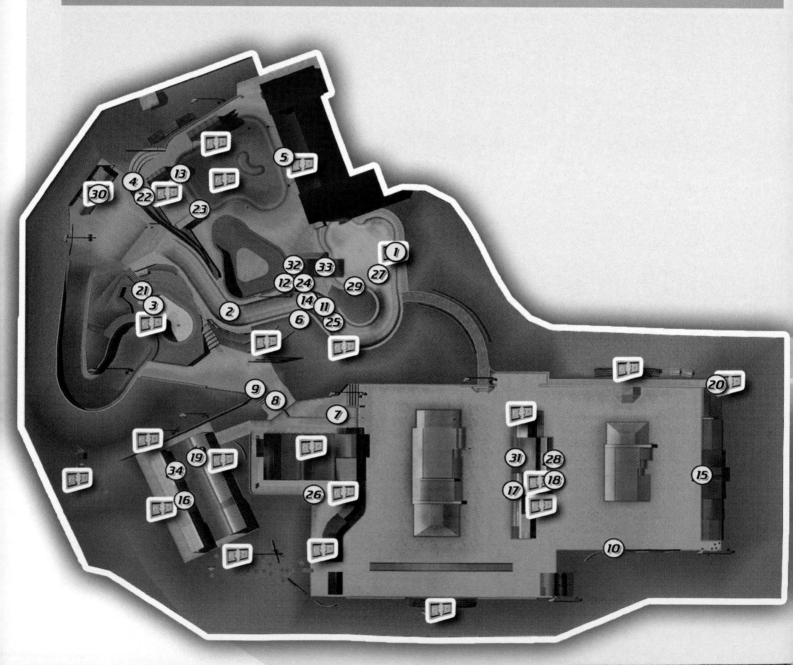

GAP CHECKLIST

[1] BIG BLOCK EXTENSION 25 POINTS
Lip trick on the concrete extension in the blue bowl.

[2] BLUE LINE TURN 1 25 POINTS
Start manualing down the snake run and stay on two wheels past the first turn. The skater must stay on the blue line.

[3] CHANNEL - KIDNEY ROLL-IN! 25 POINTS
Air over the roll-in inside the kidney-shaped pool.

[4] CRUSTY CONNECTIONS 25 POINTS
Grind the uppermost step near the concrete halfpipe onto the upper slab of concrete leading towards the park entrance.

[5] LEDGE 2 LEDGE 25 POINTS
Transfer a grind between any two ledges in the park.

[6] LEDGE 2 LIP 25 POINTS
Transfer a grind from either of the wooden retaining walls behind the first turn in the snake run onto a grind on the right-hand edge of the run.

[7] LEDGE 2 RAIL 25 POINTS
Transfer a grind from a ledge to a rail.

[8] RAIL 2 LEDGE 25 POINTS
Transfer a grind from a rail to a ledge.

[9] RAIL 2 RAIL 25 POINTS
Transfer a grind between any two rails in the park.

[10] ROBOT LINE GAPS! 25 POINTS
Transfer a grind onto or off the lengthy wooden ledge at the back corner of the street course.

[11] SIDESTEP THE SNAKE 25 POINTS
Grind an edge of the snake run and ollie into a grind on the opposite edge. This is best done at the turns.

[12] TOMBSTONE EXTENSION 25 POINTS
Lip trick on the concrete extension in the pink bowl.

[13] WILD MAN'S BOMB DROP 25 POINTS
Ollie off the deck of the concrete halfpipe (the side with the roof) and land in the shallow pool next to it.

[14] BLUE LINE TURN 2! 50 POINTS
Keep the blue line manual going all the way to the second turn!

[15] CHANNEL - DOUBLE ROLL-IN! 50 POINTS
Approach the bank of ramps along the back edge of the street course and transfer over the pair of roll-ins in the center.

[16] CHANNEL - MONSTER PIPE ROLL-IN! 50 POINTS
Transfer the roll-in in the enormous halfpipe.

[17] CHANNEL - RAMP 2 RAMP! 50 POINTS
Enter the street course and transfer over the smaller wedge built into the set of ramps nearest the path leading up to the pools. This wedge is between two quarter pipes and is not the one next to the large roll-in.

[18] CHANNEL - SINGLE WEDGE! 50 POINTS
Transfer over one of the slant ramps on the middle set of ramps in the street course. This is done on the side of the ramps facing the back of the park.

[19] HIGHWIRE ACT 50 POINTS
Leap into a grind or stall on any of the power lines in the park.

[20] LAMP EXTENSION 50 POINTS
Perform a lip trick on any of the lampposts in the corner of the street course.

[21] REDLINE 2 KIDNEY COPING! 50 POINTS
Transfer a grind from the red handrail leading down to the kidney bowl into a grind on the edge of the bowl.

[22] TC'S DECK GAP 50 POINTS
Ollie from the ground near the vert ramps at the starting point onto the deck of the concrete halfpipe.

[23] THE CRUSTY TRANSFER! 50 POINTS
Transfer out of the concrete halfpipe and into the shallow bowl. Use the side of the halfpipe without the roof.

[24] WAY TRANSFER 50 POINTS
Spine Transfer from the left side of the Tombstone Extension in the pink bowl into the turn #2 of the snake run.

[25] BLUE LINE TURN 3!! 75 POINTS
Keep the blue line manual going all the way to the third turn!

[26] 10 POINT LANDING!! 100 POINTS
Enter the street park and face the large bank of ramps nearest the mini-pipe. Hit the wedge with the staircase behind it and ollie off the ramp, over the stairs, and into a grind on the blue ledge that curves around the mini-pipe.

[27] 2 WHEELIN' THE BLUE LINE!!! 100 POINTS
You know the drill, wheelie the entire length of the snake run without straying from the blue line!

[28] DOUBLE WEDGE! 100 POINTS
This is the same as the **Channel - Single Wedge!** gap, except the skater must transfer over both wedges at once.

[29] SNAKE-HEAD 2 TAIL! 100 POINTS
Hop into a grind at the start of the snake run and hold it all the way to the bottom near the big hut.

[30] CHANNEL - TRIPLE ROLL-IN! 150 POINTS
Use the quarter pipes flanking the starting point to transfer over all three roll ins.

[31] CHANNEL - HUGE BANK N' ROLL!!! 200 POINTS
In the street park, approach the set of ramps nearest the path leading up the hill and transfer over the roll-in and the large slant ramp.

[32] BIG HUT GAP 250 POINTS
Transfer out of the pink bowl, over the hut, and into the blue bowl at the bottom of the snake run.

[33] LITTLE HUT GAP 250 POINTS
Clear the hut from the blue bowl over to the pink bowl.

[34] AIR OVER 1000 POINTS
Air over Rick Thorne in Steve's Pro Challenge.

Shipyard

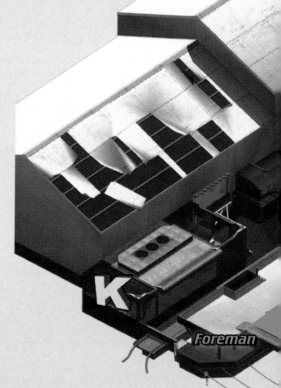

Unlocked with 32 Pro Points.

When it comes to mass amounts of exposed metal, it's tough to beat a rusty old shipyard—and the one where Jim's Shipping has been "moving junk since 1978" is no exception! The Shipyard course contains several warehouses, multiple freight cranes, barge ships, and a flatbed train. And, of course, everything is run down and nasty. Skaters will be splashing through spilled gasoline, scraping the rust off exposed beams, crashing through clapboard roofs, and gapping over toxic waterways. Tetanus shots, anyone?

When compared to the manicured landscape of Kona, the Shipyard can be both overwhelming and intimidating. Whether by crashing through a ventilation duct or by Spine Transferring into a a little lost here.

LEVEL GOALS

Unlocked Objectives

Get a High Score: 65,000 points
Collect S-K-A-T-E
Collect C-O-M-B-O
Varial Kickflip the shack water gap
Gap across the suspended containers
Slap the buoy
Welder lunch delivery
Collect the rivets
Dog Chase
Inventory the freight containers

Locked Objectives

Get a Pro Score: 150,000 points
Collect High C-O-M-B-O
Bust tricks across the rooftop gap
Heelflip FS Invert the freight container
Competition: Medal the barges
Manual combo the train

Pro Challenges

Gap the suspended containers
Get a Sick Score: 600,000 points
Collect Pro C-O-M-B-O
Rat Race: Catch the Rat
Liptrick Transfer

For this reason, it's important to study the maps and do plenty of skating around before attacking the objectives. Several of the inhabitants of the Shipyard offer up challenges that have skaters venturing throughout much of the course—knowing where to go is key! Finally, look closely at the maps to find out where the water is. There are numerous places where an unexpecting skater can slip through the cracks, and there's no worse way to spoil a lengthy scoring run than taking a swim in Jim's noxious lagoon.

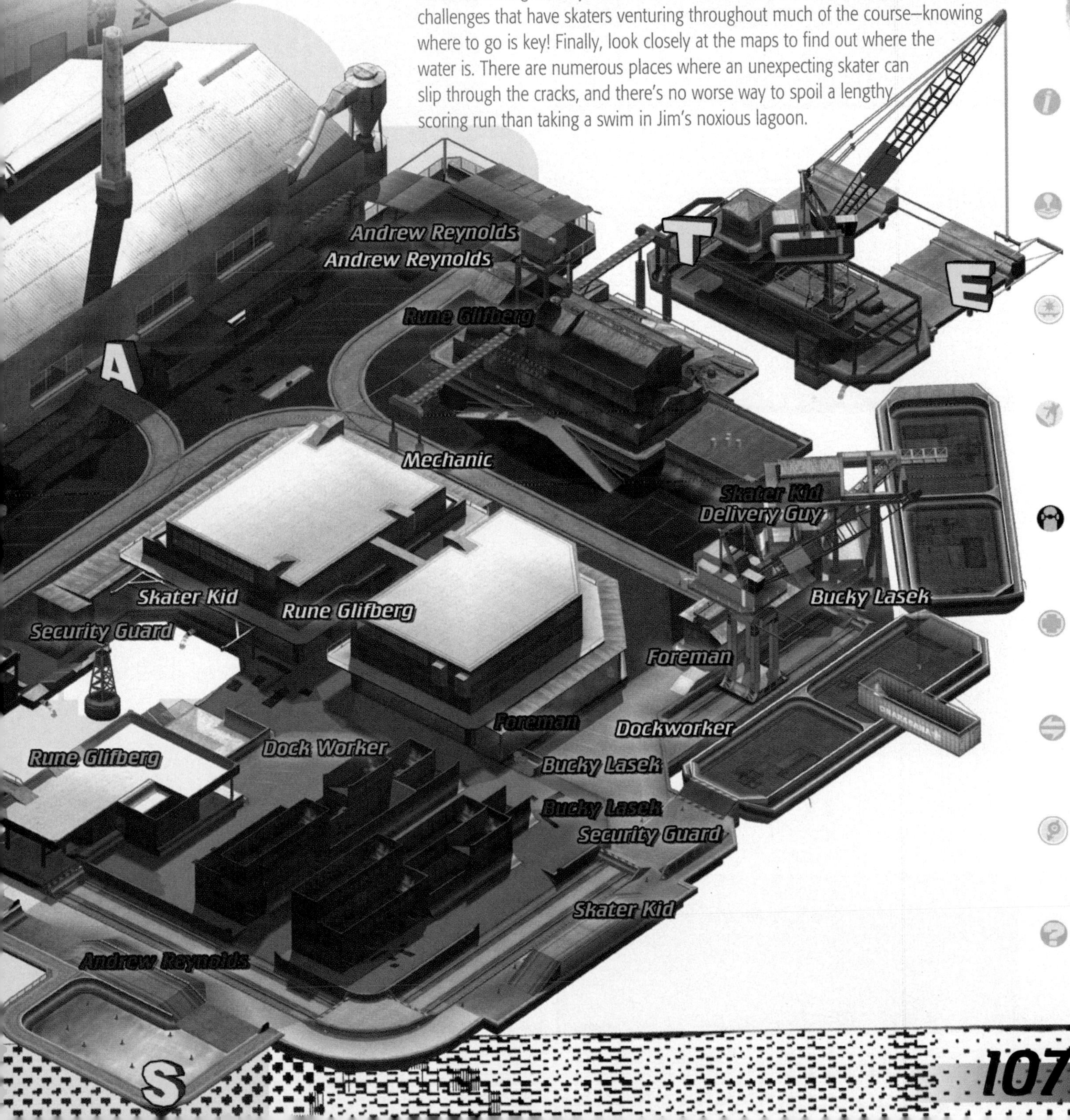

T E
A
E

Andrew Reynolds
Andrew Reynolds

Rune Glifberg

Mechanic

Skater Kid
Delivery Guy

Skater Kid

Bucky Lasek

Security Guard

Rune Glifberg

Foreman

Rune Glifberg

Dock Worker

Foreman

Dockworker

Bucky Lasek

Bucky Lasek

Security Guard

Skater Kid

Andrew Reynolds

S

Amateur Challenges

GET A HIGH SCORE 65,000 POINTS

Location	Near the large moving crane.
Time	2:00
Awards	$250 and a Stat Point
How unlocked	N/A
Unlocks	Get a Pro Score: 150,000 points

Skater Kid
"Can you bust a High Score?! Show me in the next two minutes."

Roll past the Skater Kid and trick into a grind on the lip of the quarter pipe behind him. Grind down the angled side and trick across to the first barge. Land in a Special Grind on the yellow edge and grind an entire lap around it. Trick out of the grind and back onto solid ground for one more multiplier.

COLLECT S-K-A-T-E

Location	By the barge near the stacks of containers
Time	2:00
Awards	$250 and a Stat Point
How unlocked	N/A
Unlocks	Nothing

Security Guard
"Oh no... someone's run off with the S-K-A-T-E letters! I was supposed to be watching this area. Oh man, am I in BIG trouble if I don't find them soon. Help me out will yah?"

S — Head clockwise around the perimeter of the Shipyard to the area sticking out into the water. Boneless into a grind on the outer railing to get the "S".

K — From the "S", grind across one of the ropes and enter the leaky room in the corner. Air up through the dilapidated roof and land in a grind on the beam above. The "K" is on the middle of the beam near the water.

A — Hug the outer wall of the factory and grind-hop onto the pair of trailers on either side of the railroad tracks. Gap across the trailers to snag the "A" and the **Trailer Hop** gap.

T — Jump down onto the main road and charge the "caution" launch ramps in the distance. Leap up to overhead beam and grind to the right. Ollie off the end of beam straight across to the "T" on the beams in the distance.

E — From the "T", land in a grind and hold it around the crane and towards the blue suspended container. Leap out of the grind just before it angles back towards the starting point. Don't grind the container, however. Land inside it and use its halfpipe-esque interior to snag the final letter.

WATER BAD!
Miss the container and end up in the drink? No worries, just use the ramps on the docks to transfer up and into the container for the **Dock Transfer** gap.

COLLECT C-O-M-B-O

Location	By the starting point
Time	2:00
Awards	$250 and a Stat Point
How unlocked	N/A
Unlocks	Collect High C-O-M-B-O

Andrew Reynolds
"Hey, I just got this line, man. Let's see what you got!"

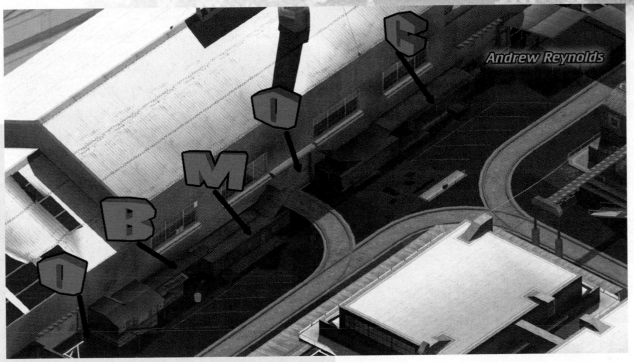

Andrew Reynolds

All the letters in this COMBO line are along the outside of the factory to the right. Collecting them all in one string requires some pretty quick finger tapping as well as an understanding of the roof line.

Head towards the trailer on the right and use the ramp near its door to leap into a grind on the roof for the "C". The grind shifts outward beyond the edge of the trailer's air conditioner. Hold the grind to the very edge of the ac unit and leap straight ahead to grind the left-hand edge of the pallet-ramp.

Grind up and over the pallet to grab the "O" and gap into a grind on the next trailer. Land in a grind on the second pallet. The grind shifts directly to the edge of the trailer to gain the "M".

Continue grinding along the trailer to the end and ollie over to a grind on the walkway railing to pick up the "B". Hop off the end of the railing into a momentary manual (don't touch down) and leap from the edge of the foreman's office for the "O".

VARIAL KICKFLIP THE SHACK WATER GAP

Location	On the walkway over the nasty water
Time	2:00
Awards	$250 and a Stat Point
How unlocked	N/A
Unlocks	Bust tricks across the rooftop gap

Charge the banked lip of the rooftop straight ahead and transfer down through the skylight to the ramp inside. This lines the skater up with the jump Rune wants to see performed. Input the commands for the Varial Kickflip while airing across the water and land it clean to complete the objective.

Rune Glifberg
"Ooh nasty, look at that water. That's a perfect place for a flip trick. Do this trick while airing across the gap."

GAP ACROSS THE SUSPENDED CONTAINERS

Location	Between the barges and the containers
Time	2:00
Awards	$250 and a Stat point
How unlocked	N/A
Unlocks	Heelflip FS Invert the freight container

This is the ultimate test of the skater's Spine Transfer skill. The skater starts in a suspended container at the opposite end of the yard and must Spine Transfer two times to reach the container near Bucky. Once there, the container spins around and the skater must survive the return trip.

Don't try to get too fancy with tricks and rotation. Instead, keep a straight line, hold the Jump Button down for speed, and Spine Transfer right after lifting off above the edge of the container.

JUST TRY IT AGAIN

Although it's possible to reenter the suspended containers from the ground by transferring out of the large stack of containers, it's just not worth the effort. Instead, select the 'Retry Last Goal' option from the Pause Menu to be placed right back into the first container with a full 2:00 on the clock!

SLAP THE BUOY

Location	Between the buoy and containers
Time	0:30
Awards	$250 and a Stat point
How unlocked	N/A
Unlocks	Nothing

The skater drops in from atop a container near the Dockworker. Hop over the banked ledge directly ahead to charge the ramp near the buoy. Ride up the center of the ramp near the water, and ollie towards the buoy. Press the Grind Button to "kiss the rail" atop the buoy. The skater must do this five times to complete the task.

The key to this objective is speed. The skater must have enough speed to clear the water, but not so much that he flies right past the buoy. Aim slightly in front of the buoy as it sways back and forth and try not to launch too high and far, else it may be missed altogether. Lastly, don't try to link up a grind on the rail in the center of the ramp with the one on the buoy—the grind takes too much speed away from the skater when going up the ramp.

STAYING GROUNDED

Having trouble getting all 5 slaps in within the time limit? This may be due to unnecessarily huge jumps on the quarter pipes on either side of the water. Instead of using the ramps to turn around, try putting on the brakes and turning around the old-fashioned way. It's possible to get enough speed to reach the top of the buoy and a lot of time is saved by not flying through the air when turning around.

WELDER LUNCH DELIVERY

Location	Between the warehouses and rusty crane
Time	0:10
Awards	$250 and a Stat Point
How unlocked	N/A
Unlocks	Nothing

Delivery Guy
"I'm here to deliver some grub for the welders. They're kinda impatient but they tip really well. Problem is those guys are always hanging out in the darndest places and I'm already late. If ya help me out, I'll split the tip with ya!"

Don't let the idea of finding 5 welders in 10 seconds scare you, they're all close at hand. That isn't to say that making the delivery in time is easy, just that it's possible.

Cross the street and leap into a grind on the edge of the roof above the ramp to find the first welder. Transfer the grind to the railing of the building to the right for the **Building Hop** gap and immediately ollie into a grind on the ledge beside it. Grind past the next two welders and down onto the roof below. Skate past the fourth welder and quickly leap across the gap to the next rooftop. The final welder is in the back left corner.

COLLECT THE RIVETS

Location	Near the ropes over the water
Time	0:30
Awards	$250
How unlocked	N/A
Unlocks	Competition: Medal the barges

Foreman
"Hey, I need someone to gather up a bunch of rivets for the guys working on the barges. You look like just the man for the job. Those guys need those rivets ASAP!"

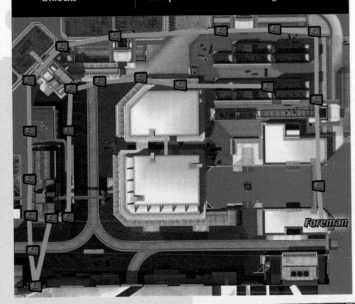

This objective challenges the skater to collect 21 rivets in under half a minute, and although they are all in a relatively easy-to-follow line (see map) there is no time to waste. Collecting all of the rivets needn't be done in a single combo, but it is possible. There is a break between the first 15 and the final 6 that can be hard to connect at times, but those who do are rewarded with a very high score.

Trick into a grind on the left-hand rope to grab the first rivet and ollie ahead to a grind on the short wall. Hop-n-grind around the bend and past the breaks in the wall to collect four more rivets and head over to the barge on the right. Grind the left side of the uppermost edge of the barge to snag another rivet and leap down into a grind on the edge of the concrete near the second barge. The skater grabs the 7th rivet here.

Balance past the bend and up and onto the wall alongside the water. Ollie the gap in the wall after picking up the 8th and 9th rivets and keep grinding towards the course's initial starting point. Follow the trail of rivets to the large quarter pipe against the factory and sky up into the air to grab the 13th rivet.

Cross back over the tracks and leap into a grind on the rail of the rusty building directly ahead. Grind the rail off to the right to pick up two more rivets and ollie the pair of gaps in the railing to continue grinding straight ahead. Ollie off the railing just before it banks to the left to pick up the 16th rivet. Grind the edge above the mini-ramps near the building ahead to pick up some more rivets and gap across to the ledge across the street.

Grab the rivet on the edge and immediately hop into a grind on the metal rail in the center of the sidewalk to obtain the 20th rivet. Skate straight towards the open container directly ahead and use the ramp at the far end to leap up and grab the final rivet.

DOG CHASE

Location	At the other end of the road from the starting point
Time	0:02
Awards	$250
How unlocked	N/A
Unlocks	Nothing

The Security Guard, er, lets the dogs out, and they've been trained to chow on trespassing skaters! Gather up their 5 bones (+2 seconds per bone) before time runs out. This challenge requires some fast thinking and even faster finger tapping; get ready, it'll be over before you know it!

Quickly hop into a grind on the ledge near the Security Guard and ollie across to the next ledge for the **Ledge 2 Ledge** gap and snag the first bone. Hop across the second gap to continue grinding around the bend to the right. Grab the second bone, then jump down and head for the ledge on the neighboring building. Grind through the third bone and cross over to the rail near the barge on the left to find the fourth bone. Time is ticking away, so act quickly: the last bone is between the two quarter pipes near the water. Head to the right of the barge and transfer the ramps to grab it and the **Transfer** gap before time runs out!

Security Guard
"Looks like the dogs are feeling ornery. Must be that hot sun that drives them crazy! Better get to those bones before they get to you!"

WALKING THE DOG

Although the bones don't have to be collected in one combination, doing so not only nets the **5 bones 1 combo** gap, but the added momentum arguably makes it easier.

INVENTORY THE FREIGHT CONTAINERS

Location	By the crane next to the barges
Time	2:00
Awards	$250
How unlocked	N/A
Unlocks	Manual combo the train

This objective plays exactly like the multiplayer game 'Graffiti' only there are no other skaters and only a select group of objects can be "tagged". There are 21 freight containers divided up between two lengthy stacks. The skater

Foreman
"I need to get those freight containers inventoried. If you help me out I'll, uh, throw some money your way. All you have to do is trick on each container to mark it. What do you say?"

has 2:00 to trick off of each one of these containers, thereby successfully inventorying it for the Foreman. Containers that have been successfully tricked on (tricks must be landed) are painted red to prevent confusion.

The hardest containers to inventory are those at the top of the stacks. Start the run by entering the open-ended container straight ahead and the Spine Transfer down the row to the blue container piled three-high. Transfer to the blue container to the left of it and Spine Transfer back towards the starting point. Many of the containers at the bottom of the left-hand stack are open on the bottom and contain rails in their center. Head around the side of these containers, grind the rail inside. Two of those on the bottom of the other stack are of the same shape and it's possible to gap across to the rail inside the other container to string together multiple containers.

Once the upper containers and those on the ground have been inventoried, begin methodically attacking those remaining, all of which have a quarter pipe alongside them. Use the ramp to leap up into an aerial trick, a grind on the edge, or even a lip trick to finish the task. Multiple containers can be inventoried at once by launching off the ramp next to one container and tricking through the air to another.

MONEY ON THE SIDE

Sure, the Foreman is going to throw you $250 when the job is done, but how's about earning some dough in the meantime? From the starting point, skate around to the right-hand side of the stacks and turn and face the warehouse near the Foreman. Leap into a grind on the pink container piled two-high and transfer the grind to the green container nearest the warehouse. Kick off the lip at the end of the container and smash through the ventilation duct. Grind the rail inside for cash prizes and the **Ventilation Claustrophobia** gap. Try to leap across to the right-hand ventilation duct for even more cash!

GET A PRO SCORE: 150,000 POINTS

Location	Near the buoy
Time	2:00
Awards	$250
How unlocked	Complete 'Get a High Score: 65,000 points'
Unlocks	Nothing

Skater Kid
"You're pretty good! Now let's see you pull a Pro Score!"

This line leads down the rail yard towards the initial starting point on the course and back along the factory wall. This line has many quick hops that require some fast reflexes, but the multiplier just grows and grows. This line can be put to use to score 150,000 points or it can be extended to net well over 500,000 points!

Round the corner past the Skater Kid and trick into a grind on the yellow handrail to the right. Manual over to the yellow rail with the lever on the left, grind the rail, and trick into a Special Grind on the railroad tracks for the **Rail 2 Track** gap. Manual at the quarter pipe and bust a Special Trick while drifting to the left. Instead of landing on the ramp below, press the Grind Button to land in a grind on the rail curling back towards the factory above the trailers. Transfer the grind to the ledge on the factory and hop-n-grind down the side of the building, picking up multiple **Ledge 2 Ledge** gap bonuses. Make it all the way to the black and yellow striped ledge—the 5th one—to claim the **Warehouse Ledge Madness!** gap. Try to incorporate a quick 180-degree rotation and a flip trick between grinds. For even more points, mix in some quick Special Grinds.

By following this line, the multiplier quickly grows to over 20 and the base points to at least 7,500 pts, which just so happens to be equal to 150,000 points! Why stop there? Practice wrapping the grind around the leaky roof in the distance, across to the other building, and even onto the roofs of the warehouses!

COLLECT HIGH C-O-M-B-O

Location	Near the starting point
Time	2:00
Awards	$250
How unlocked	Complete 'Collect C-O-M-B-O'
Unlocks	Nothing

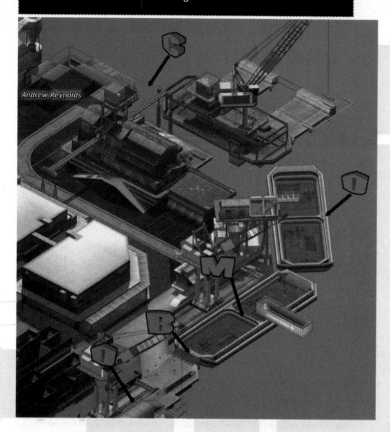

That's right, a second C-O-M-B-O letter objective on the same course! This line is the antithesis of Andrew's earlier line as it stretches out across half of the course! The skater's ability to maintain lengthy grinds is put to the test here.

Skate towards either of the quarter pipes straight ahead and leap into a grind to the right on the rail above. Gap across to the rail of the rusty structure beyond the "C" and drop off into a manual in the barge below. Grind the outer edge of the barge for the "O" and hold it as the edge angles towards the next barge. Leap off into a manual and Spine Transfer the divide in the barge to grab the "M". Revert into a manual and ride up the ramp at the end of the barge to snag the "B". Leap into a manual and ollie into a grind on the left side of the crane's tracks to collect the final "O".

BUST TRICKS ACROSS THE ROOFTOP GAP

Location	On the elevated walkway between the warehouses
Time	1:00
Awards	$250
How unlocked	Complete 'Varial Kickflip the shack water gap'
Unlocks	ProSet1

Rune Glifberg
"What's up, you ready to take some photos? Do the tricks as they appear, but here's the deal, they only count if you do 'em across the roof gap. Let's see it."

Rune has set up a series of ramps on the rooftop of the warehouses and he wants to see some tricks get performed while gapping from roof to roof. Although the number of the tricks hasn't changed, the difficulty of the button presses has certainly increased. Unlike the previous falling trick challenges, this one incorporates double-tap tricks and numerous tricks that require a diagonal direction press.

In addition to the added complexity of the trick commands, the angle of the ramps is not conducive for more than one grab trick. While it may look as if there's plenty of clearance to link up a Nosegrab and Indy in one jump, it's highly unlikely and more than one failed attempt will likely ruin any chance at success. It's going to take some discipline, but those who only attempt to link tricks when its between two simple flip tricks (Kickflip, Heelflip, Shove-It, and Pop Shove-It) will have the least difficulty.

HEELFLIP FS INVERT THE FREIGHT CONTAINER

Location	Near the two barges
Time	2:00
Awards	$250 and a Special Trick slot
How unlocked	Complete 'Gap across the suspended containers'
Unlocks	Nothing

Drop into the barge and, without turning, go big off the opposite side. Link a few tricks together to max out the Special Meter and travel back to the other side of the barge and jump one more time where the skater dropped in. Again, without turning, launch off the far side of the barge and input the commands for the Heelflip FS Invert. Hold the lip trick on the edge of the container for at least 5 seconds while it moves over the other bowl. Release the trick and drop down into the bowl below to complete the objective.

Bucky Lasek

"All right here's a crazy lip trick for you. Get SPECIAL, then Heelflip Front Side Invert on the suspended freight container. But here's the catch: you've got to hold the invert as the container mooooves from bowl to bowl."

LEAN HOLDER

Don't sweat it if the skater starts wobbling during the lip trick. If the skater leans too far to the right and lets go, he's not going to automatically wipe out. Adjust his direction during the free fall so that he rolls through the landing. He might have let go before you wanted him to, but if he lands in the next bowl without bailing, it counts just the same.

COMPETITION: MEDAL THE BARGES

Location	Near the two barges
Time	1:00
Awards	$250
How unlocked	Complete 'Collect the rivets'
Unlocks	Nothing

Dockworker

"My foreman had me put up all this stuff for some kind of competition. You're pretty good, you should give it a try!"

The two barges have been transformed into a pair of towering bowls, complete with a roll-in, multiple ledges to grind, and several feet of vert! The tight nature of bowl skating is in sharp contrast to street competitions, as well-defined scoring lines aren't practical. Much of the skating done in this competition will be more improvisational.

The design of the bowls makes linking air-based Special Tricks commonplace. Boost the Special Meter with several quick flip and grab tricks and be sure to Revert the landing to carry the string across the bowl. Work the bowl back and forth with different Special Tricks. Once it looks as if there's not going to be enough speed to leap too high out of the bowl, slide up the bowl into a Special Lip Trick.

Another option is to incorporate the Special Lip Trick earlier into the run and follow it up with a grind on the lower ledge. Ollie into a Special Grind on the ledge of the other bowl to extend the string and trick back to the original bowl's ledge to finish it off.

Arguably, the best line on the barges is one that puts the kinked ledges to use for one lengthy grind. Trick out in the bowl near the roll-in to get the Special Meter fully lit and to grow the multiplier quickly. Ride up the left side of the pool (back to the roll-in) and slide into a Special Grind on the upper ledge. Trick across the gap after the ramped part of the ledge and into a second Special Grind on the other bowl. Continue grinding all the way around the bowl to where the ledge tapers off and ollie across to where the other ledge starts up again. Land in yet another Special Grind but be sure to hit the Revert Button to end the grind before the roll-in. Trying to gap across the roll-in at this speed will likely land the skater on the asphalt and out of the competition area.

MANUAL COMBO THE TRAIN

Location	Beside the white warehouses
Time	0:40
Awards	$250
How unlocked	Complete 'Inventory the freight containers'
Unlocks	Nothing

Mechanic
"I just finished putting this old train back together again. I need someone to make sure it's not gonna fall apart. See if you can manual from one end of the train to the other."

The Mechanic needs to have a skater manual from one end to the other on the train, but there are no rules as to how much of the train the skater must touch. The skater can easily get enough speed so as to pop off the first train bed and quickly hop and manual all the way to the end with very little actual manualing.

Drop down the ramp that's been set up and come to a stop near the cones. Wait at least ten seconds for most of the train to round the bend and go for it. Ollie into a manual on the first car and hold the Jump Button down for speed. Ollie across to the next car, land in a quick manual, ollie again, and so on. Manual off the back of the train to complete the objective.

Pro Challenges

GAP THE SUSPENDED CONTAINERS

Location	Between the barges and the containers
Time	2:00
Awards	$500
How unlocked	Complete a Pro-Specific Challenge
Unlocks	Nothing

Foreman
"Well, you really impressed the crane operators. Now they want to see something tougher. Gap from one suspended container to the other."

The crane operators have positioned two yellow containers near the stacks and the Foreman wants to see them gapped. The first step in completing this high-flying stunt is to ascend the mountain of containers. Perform a couple of quick Pop Shove-Its to gain speed and enter the open container straight ahead. Spine Transfer up to the blue one atop the pile. Slow the skater down and transfer to the container to the left (the one hanging between the two upper blue containers).

Take some time tricking out the Special Meter on the ramps inside the container to maximize the skater's speed. Dash towards the ramp on the end of the container near the Foreman and fly off it on an angle to the left. Rotate to the left while flying through air to help pull the skater the full distance. Set up to land in the other yellow container for the **Container Combo** bonus and to complete the Foreman's challenge.

GET A SICK SCORE: 600,000 POINTS

Location	Near the barge and the rusty structure
Time	2:00
Awards	$500
How unlocked	Complete a Pro-Specific Challenge
Unlocks	Nothing

Skater Kid
"Your moves are tight! Think you have a Sick Score you can bust out?"

Cross the street towards the warehouse near the first welder and perform a couple of quick grabs and flips to max out the Special Meter. Revert the landing and manual towards the rusty quarter pipe across the street. Throw down a Special Trick, Revert on the ramp, and manual back towards the ramp across the street. Leap into a right-hand grind on the awning and transfer it into a Special Grind on the railing of the neighboring building for the **Building Hop** gap. Hop off the end into a quick manual and trick across the gap to the other building. Manual across the roof towards the welder near the catwalk and slide into a clockwise grind on the edge of the roof.

Trick down onto the left-hand railroad track below and Special Grind down the road. Transfer the grind across the rail near the lever and onto the next set of tracks for the **Track 2 Rail** and **Rail 2 Track** gaps. Manual towards the quarter pipe at the end of the road and leap into a right-hand grind on the beam above. Ollie off the end onto the ledge directly ahead just as was done in the 'Collect High C-O-M-B-O' objective, and trick down into the barge below to end the chain.

COLLECT PRO C-O-M-B-O

Location	Near the bowl beyond the container stacks
Time	2:00
Awards	$500
How unlocked	Complete a Pro-Specific Challenge
Unlocks	Nothing

Andrew Reynolds
"You again! All right this next line is insanely hard. Let's see if you got this one."

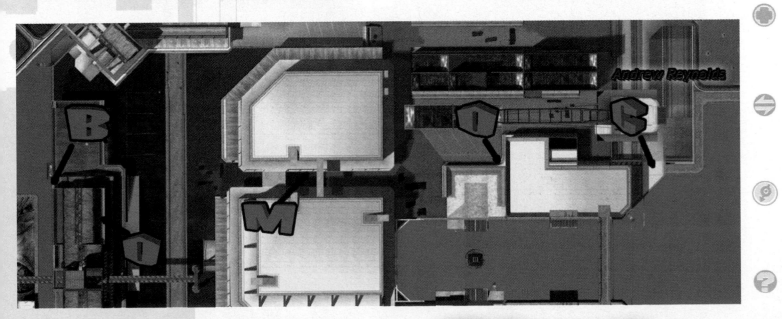

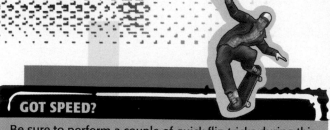

Roll down the ramp straight ahead and hop into a grind on the white rail to the left. Air off the blue light to grab the "C" out of the air and land in a grind on the roof of the building to the right.

GOT SPEED?

Be sure to perform a couple of quick flip tricks during this leap to gain speed for the next couple of jumps.

Manual out of the grind and ollie over the edge of the building to grab the "O". Land in a manual on the street below and balance it straight ahead to the series of ledges. Transfer a grind across the ledges to pick up the "M" and ollie into a manual towards the rusty quarter pipe across the tracks. Spine Transfer onto the roof and manual out of a Revert towards the left. Hit the ramp across the roof on an angle so as to grab the "B" while airing onto the upper rooftop for the **Conveyor QP Transfer** gap. Revert into one final manual and cross the rooftop to the ramp on the other side. Air up from the center of the ramp to snag the final "O".

RAT RACE: CATCH THE RAT

Location	On the balcony of the rusty building
Time	0:15
Awards	$500
How unlocked	Complete a Pro-Specific Challenge
Unlocks	Nothing

Rune Glifberg
"Woah, look at that bastard rat! He's making fun of you. You better go get him. Smash him!"

There's a rat on the loose and Rune wants to see you hunt him down. Although the rat takes off running, he often stops for a breather. Catch up to him at each of these spots to gain additional seconds on the clock.

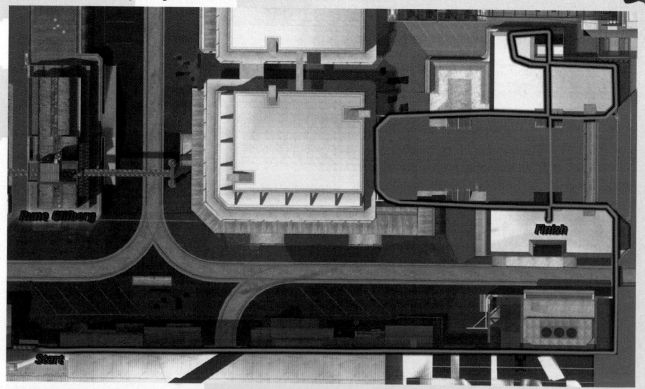

From the start air up off the quarter pipe near the factory and land in a left-hand grind on the ledge above. Transfer the grind across the ledges to get the rat off and running and continue hitting the **Ledge 2 Ledge** gap, then ollie to the black and yellow rail for the **Warehouse Ledge Madness!** gap.

Keep after the rat by grinding the rusty beams of the building in the corner, ollieing across to the ledge near the welder, and continuing over the yellow swinging rail back towards the main warehouses. Grind the metal beams beside the handrail to make a u-turn towards the roof on the other side of the catwalk and ollie across the gap.

The rat takes a rest near the catwalk, then moves to the hole leading to the secret ramp below. The rat then leaps down the hole and across the water to his final resting spot in the building across the water. Transfer off the rooftop into the hole and across the **Dirty Water** gap to complete the objective. Splat!

LIPTRICK TRANSFER

Location	Near the barges
Time	2:00
Awards	$500
How unlocked	Complete a Pro-Specific Challenge
Unlocks	Nothing

Bucky Lasek
"You again? Let's see you try this one. Lip trick on the crane over there. Chill. Then, once it gets to the other side, snap off! Let's see it."

Max out the Lip Balance rating, it's time for an uber-long lip trick on a moving object! Bucky wants to see the skater air up into a lip trick on the railing of the crane and hold it as the crane lumbers down the tracks towards the barges. Once it gets over the ramps at the other end, the skater must freefall back to ground level and land it cleanly.

Since the crane isn't going to start moving until the skater is firmly lip tricking on the rail, take your time maxing out the Special Meter on the ramp below the crane and on the mini-verts on the other side of the nearby container. Grind the rail through the container to pick up speed and leap into the lip trick on

the crane. The skater must hold the stall a full 7 seconds while the crane moves over the landing ramp. Once it stops, let go and land it to complete the objective.

JIM'S SHIPPING
Moving Junk Since 1978

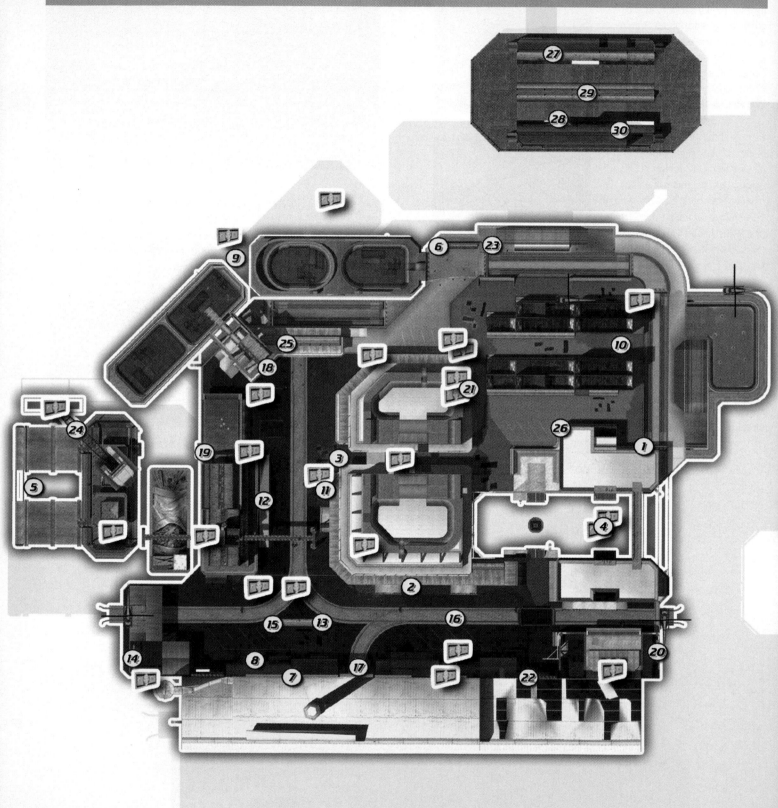

GAP CHECKLIST

[1] TRANSFER   25 POINTS
Follow the crane tracks towards the ropes over the water and transfer from the "caution" mini ramp to the quarter pipe near the building beside it.

[2] AWNING HOP   50 POINTS
Leap from the angled walkways on the side of the warehouse near the barges and land in a grind on the edge of the awning.

[3] BUILDING HOP   50 POINTS
Transfer a grind from the awning of one warehouse to a grind on the handrail of the other. It's best done near the welders.

[4] DIRTY WATER   50 POINTS
Gap across the nasty water using the wooden ramps near the two smaller buildings with the holes in their roofs.

[5] DOCK TRANSFER   50 POINTS
Transfer over the water between the quarter pipes on the docks. This gap also triggers if the skater transfers from the right-hand dock into the blue container suspended above.

[6] INTO THE BARGES   50 POINTS
Transfer from the quarter pipe to the right of the barge near the containers and land inside the barge.

[7] LEDGE 2 LEDGE   50 POINTS
Transfer a grind between any two ledges.

[8] LEDGE 2 RAIL   50 POINTS
Transfer a grind between any ledge and rail.

[9] MORE BARGE FUN   50 POINTS
Use the banked walls of the barges to transfer from one to the other. Do this on the outer side of the barges, over the wide water gap.

[10] ONARABANA   50 POINTS
Gap between the blue containers on top of the stacks of freight.

[11] RAIL 2 LEDGE   50 POINTS
Transfer a grind from any rail to a ledge.

[12] RAIL 2 RAIL   50 POINTS
Transfer a grind between most any two rails.

[13] RAIL 2 TRACK   50 POINTS
Grind the rail near the lever by the railroad tracks and transfer the grind onto one of the tracks.

[14] RUSTY LIP   50 POINTS
Leap off either of the "Caution" ramps at the starting point and lip trick on the beam directly above.

[15] TRACK 2 RAIL   50 POINTS
Transfer a grind from one of the railroad tracks onto the rail near the lever.

[16] TRACK 2 TRACK   50 POINTS
Transfer a grind between two parallel railroad tracks.

[17] TRAILER HOP   50 POINTS
Gap across the roofs of the trailers set up by the large rundown factory near the starting point.

[18] CIRCLE T   100 POINTS
Grind the train tracks towards the dead end near the barges to gain speed and leap off the ramp straight ahead and into a lip trick on the metal platform near the elevated office.

[19] CONVEYOR QP TRANSFER   100 POINTS
Transfer from the lower level rooftop to the upper one on the rusty old building near the garbage barge.

[20] ROOF SMASH TRANSFER   100 POINTS
Transfer between the pairs of quarter pipes at either end of the main road (near the starting point). Be sure to air up and through the wooden roofs during the transfer.

[21] VENTILATION CLAUSTROPHOBIA   100 POINTS
Grind the upper containers near the warehouse and ollie through the ventilation duct and land in a grind on the rail inside. Grind the entire rail to the other end of the ventilation unit to score the gap.

[22] WAREHOUSE LEDGE MADNESS!   100 POINTS
Use the quarter pipe near the factory that runs the entire length of the course and hop into a grind on the upper ledge. Transfer a grind along the entire side of the building via the numerous ledges and, finally, gap into a grind on the black and yellow striped ledge past the last trailer.

[23] 5 BONES 1 COMBO   200 POINTS
Gather up all of the dogs' bones in one combo during the 'Dog Chase' objective.

[24] RUN 1!!!   500 POINTS
Complete the first cable grind in Eric's Pro Challenge.

[25] RUN 2!!!   500 POINTS
Complete the second cable grind in Eric's Pro Challenge.

[26] RUN 3!!!   500 POINTS
Complete the third cable grind in Eric's Pro Challenge.

[27] RUSTY ROOST   500 POINTS
Lip trick on the lower roof during Bucky's Pro Challenge.

[28] BIG HOLE GAP   1000 POINTS
Transfer the white vert ramps after they start falling apart during Bucky's Pro Challenge.

[29] RUSTY OLD RAMP CHANNEL GAP   1000 POINTS
Transfer between the spines after they start breaking apart during Bucky's Pro Challenge.

[30] RUSTY ROOST II   1000 POINTS
Lip trick on the upper roof during Bucky's Pro Challenge.

London

Unlocked with 40 Pro Points.

Welcome to Trafalgar Square, one of the most popular tourist spots in all of London. It's an unusually sunny day here in the UK, so take advantage of the weather and get out and see the sights. The Square is home to two fabulous fountains near Nelsons Column, the National Gallery museum to the north, and several other key diplomatic buildings. Just as ubiquitous as the fine architecture, are the pigeons, double-decker buses, and the coppers. While the buses and the pigeons do their best to stay out of your way, the coppers are always looking to belt a skater—don't give them the satisfaction!

LEVEL GOALS

Unlocked Objectives

Get a High Score: 75,000 points
Collect the S-K-A-T-E letters
Collect the C-O-M-B-O letters
Wallride Tag 5 buses
Grab 5 Coppers hats
Land a 100,000 point combo
Rodney's flatland training
Do a Grab trick over the fountains
Race the Coppers around London
Free Stompy! Destroy the traps

Locked Objectives

Get a Pro Score: 175,000 points
Ghetto Tag the SB light line
Skitch the Police Bike
Nail the combos as they come up
Land the Flatland tricks as they appear
Medal in the Competition

Pro Challenges

Get the Sick Score: 700,000 points
Pro C-O-M-B-O letters
Beat Muska's best 6 Combos
Grind American cars for Parking Guy
Trick on every object in the Southbank

Rodney Mullen
Geoff Rowley

Competition Judge

While the many ramps, cables and ledges that criss cross all over the Square make it the course's hotspot for skating, there is plenty to see and shred down by the river. Drop off either side of the bridge onto the popular river walk to partake in some of London's best rails and quarter pipes. Finally, those looking for pure vertical bliss will find it atop the building near the river. The large gap between the two raised portions of the building makes an excellent halfpipe. Then again, the ramps atop the National Gallery and Canada House offer up plenty of high-flying opportunities as well!

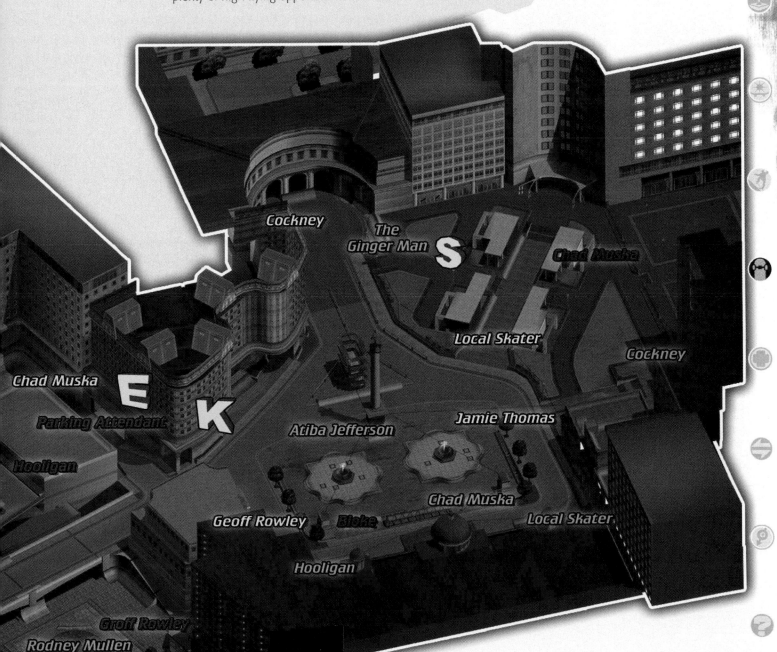

Amateur Challenges

GET A HIGH SCORE: 75,000 POINTS

Location	In the corner of the Square opposite the parking garage
Time	2:00
Awards	$250 and a Stat Point
How unlocked	N/A
Unlocks	Get a Pro Score: 175,000 points

Cockney
"Eh-up? Care to attempt a High Score, bloke?"

Hook a left turn and light the Special Meter with a big leap off the concrete quarter pipe there. Revert the landing and manual towards the steps near Cockney. Grind down the steps, trick into a manual, and head for the fountain. Leap into a Special Grind on the right-hand edge of the first fountain and ollie across to the second fountain for the **Ledge 2 Ledge** gap. Perform a different Special Grind on its edge and Varial Kickflip out of the grind and onto the street.

COLLECT THE S-K-A-T-E LETTERS

Location	In Trafalgar Square near the shops
Time	2:00
Awards	$250 and a Stat Point
How unlocked	N/A
Unlocks	Nothing

The Ginger Man
"Why don't you try and get those letters up there!"

S — Skate forward to the concrete halfpipe set up near the four red buildings. Use the far left ramp to leap into a counter-clockwise grind on the edge of the building. Transfer the grind to the flags for the **Onto the Flags** gap, and off the flags onto the beige brick wall for the **Off the Flags** gap. Quickly hop into a grind on the power line to the right to grab the "S".

K — From the "S", drop into the road near the fountain and bear to the right. Use the quarter pipe against the brown building to leap into a left-hand grind on the ledge above. Grind around the front of the building towards the bridge to find the "K".

A — Circle around the large concrete buildings on the South Bank in a counter-clockwise direction and use one of the quarter pipes to air up into a grind on the lengthy strand of lights. Transfer the grind across the gap in the lights for the **Rail 2 Rail** gap, and to snag the "A" before passing under the bridge.

T — Hop onto the elevated walkway that wraps around the front of the large concrete buildings and use the ramp to Spine Transfer into the bowls on top. Gap across to the upper bowl and come to a stop. Line the skater up with the "T" floating high above and charge the edge of the bowl nearest it. Hold Up so as to leap out of the bowl and towards the letter—just like when gapping the Big Hut at Kona!

E — Drop down out of the bowls and grind the walkway's outer ledge clockwise to the cable leading to the brown building. Ride along the ledge and Wallride the face of the building to snag the "E".

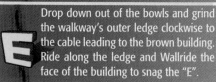

COLLECT THE C-O-M-B-O LETTERS

Location	Near the fountains
Time	0:30
Awards	$250 and a Stat Point
How unlocked	N/A
Unlocks	Nothing

Bloke
"Get all the C-O-M-B-O letters in one single combo!"

Grind the park bench behind the Bloke and quickly transfer it to the ledge on the left after grabbing the "C". Grind off the kinked end of the ledge and onto the bus stop for the **Bus Stop** gap. Leap off the end of the bus stop and onto the ledge at the corner to snag the first "O". Manual across the street towards the ramp between the two planters and leap into a right-hand grind on the ledge above to snag the "M". Get comfortable with this grind, as it's got to be held across the cable to the building that bridges the road and all the way to the other end. Hold the grind all the way to the end to collect the "B" and the other "O".

WALLRIDE TAG 5 BUSES

Location	Near the bus stops
Time	2:00
Awards	$250 and a Stat Point
How unlocked	N/A
Unlocks	Ghetto Tag the SB light line

Chad Muska
"Hey man, see those double-decker buses moving around London? Let's tag 'em with the boards and cans, kid. See if you can wallride 5 different buses. I don't think so."

There are 5 different buses rolling around and the skater's job is to wallride each and every one of them. The buses don't all follow the same route, so the skater is going to have to roll around looking for them. Hang out near the bus stops and wallride the three buses that drive that road and head downhill to the white building that bridges the road. The other two buses come down the road by the river and head under this building.

Each time a successful Wallride is performed, the **Bloody Tourists!** bonus (500 pts) is awarded. Keep an eye out for buses plastered in graffiti as those have already been tagged. Grinding these buses triggers the **You Already Got this Bus** warning and won't help in completing the objective.

GRAB 5 COPPERS HATS

Location	On the brick walkway by the river
Time	2:00
Awards	$250 and a Stat point
How unlocked	N/A
Unlocks	Skitch the Police Bike

A FISTFUL OF HAT

Ollieing into a grab trick isn't the easiest thing to do, but it's the only way to grab the bloody coppers' hats. Be sure to avoid the more elaborate grab tricks such as the Airwalk, Benihana, and Madonna and stick, instead, to the Indy, Nosegrab, or Melon. The chance of bailing is reduced when doing these simpler, quick grabs.

The first copper is just beyond Geoff, on the brick river walkway. Keep the Jump Button depressed for speed and ollie over him while getting in a quick Nosegrab or Indy. Reveal his bald noggin for the **Oi, Gimme Me Hat!** bonus.

Cut through the underground parking garage to the white building built over the road. The next copper is patrolling the sidewalk across the street.

Circle around the Square towards the National Gallery on the far side of the fountains. The next unsuspecting officer is on the sidewalk by the "Gallery of the Dead" banners.

Continue clockwise around the square, past the South Africa House and over to the brown building across the street. Grab some deck while ollieing over the copper on the sidewall.

The final cop cap to be had is in the small plaza overlooking the river. Head down the ramp leading to the café and seek him out amongst the crowd of animal rights activists.

POST PACHYDERM

If you are attempting this challenge after freeing Stompy, the final cop's location is slightly different.

LAND A 100,000 POINT COMBO

Location	Left-hand corner of the National Gallery
Time	2:00
Awards	$250 and a Stat point
How unlocked	N/A
Unlocks	Nail the combos as they come up

The challenge starts in a perfect spot—right next to a series of lengthy ledges. Trick onto the ledge on the side of the building and transfer the grind to the ledge near the street for the **Ledge 2 Ledge** gap. Continue tricking and grinding the ledges around the mall for a couple more **Ledge 2 Ledge** gaps and land in a Special Grind on the ledge that curves back to the right. Trick over to the rail on the edge of the sidewalk, manual towards the ramp between the arches and either Special Grind the ledge above or go big with an aerial Special Trick and Revert the landing.

RODNEY'S FLATLAND TRAINING

Location	Outside the café by the river
Time	1:20
Awards	$250 and a Stat Point
How unlocked	N/A
Unlocks	'Land the Flatland tricks as they appear' and 'Medal in the Competition'

At this stage of the game, you've likely got a handle on aerials, grinding, and lip tricks—it's time to start putting those flatland tricks to use. And Rodney Mullen is going to show you how!

Rodney has assembled a three-part test that introduces the basic flatland tricks. First things first, tap into a manual, hold it for a second in place, then ollie out of it to land. This proves to him that you're ready.

The second step is performing a Pogo. Get into a manual once again and tap the Grind Button twice to start the Pogo. Ollie out of the Pogo to move on to the next step.

The third test is to perform a Wrap Around during the Pogo. Tap back into the Pogo just as before, but this time press the Flip Button twice to perform the Wrap Around. Manage the Balance Meter carefully and ollie out of it to land it. Rodney's final challenge is to do an 8,000 point flatland combo. First, change to Switch stance to earn the 20% scoring bonus. Now start manualling and watch the balance meter while switching between tricks. If the 8,000 points

Rodney Mullen
"Hey, you can rack up a lot of points doing flatground tricks! Just lock in to a manual, then go into combos without actually ollieing into 'em."

remains elusive, add a Special Manual to the skater's trick list. Completing these tests proves to Rodney that you're ready for more sophisticated tricks. Be sure to meet up with him on the other side of the bridge later on for further instruction!

DO A GRAB TRICK OVER THE FOUNTAINS

Location	Near the fountains
Time	1:00
Awards	$250
How unlocked	N/A
Unlocks	ProSet2

Atiba Jefferson
"Yo! Let's show these Brits what we got, man. Bust a phatty over them fountains. Ain't nobody playing with them."

Atiba has dragged a couple of lengthy quarter pipes over towards the fountains. Use these to gain speed and air off the banked ledge encircling each of the fountains. Launch over the center of the fountain and perform the grab trick specified (Up/Left + Grab Button). The skater must clear the entire fountain and land outside of the pool of water to get credit for the jump Perform the trick while hitting the **Ye Old Fountain** gap for each of the two fountains to complete the objective.

RACE THE COPPERS AROUND LONDON

Location	On the right side of the National Gallery
Time	2:00
Awards	$250
How unlocked	N/A
Unlocks	Nothing

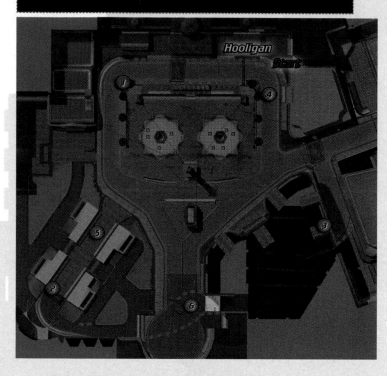

It's time for the annual Beat-a-Copper races! Trafalgar Square has been lined with hay bales and an assortment of barriers has been set up on the road to funnel racers through narrow chutes. It's a one-on-one race with skaters and cops, and the first to the finish line after two laps wins! Although skaters can Luge Hop over the barriers, any contact with a concrete wall or hay bale means automatic disqualification.

The key to winning the race is to get out to a big lead right from the start. The following tips refer to the numbered areas on the maps and show how to navigate the course as fast as possible.

Hooligan
"Race these Coppers around London. You'll need to dodge or jump the barriers. Don't run into any walls or bails of hay. 2 laps oughta show 'em."

[1]Take this turn close to the trees on the inside so as to be in position to slip past the barriers around the bend.

[2]Stick to the right when going up the wooden ramps and cut hard to the left. The fastest line through this hard turn is to aim at the stone ledge inside the turn. The skater uses the very bottom of the banked wall and has a lot of speed heading downhill to the parking garage.

[3]Head to the left of the parking attendant's booth during the first lap. Allow the skater to drift into a wide U-turn to make the next turn easier.

[4]Tap Down to slow down a touch before the turn leading to the finish line. Take this turn tight in order to avoid the barriers that have been set up.

[5]Stick to the center through this area to avoid the many barriers that have been set up. Tap the brakes just before the wooden ramp to adjust the skater's speed since the barriers have taken away the line used in the first lap.

[6]Swing through the first set of barriers after the jump and angle back to the right to line up for the opening leading down to the parking garage. Don't fret if you're out of position, just Luge Hop right into the garage.

FREE STOMPY! DESTROY THE TRAPS

Location	The crowd of activists by the river
Time	Until Stompy gets caught!
Awards	$250
How unlocked	N/A
Unlocks	Nothing

Elephant Lover
"We're about to free Stompy the Elephant, but these damn zoo keepers will find a way to recapture her. Destroy whatever they put out to trap her."

The Elephant Lover has done his job and let Stompy loose, now it's up to you to tear down the four traps that the zoo keepers have set up. Each trap has two cables that run up and over the frame on each side of the road. Gather up some speed and grind up one side, across the top of the net, and down the other side to cut the cables. The **Netting Destroyed** gap triggers with the slicing of each cable.

The first two traps are on the road leading into town from the river. Quickly cut these two traps and head up the road to the right. The third net is in front of the National Gallery. Grind the cables on one side, turn around, and put the board's trucks to use on the other. The final trap is near the building with the arches over the road. Stay one step ahead of Stompy and cut it down so she can go free.

GET A PRO SCORE: 175,000 POINTS

Location	Near the building with the arches
Time	2:00
Awards	$250
How unlocked	Complete 'Get a High Score: 75,000 points'
Unlocks	Nothing

Cockney
"Blimey! A Pro Score will be quite difficult."

Cross the road and start the combo off big on the quarter pipe to the right of the building. Revert the landing and manual back across the street to the ramp near the Cockney. Launch into a Special Trick and Revert into a manual. Head back across the street and hop into a Special Grind on the ledge near the grass. Trick across the gap in the ledge and land in a second Special Grind for the **Ledge 2 Ledge** gap. Hop across to the third ledge for one more gap bonus, and bring the string to an end near the National Gallery building.

GHETTO TAG THE SB LIGHT LINE

Location	On the brick walkway near the river
Time	0:20
Awards	$250 and a Special Trick slot
How unlocked	Complete 'Wallride Tag 5 Buses'
Unlocks	ProSet4

Chad Muska
"Yeaah! Let's light it up! Get Special first, then bust a Ghetto Tag grind on the South Bank light line. Grind the lights all the way from end to end. That's how we do it."

CONGRATULATIONS

Freeing Stompy marks the conclusion of the 90th amateur goal in the game. You're now qualified to attempt one of the pro-specific challenges. Each skater's specific challenge is covered in the Pro Skater's section of this guide. Complete any of those challenges to gain access to the hidden Pro Challenges on each of the courses in the game! That's right, each course (except Carnival and Chicago) has 5 more Pro-level objectives to tackle!

BALANCING ACT

Not only is the South Bank Light grind a heck of a long grind, but it's a very bumpy ride too. Readjust one or two Stat Points to maximize the skater's Grind Balance rating.

Put Chad's spine to use and trick out the Special Meter on it. Ride up into a grind on the concrete quarter pipe at the end of the river walk and trick from it into a Ghetto Tag Special Grind on the lights. Hold the grind around the turn to the left and prepare to gap across a break in the lights. Continue the Ghetto Tag after clearing the break and picking up the **Rail 2 Rail** gap. Tap Left and Right carefully to maintain balance when going under the bridge and around the plaza on the other side. Keep the skater grinding all the way to the café to snag the **South Bank Lights** gap and the successful completion of this difficult challenge!

SKITCH THE POLICE BIKE

Location	Outside the South Africa House
Time	One lap around town
Awards	$250
How unlocked	Complete 'Grab 5 coppers hats'
Unlocks	Nothing

Geoff Rowley
"Ah – it's the bloody cops! Let's have some fun with these bleedin' wankers. Skitch their bike all the way around the city. They'll wack you, so you'll need to switch from side to side."

You've already beaten them in a race, now it's time to Skitch a ride around town on the back of their buggy! Ride up to the back of the police bike and press up to grab it. Although maintaining balance throughout the many tight turns is a challenge in and of itself, the coppers take turns swiping at you with their nightsticks.

Use the Rotate Left and Rotate Right Buttons to shift the Skitch from behind the motorcycle to behind the sidecar so as to avoid being cracked in the head.

Thankfully, the cops don't just swing blindly. Each swing of the nightstick is preceded by the cop glancing over his shoulder. This is the signal to slide over! Keep one eye on the Balance Meter and the other on the cops. Since the skater only gets 2-3 seconds of Skitchin' in before the cop turns around and starts swinging, it's important to use this time to quickly adjust the skater's balance. Then move!

NAIL THE COMBOS AS THEY COME UP

Location	By the red buildings in the Square
Time	1:00
Awards	$250
How unlocked	Complete 'Land a 100,000 Point Combo'
Unlocks	Nothing

Local Skater
"Us locals love to do mad combos here. The tricks'll appear two at a time. Make sure you nail 'em both before you land."

It's time once again for another game of falling tricks. Use the banked walls of the mall as a half pipe and boost enough air to perform the combos that appear. That's right, the tricks that appear must be performed together in one jump! There are a total of 9 combos, representing 18 tricks that must be performed. Unlike the previous falling trick objectives, there's little to no chance of having identical combos appearing on the list, so don't count on getting any freebies!

Start working the pipe to get the Special Meter fully lit; this guarantees enough hangtime to perform any combo the Local Skater throws out. Avoid lateral motion and rotation as either could cause the skater to drift out of the pipe. If the skater does start to soar out of the pipe or towards the gap near the stairs, be sure to tap the Revert Button to recover. Finally, the order in which the pair of tricks is performed is inconsequential. Although there's no real benefit to performing one before the other, it is acceptable to do the bottom trick first.

MIXIN' UP THE SKITCHIN'

The coppers may be a bunch of wankers, but even they can pick up on the skater's pattern. Skaters eventually get whacked in the head if they shift back and forth at regular intervals. Try shifting back and forth between the two cops sporadically, sometimes before they even turn around to see if the skater is there. This throws them off as they must spend more time looking and less time swinging!

LAND THE FLATLAND TRICKS AS THEY APPEAR

Location	On the walkway by the river
Time	1:00
Awards	$250
How unlocked	Complete 'Rodney's flatland training'
Unlocks	Nothing

Rodney Mullen
"Hey, remember those flatground tricks from before? OK, here's a new one. Lock in to a manual, and nail the tricks as they show up."

Got time for another game of falling tricks? This one contains strictly flatland tricks and is not only a fun objective, but it really helps introduce the various flatland tricks and how they can be linked together. Tap into a manual and start performing the flatland tricks that Rodney calls out. Since the trick string extends until the skater either bails or ollies out of it, be sure to touch down and "cash in" after every 3 or 4 tricks. The skater must perform—and land—a total of 10 tricks to complete the objective.

CAN'T STOP ROLLING?

One of the common problems for beginning flatland skaters is that they can't stop rolling around while in the manual. One way to prevent this is to come to a complete stop before tapping into the manual. Another way, specific to this challenge, is to position the skater over the sewer grate before initiating the manual. The ground slopes down towards the grate very slightly; just enough to keep the skater from rolling while trying to flatland.

MEDAL THE COMPETITION

Location	Under the bridge near the river
Time	1:00
Awards	$250
How unlocked	Complete 'Rodney's flatland training'
Unlocks	Nothing

Competition Judge
"There's not a lot of stuff to trick off of down here... This Comp is gonna really test your Flatland skills! Let's see you medal in this competition!"

PREPARING FOR BATTLE

Be sure to enter the 'Edit Tricks' menu before starting this objective so as to assign at least one Special Manual to a Special Trick Slot. There's nothing to grind or jump from in this contest—a Special Manual helps rack up some points.
Another absolute must in terms of preparation is assigning as many Stat Points to the Manual Balance and Ollie categories as needed to max them out.

Welcome to the flatland contest. There are no rails, no half pipes, and no kickers—nothing but smooth, flat concrete! This contest is all about launching an epic ground attack that strings together as many flatland tricks as possible. It may seem out of reach at first, but skaters can score well over 100,000 points during each run—and if their eyes are set on the gold medal, it's a must. The judges only give out scores of 98 and 99 to those who score at least 110,000 points.

PREREQUISITES

This 'Medal the Competition' objective may have become available after completing Rodney's first flatland lesson, but it's recommended that all skaters complete Rodney's second flatland challenge before entering the competition. The 'Land the Flatland Tricks as they Appear' goal does an excellent job of preparing skaters for this competition.

One of the great things about flatland tricks is that many can be linked together in a very short period of time. Since the tricks themselves aren't worth very many points, it's important to grow the multiplier as fast as possible. One of the best ways to go about doing this is by tapping into a Handstand and performing multiple Handflips. The same is true if the Wrap Around is performed repeatedly while in the Pogo position.

Regardless of how many flatland tricks the skater links together, the base points aren't likely to get too high without some Special Tricks. Kickflipping into a Special Manual after a handful of flatland tricks is a great way to boost the base points and to reduce the number of times a trick is repeated. Try to Pop Shove-It out of the Special Manual and tack on some more flatland tricks after that.

Other ways to rack up the points, and the multipliers, is to start a second scoring string from the switch stance, or even from a Nollie. Perform multiple Heelflips and Kickflips to increase the multiplier rapidly.

Another way to really boost the points total is to use the Revert Button to Pivot. Depending on the flatland trick the skater is in, tapping the Revert Button results in a Pivot, Nosepivot, or even Truckspin if in the Truckstand position. Repeatedly pressing the Revert Button can take a normal Truckstand and tack on a 5040 Truckspin! Although these spins and pivots only increase the multiplier once, there are many points to be gained from 14 complete rotations!

Pro Challenges

GET THE SICK SCORE: 700,000 POINTS

Location	On the roof of the large white building by the river
Time	2:00
Awards	$500
How unlocked	Complete a Pro-Specific Challenge
Unlocks	Nothing

Thanks to the skater-friendly starting position, this 700,000 point Sick Score is well within reach of a single combination. He might be a Hooligan, but he sure knows a good skate spot when he sees one. The two roofs that rise up beside the Hooligan not only make a perfect halfpipe, but the upper areas offer plenty of lengthy grinding opportunities as well.

Start the combo with a big aerial off the taller side of the halfpipe, Revert the landing, and go right into an aerial Special Trick on the other side. Revert back towards the taller portion and unleash another Special Trick. Revert the landing to keep the string going and perform one more aerial Special Trick, but this time while Spine Transferring onto the lower roof. Revert into a

Hooligan
"Oi, don't get your knickers in a twist! All you have to do is nail down this Sick Score!"

manual and two-wheel it across the roof towards the edge parallel to the river. Ollie into a clockwise Special Grind on the ledge, hold it around the bend, and trick down onto the walkway below. Land in a Special Grind on the outer ledge of the walkway and balance the grind up the cable to the other building and trick into another grind on the ledge and carry it across the street to the South Africa building. Trick across the gap in the railing for the **Rail 2 Rail** gap and trick down onto the ground to end the string.

COLLECT PRO C-O-M-B-O

Location	Near the bus stop
Time	0:30
Awards	$500
How unlocked	Complete a Pro-Specific Challenge
Unlocks	ProSet1

Bloke
"All right, mate, I've got a tougher one for ya, this time. Let's see if you can get all of these letters in one C-O-M-B-O."

Cross the street towards the quarter pipe near the Gallery and pluck the "C" out of the air while transferring onto the balcony ramp. Quickly tap into a left-hand grind on the edge of the ramp near the edge to grind onto the cable leading to the South Africa house. Snag the "O", hop across the gap in the rail to grab the "M" and the **Rail 2 Rail** gap and continue the grind. As soon as the skater makes it onto the wire running across the street, ollie off to the left to land in another grind on the wire with the "B". Hop into a manual on the roof, Spine Transfer down into the halfpipe gully between the two roofs, and Spine Transfer up to the other side. Manual across the roof and leap off the ramp near the edge to get the final "O".

BEAT MUSKA'S BEST 6 COMBOS

Location	In the mall area
Time	0:30
Awards	$500
How unlocked	Complete a Pro-Specific Challenge
Unlocks	Nothing

Chad Muska

"Good day mate! Cheerio! We're over here in London, trying to bust mad tricks. Let's cruise around and check your skills. Beat my best six combos... I don't think so."

Chad has laid down six combos ranging from 20,000 points to 70,000 points and he wants to see if you can beat every one of them. Each combo takes place at a different spot around London and he's giving a generous 30 seconds to get started on each of them.

The first combo must exceed 20,000 points and begins in the pedestrian mall. Heelflip into a grind on the benches, trick across to the other benches for the **Bench Gap** and ollie down into a manual. Go big off the quarter pipe near the Canada House with plenty of rotation to nail the first combo.

The party moves over to the arches for the second combo, worth 30,000 points. Turn to the right and leap into a Special Trick on the ramp there. Revert into a manual and roll across the street to the ramps on the other side. Launch into another Special Trick to put the base score over the top.

The third location is on the walkway of the large building near the river. Treat the little ramp to the right (near the street) and the large banked wall of the building as a halfpipe and link up several flips and grabs with a Special Trick to get the required 40,000 points.

It's time to shift away from air-based combos to a focus on street lines. The fourth combo, worth 50,000 points, starts on the street up the hill from the parking garage. Charge the right-hand edge of the bridge and Special Grind on it towards the river. Trick off the right and land in another Special Grind on the walkway below (land in a manual and quickly hop into the Special Grind if necessary). Grind around the turn and down towards the quarter pipe near the river. Finish off the line with a big trick on the ramp.

The fifth combo is for 60,000 points and begins on the bridge near the stairs leading down to the river. Hop into a Special Grind on the right-hand railing and hold it all the way to the gap near the quarter pipe. Trick straight across the gap and into another Special Grind and hold this one around the bend. Trick across the break in the rail near the quarter pipe for the **Rail 2 Rail** gap and pick up the Special Grind on the other side. Hold it up and over the curved quarter pipe in the corner and trick down onto the ground by the parking attendant to end the chain.

The final combo takes place along the ledges near the National Gallery and is best suited to those with very fast reflexes. Hop into a grind on the ledge near the starting spot, trick across the gap and land in a Special Grind for the **Ledge 2 Ledge** gap and quickly trick down onto the curb for another hit of the **Ledge 2 Ledge** bonus. Grind around the curve and up onto the top of the quarter pipe in the corner. Continue tricking across the gaps and landing in different grinds on the ledges to build the multiplier with multiple **Ledge 2 Ledge** gaps and flip tricks. End the combo with a lengthy grind near the pedestrian mall—the score should be well over 70,000 points by then.

GRIND AMERICAN CARS FOR PARKING GUY

Location	At the parking garage booth
Time	0:30
Awards	$500
How unlocked	Complete a Pro-Specific Challenge
Unlocks	Nothing

Parking Attendant
"Help me! Crazy Americans have parked here. Grind their cars in the order shown to teach them a lesson!"

There are four illegally parked cars in the parking garage that must be grinded on in one continuous trick string. Each car turns pink after being grinded on and the **Crazy Americans** bonus triggers.

Hop into a grind on the left side of the silver car straight ahead and hold the grind right onto the curb. Grind the curb towards the blue sports car and ollie over the hood of the black car and into a grind on the **Crazy Americans'** car. Manual around the turn and towards the black sports car in the distance. Grind the driver's side of the black car right onto the curb and continue the grind to the right. Ollie off the curb and into a grind on the blue car near the parking attendant to complete the challenge.

TRICK ON EVERY OBJECT IN THE SOUTHBANK

Location	Near the café by the river
Time	2:00
Awards	$500
How unlocked	Complete a Pro-Specific Challenge
Unlocks	Nothing

Geoff Rowley
"This, my friend, is the South Bank! Let's see if you can do a trick off every object."

All told, there are 40 objects in the South Bank area that must be tricked on. This includes the area near the café, the rails and ledges on the bridge, the walls and ledges below the large building by the river, and all of the ramps and lights near the river walk. In this Graffiti-inspired objective, an object becomes painted red once a trick has been performed on it. Everything from a Revert to a grind to a Kickflip can be used to "tag" an object—the only thing that doesn't is an ordinary ollie. The key to tackling this objective is efficiency. Line up a few ramps and rails at a time, hit them with basic tricks—this is no time for Special Tricks—and land cleanly to make 'em count!

Start the assault on the Southbank by clearing out the objects near the café. Grind the 3 stone blocks in the center and head to the curved wall near the

café. Transfer a grind from the wall to the café and onto the rail near the river. Grind the railing along the river onto the rail leading up to the bridge and descend the other railing. Trick off the quarter pipe into a left-hand grind on the lights and trick off the ramps atop the café.

Leap into another grind on the lights and balance it under the bridge to the other side of the river walk. Hit the **Rail 2 Rail** gap while transferring a grind across the various sections of railing by the water and come back

and hit each of the three quarter pipes as well. Grind on the ledges of the walkway and the bridge and Spine Transfer off the small ramps near the street to drop into the area below the building.

Although it may seem as if there's little to trick on under the building, there are numerous U-shaped benches and ledges near the Pimp that can be gapped across quickly. There's also the lengthy wall opposite the river and the smaller handrails by the steps.

Regain the walkway and Spine Transfer up to the roof. Trick off the ramps and Spine Transfer between the two raised portions to paint the entire rooftop sections red. Should there still be some missing, do a quick lap on the walkway or check to make sure that all of the ramps on the street have been turned red

SIDE MONEY

PIMP DADDY

Time	N/A
Award	$100

Pimp
"Oi, wanna bet on one of these lovely ladies?"

Skate up to the group under the bridge and talk to the Pimp to get the opportunity to bet one of the lovely slappers. The ladies take turns slapping each other and if the one you select stays on her feet, the Pimp pays you $100.

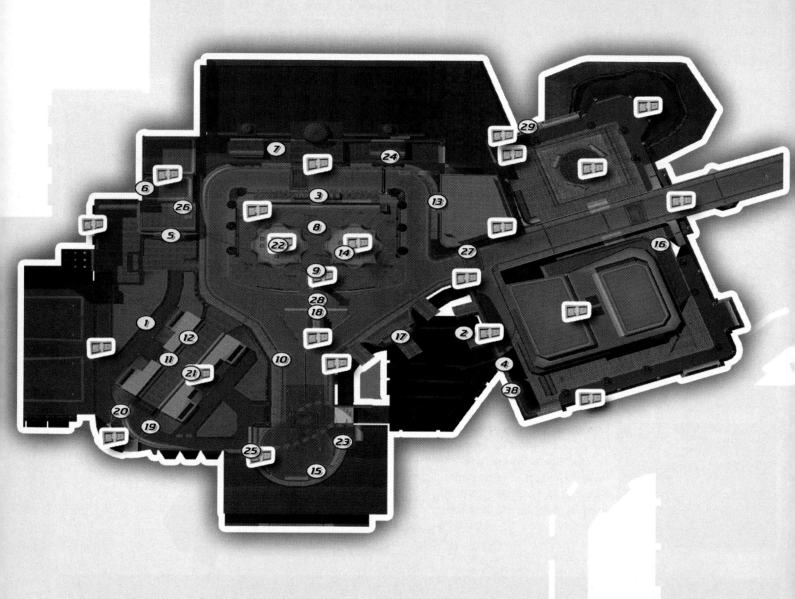

GAP CHECKLIST

[1] BENCH GAP — 25 POINTS
Hop into a grind on the benches in the pedestrian mall and transfer it across the gap to continue grinding on the other benches.

[2] GARAGE HOP — 25 POINTS
Transfer a grind between the curbs in the parking garage.

[3] BUS STOP — 50 POINTS
Leap into a grind atop either of the bus stops.

[4] CHEESE LEDGE — 50 POINTS
Grind the curved quarter pipe in the corner near the river and transfer the grind to the ledge above the entrance to the parking garage.

[5] EH? CANADA... — 50 POINTS
Leap into a lip trick on the roof of the Canada House (the brown building near the pedestrian mall).

[6] EH? NOKIA... — 50 POINTS
Spine Transfer up to the bowl on the uppermost roof of the Canada House and lip trick on the neon Nokia sign.

[7] GALLERY GAP — 50 POINTS
Ride up onto one of the three front porch areas of the Gallery and ollie over the sloped walkway to one of the other porches.

[8] LEDGE 2 LEDGE — 50 POINTS
Transfer a grind between any two adjacent ledges.

[9] NELSON'S LIP — 50 POINTS
Use the quarter pipe at the base of the statue in the Square to lip trick on the statue.

[10] RAIL 2 RAIL — 50 POINTS
Transfer a grind between any two adjacent handrails.

[11] SHELL BUILDING HOP — 50 POINTS
Transfer a grind between the roofs of the red buildings in the pedestrian mall.

[12] SHELL EDGE — 50 POINTS
Lip trick on any of the roofs in the pedestrian mall area.

[13] SOUTH AFRIKA — 50 POINTS
Lip trick on the roof of the South Africa House (white building beside the National Gallery).

[14] YET ANOTHER WIRE — 50 POINTS
Leap from the fountain's ledge and land in a grind on the wires that criss cross over the fountain.

[15] ADMIRALTY — 100 POINTS
Transfer the quarter pipes in front of the building with the arches.

[16] BIG RAIL 2 RAIL — 100 POINTS
Grind the ledge of the lower walkway by the building near the bridge and transfer it to a grind on the railing near the river.

[17] LIP GAP — 100 POINTS
Lip trick on the brown or white building up the hill from the parking garage, near the arches.

[18] ME SCAFFOLDING — 100 POINTS
Lip trick on the uppermost piece of scaffolding on the statue that's under construction in the Square.

[19] OFF THE FLAGS — 100 POINTS
Transfer a grind from one of the outstretched flagpoles onto a booth in the pedestrian mall

[20] ONTO THE FLAGS — 100 POINTS
Transfer a grind from one of the booths in the pedestrian mall onto the outstretched flagpoles.

[21] SHELL TRANSFER — 100 POINTS
Use the ramps in the pedestrian mall to transfer over the stairs between the red booths.

[22] YE OLD FOUNTAIN — 100 POINTS
Gap over either of the fountains by leaping from the ledge. The skater must leap over the center of the fountain.

[23] 'ROUND THE ARCHES — 200 POINTS
Grind from the **Shell Mega Wire** onto the white ledge above the arches and hold the grind around the entire curving face of the building.

[24] TOP 'O THE GALLERY — 200 POINTS
Grind the edge of the three roofs of the National Gallery in one continuous grind.

[25] SHELL MEGA WIRE — 250 POINTS
Grind the full length of the cable that extends from the Canada House to the white arches.

[26] CANADA BOMB — 500 POINTS
Leap onto the lower rooftop of the Canada House (over the front of the building) and transfer from the quarter pipe against the wall to the quarter pipe in the Square between the bus stops and fountains.

[27] NETTING DESTROYED! — 500 POINTS
Grind up the cables and across the top of the traps in the 'Free Stompy! Destroy the Traps' objective.

[28] RING AROUND THE COLUMN — 500 POINTS
Starting near Nelson's Column, Skitch a ride on a bus for an entire lap around Trafalgar Square and back to the statue.

[29] SOUTH BANK LIGHTS — 500 POINTS
Grind the entire strand of lights near the river, all the way from the café to the corner near the parking garage.

ZOO

Field trip!!!

Listen up class, today's trip is to a Zoo unlike any other. Oh, sure, it has the same animals as other Zoos, but it's much more interactive. For instance, this Zoo allows its visitors to Skitch the tail of elephants, get into a foot race with a monkey, and even grind on the edge of a shark tank. And if that doesn't sound exciting enough, then maybe a rampaging elephant and a pair of escaping lions is!

The Zoo isn't all about playing with the animals though. There's some serious skating to be had here as well. Numerous quarter pipes and spines are found on many of the rooftops and miles of cables offer

LEVEL GOALS

Unlocked Objectives

Get a High Score: 80,000 points
Collect the S-K-A-T-E letters
Collect the C-O-M-B-O letters
Hardflip and Heelflip over Kenny
Nail the tricks they yell out
Help the Lion Tamer escape
Beat Bob's 3 best combos
Stop the Monkey from escaping
Feed the Hippos
Skitch the Elephant
Catch the 5 runaway Penguins

Locked Objectives

Get a Pro Score: 200,000 points
Medal the Competition
Grind the 4 Zoo banners
Do a Sit Down Air over the Lion's cage

Pro Challenges

Get the Sick Score: 800,000 points
Collect Pro C-O-M-B-O
Transfer Over Elephant Rock
Get Kong Back in his Cage
Combo scare 40 birds

plenty of grinding action. Finally, those looking for pure vertical action can get their fill in the empty moat that surrounds the rhino and elephant exhibits—it's the next best thing to an endless halfpipe. Throw in an assortment of handrails, picnic tables, and a chance to harass Kenny the Koala, and it becomes easy to see that this Zoo warrants frequent visits.

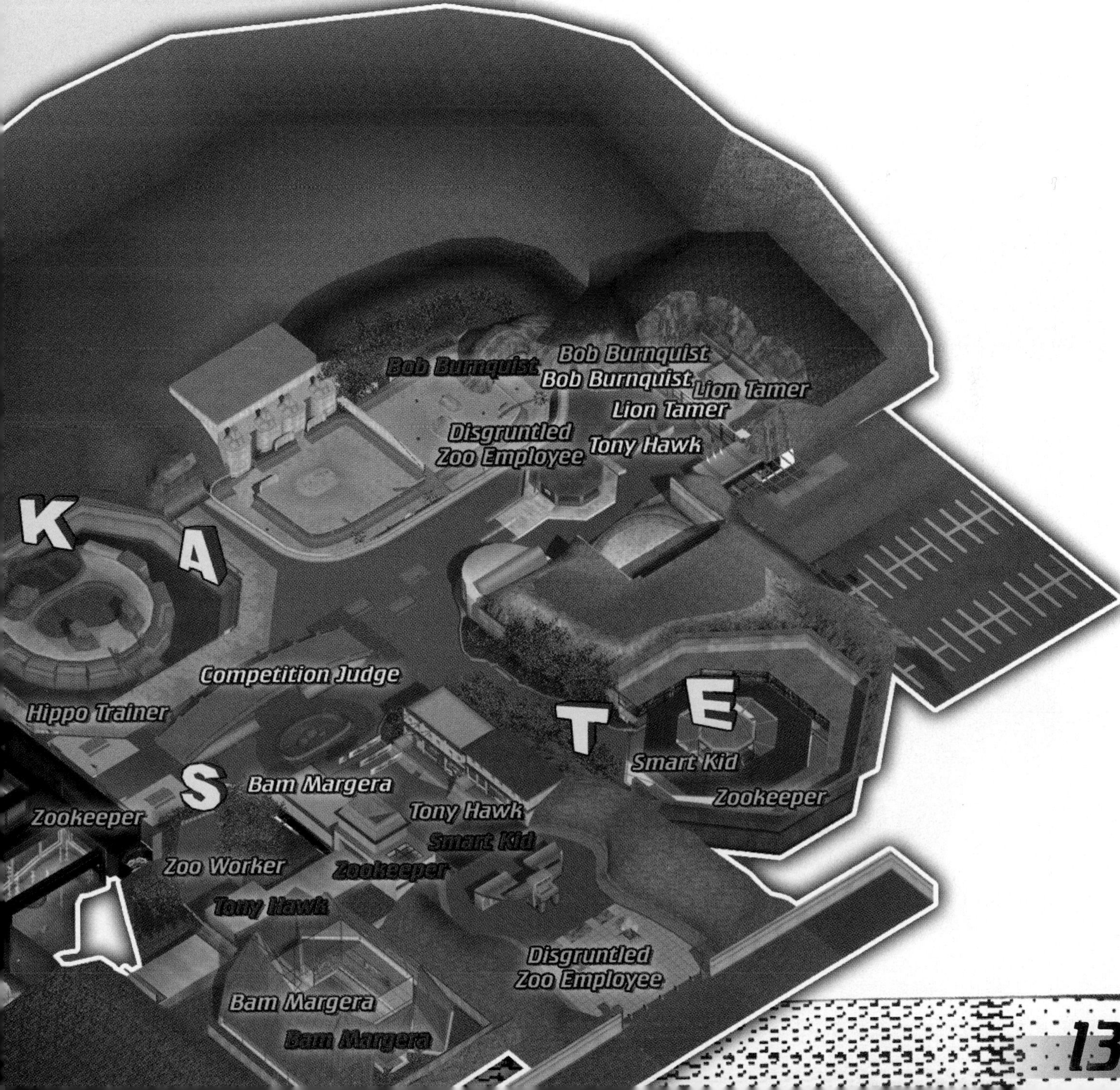

Bob Burnquist
Bob Burnquist
Bob Burnquist
Lion Tamer
Lion Tamer
Disgruntled
Zoo Employee
Tony Hawk

K
A
Competition Judge
Hippo Trainer
T
E
S
Smart Kid
Bam Margera
Zookeeper
Zookeeper
Tony Hawk
Zoo Worker
Smart Kid
Zookeeper
Tony Hawk
Disgruntled
Zoo Employee
Bam Margera
Bam Margera

Amateur Challenges

GET A HIGH SCORE: 80,000 POINTS

Location	By the main entrance
Time	2:00
Awards	$250 and a Stat Point
How unlocked	N/A
Unlocks	Get a Pro Score: 200,000 points and ProSet4

Tony Hawk
"The Zoo's a killer place to skate. Try to bust out a High Score and don't feed the animals."

Ollie off the angled ledge behind Tony and land in a grind on the lower green ledge. Hold the grind across the banner at the end for the **Banner Gap 4!** gap and continue around towards the monkey cages. Switch up the grind once or twice and flip trick into a Special Grind on the shingled roof in the center of the exhibit. Trick out of the grind and land in a manual on the street below to gain an extra multiplier before touching down.

COLLECT THE S-K-A-T-E LETTERS!

Location	Outside the aviary
Time	2:00
Awards	$250 and a Stat Point
How unlocked	N/A
Unlocks	ProSet1

Zoo Worker
"Hey you! Help me clean this place up. Collect the S-K-A-T-E letters!"

S — Boneless over the rail and the bushes near the picnic table to snag the "S" out of the air en route to the hippo exhibit.

K — Cross the moat into the hippo exhibit (Hippo Plant on the hippo in the center of the moat to open the bridge for later) and Spine Transfer into the upper pool. Air off the back of this pool to grab the letter out of the air.

A — Exit the **Hungry, Hungry Hippo Pool** and approach the moat to the left of the bridge. Ollie towards the "A" and Hippo Plant off the surfacing hippo to clear the moat safely.

T — Head up the path towards the monkeys and hop into a grind atop the snack hut. Ollie off the hut to grab the "T".

E — The "E" is floating above the monkey exhibit. Spine Transfer onto the monkey cages and jump onto the shingled roof in the center. Ollie off the front of this roof towards the snack hut to get the letter.

COLLECT THE C-O-M-B-O LETTERS!

Location	Near the monkeys
Time	2:00
Awards	$250 and a Stat Point
How unlocked	N/A
Unlocks	Medal the Competition

Smart Kid
"Hey skater-person! My dad says there's no way you can get all the C-O-M-B-O letters in one combo."

This batch of C-O-M-B-O letters are all near the monkey exhibit. Even better is that once you make the link from the "C" to the first "O", the whole chain becomes very straightforward.

Air off the banked ledge below the center exhibit to pluck the "C" out of the air and quickly Revert the landing. Angle towards the "O" directly across the way and hop into a grind on the rail to the right of the letter. Grind the rail and transfer across the gaps near the brick ledges to pick up the "M" and the **Hear No Evil** gap and the "B" and the **Speak No Evil** gap. Grind off the end of the rail to collect the final "O" and touch down to end the combo.

HARDFLIP AND HEELFLIP OVER KENNY

Location	By the main entrance to the Zoo
Time	2:00
Awards	$250 and a Stat Point
How unlocked	N/A
Unlocks	Nothing

Disgruntled Zoo Employee
"You know what would be funny? You should do a [flip trick] and a [flip trick] over Kenny the Koala!"

The Disgruntled Zoo Employee specifies two flip tricks (Up/Left + Flip Button and Right + Flip Button) that must be done over Kenny while he stands and waves at the visitors. Ride up to Kenny, ollie over him, and perform the more complex of the two tricks.

As you'll quickly see, Kenny doesn't like the prank and takes off running around the Zoo. Although he won't go much further than the bridge, he can be rather tricky to catch. Chase him past the turnstiles and wait for him to turn around and run back towards the entrance. Once he does skate out towards him and perform the other trick over his head.

NAIL THE TRICKS THEY YELL OUT

Location	In the aviary
Time	1:00
Awards	$250 and a Stat point
How unlocked	N/A
Unlocks	Grind the 4 Zoo banners

Bam Margera

"All right these birds know a lot about skating, AND they can talk. So do the tricks that they yell out."

This falling tricks challenge features numerous lip tricks in addition to the standard fare of flips and grabs. Get lined up with the spine and the quarter pipe to the right and try to stay as straight as possible. There's no reason to rotate and missing the spine too often could cost precious seconds. There are a total of 18 tricks to perform but none of them require diagonal presses. One thing's for certain, future falling tricks challenges are much tougher!

HELP THE LION TAMER ESCAPE

Location	The lions den
Time	2:00
Awards	$250 and a Stat point
How unlocked	N/A
Unlocks	Lure the Lions back the cage

Lion Tamer

"Crikey! Help me! If you can get in here and do a big combo, I bet it will give me enough time to escape!"

Surely you've heard the old adage that "skating soothes the savage beast". Oh, you haven't? Well, that's because nobody ever pulled off a 50,000 point combo in a lion's den before!

Drop into the den and trick out the Special Meter with a few quick flips and grabs off the vert ramp against the rear of the cage. Revert to a manual back towards the front fencing and launch into a Special Trick. Revert and manual back across to the rear ramp again

and add some more tricks to the string to further boost the multiplier. Revert the landing and roll it out to end the scoring combo.

BEAT BOB'S 3 BEST COMBOS

Location	Near the elephant exhibit
Time	0:30
Awards	$250 and a Stat Point
How unlocked	N/A
Unlocks	Do a Sit Down Air over the Lion's cage

Bob Burnquist

"Hey – I've scoped out three great spots to skate in this zoo. Follow along and see if you can beat my combo."

Bob has laid down three moderately impressive combos and wants to see someone top them. There's plenty of time to go exploring and start a combo at nearly any place in the Zoo, but the three lines described here are both straightforward and begin right where Bob says.

The first combo must exceed 40,000 points and begins just outside the lion's den. Launch off the rocks to the left of the den and perform multiple flip tricks and grabs while rotating through a 540. Revert the landing and trick into a Special Manual. Balance the Special Manual clear across the Zoo towards the aquarium to get the requisite points.

WHY NOT GRIND?

The second and third combos feature lots of grinds and it's a good idea to leave the full point value of the Special Grinds for those combos that require higher scores.

The second combo is for 50,000 points and begins atop the Koala Café. Trick down off the roof into a Special Grind on one of the rails near Stompy and manual towards the rail near the rhinos. Special Grind the rail towards the vert ramp at the dead end and Special Trick off the ramp while transferring into the moat for the **Big Moat Transfer** gap.

The final combo location is on the edge of the monkey cages near the snack hut. This one has to be for over 60,000 points, or else all three must be repeated. Turn around and hop into a Special Grind on the edge of the monkey cage. Trick off the other end and Special Manual down the hill out of the monkey exhibit. Trick into another Special Grind on the ledge near the gorillas for some extra quick points and touch the wheels down to end the string.

STOP THE MONKEY FROM ESCAPING

Location	Near the monkeys
Time	0:15
Awards	$250
How unlocked	N/A
Unlocks	ProSet3

Zookeeper
"This monkey is trying to escape! Get to the tram gate and the main gate and warn security before he gets away!"

The monkey is going to escape and it's up to a speedy skater to alert security at both exits. The monkey is going to make a beeline for the tram gate first, so that's the first stop! Hop into a grind on the ledge near the gorillas to gain speed off the **You Drive Me Ape!** gap and continue grinding towards the gate near the lion's den.

CHEATERS, GO HOME!

Those thinking they could just exit the park at the tram gate to be whisked away to the main entrance are sorely mistaken. Passing through the tram gate automatically forfeits the objective.

Once the guard at the tram gate has been notified of the fleeing monkey, quickly skate to the main entrance. Grind the rail beside the Koala Café to gain some more speed and head up the hill to the left of the bridge. Jump the turnstiles and head past the ticket counters to the guard standing near the street.

FEED THE HIPPOS

Location	To the right of the hippos' moat
Time	0:05
Awards	$250
How unlocked	N/A
Unlocks	Nothing

Hippo Trainer
"Hey – help me feed the hippos, right! See if you can knock these pumpkins into the water!"

There are four pumpkins placed precariously around the hippo's moat and they must be knocked into the water to feed the hungry beasts. There's only one good way to do this and that's via the **Backwoods Path** gap.

Hop into a grind on the rail to the left and transfer the grind to the log on the grassy hill. Grind up the first log and ollie onto the second log to knock the first pumpkin into the water. Carry the grind onto the back ledge to feed a second hippo and hop into a grind on the lone log on the grass. Transfer the grind to the railing beside the moat to knock another pumpkin into the water and continue grinding around towards the bridge. Trick over the gap in the railing near the bridge and pick up the grind near the snack hut to feed the final hippo.

SWEET HIPPO LOVIN'

Skate up to one of the telescopes near the hippo exhibit to get a sneak peak at what goes on after hours at the Zoo. Ahhh Yeahhh!

SKITCH THE ELEPHANT

Location	Near the elephant exhibit
Time	2:00
Awards	$250
How unlocked	N/A
Unlocks	Nothing

Disgruntled Zoo Employee
"I bet you can't skitch on that elephant's tail for 30 seconds!"

Transfer over the moat and roll up behind the elephant in the center of the exhibit. Press Up to grab a hold of its tail and focus on the Balance Meter. The skater must maintain a Skitch for 30 full seconds. Although the elephant starts off relatively slow, he picks up speed with each passing second. Although the constant left-turn makes balance slightly tricky, it's the elephants dung-bombs that really, err, pile on the difficulty.

Tap the controls to the Left and Right to keep the Balance Meter as centered as possible and act quickly to regain a firm handle on the elephant's tail after each "surprise". Once the 15 second mark passes, the elephant bombs come more frequently. Continue to hold on until the full 30 seconds passes.

CATCH THE 5 RUNAWAY PENGUINS

Location	Inside the aquarium
Time	2:00
Awards	$250
How unlocked	N/A
Unlocks	ProSet2

Elephant Trainer
"Be careful around old Stompy here! Skate too close to her head, and there's no telling what she'll do!"

Before one can skate into the aquarium, the doors have to be busted open—it's time to find out why they call that elephant Stompy! Hop up onto the roof of the Koala Café and ollie off the front of it on an angle to land on poor Stompy for the **Elephant Hop** gap. This sends the elephant into a rampage, during which she destroys picnic tables, the bridge, and even the aquarium entrance. Head inside and talk to the Zookeeper to see if there's anything to be done.

Zookeeper
"There are 5 penguins on the loose. You knock 'em over, and I'll catch 'em!"

Skate past the Zookeeper and down the hill towards the shark tank. Make a right at the tank to find the first tuxedo-wearing escapee.

Return to the Zookeeper and make a left at the aquarium's main entrance to take out a second escaping penguin.

The third penguin is on the bridge outside the aquarium. He's on the half near the aquarium.

Skate past the snack hut by the hippo pool and keep an eye out for the penguin near the vert ramp. Skate into him to knock him down.

The final runaway penguin is on the path leading to the aviary. Looks like he wants to earn his wings. Ground him for good with a swift Kickflip to the beak.

GET A PRO SCORE: 200,000 POINTS

Location	Atop the Koala Cafe
Time	2:00
Awards	$250
How unlocked	Complete 'Get a High Score: 80,000 points'
Unlocks	Nothing

Tony hawk
"OK, try this one. Start a run from up here on top of the snack bar, and try to beat my Pro Score."

Tony has set up some ramps atop the Koala Café and they make for a potent start to this quick combo. Roll out onto the kicker and turn around to face the vert ramp to start the run.

Use the vert to get the combo off to a good start with a pair of tricks such as a 540 Varial Heelflip to Airwalk. Revert the landing and trick off the kicker into the giraffe exhibit. Manual towards the right-hand quarter pipe and launch into a Special Trick. Revert into another manual and trick off the front ledge of the exhibit into a grind on the rails to the left of the café. Trick off the end of the rail and land in a Special Grind on the ledge near the gorillas. Hold the grind around the bend towards the monkeys and Special Manual and Special Grind up the path until there's enough points to touch down with over 200,000.

MEDAL THE COMPETITION

Location	Atop the bridge
Time	0:30
Awards	$250
How unlocked	Complete 'Collect the C-O-M-B-O letters'
Unlocks	Nothing

Competition Judge
"We're about to hold a competition. Would you like to enter? Best two out of three runs will take the gold medal!"

The competition at the Zoo consists of three 30 second runs. Although it might sound like a lot of points for such a short period, it's going to take scores of at least 275,000 to earn a perfect mark from the judges. That having been said, the course is very conducive to linking together big chains and, as far as winning a medal is concerned, a pair of scores above 190,000 points each will do nicely.

There's essentially three areas to the contest spot: the large halfpipe where each run begins, there's the rails on the bridge, and there is the vert ramps at either end of the bridge. Although it's possible to incorporate some tricks in each of these areas into one combo, it's best to not risk the bail.

A good way to start a run is to drop into the halfpipe and link up a couple of grabs and flips off the banked wall directly across from the starting spot. Revert into a manual and take it straight across the pipe to launch into a double-tap grab trick with 720 rotation or more. Revert back across the flatbottom and unleash a high-scoring Special Trick. Cap the string off by reverting one more time and leaping into a Special Lip Trick on the rail below the Neversoft banner on the bridge. Hold the lip trick as long as possible and Revert the landing for one extra multiplier.

Another good way to incorporate the halfpipe and the bridge into the same line is to trick out the Special Meter on the initial jump, Revert back across the pipe and perform an aerial Special Trick. Revert and manual on an angle to the other side and perform another air-based Special Trick. This time, Revert the landing and slide up into a Special grind on the rail of the bridge. Transfer the gap in the bridge (if Stompy broke it already) and land in a different Special Grind on the other side. Manual off the bridge and pop into a Special Lip Trick on the coping of either vert ramp.

Time to put the rails on the deck of the bridge to use. Start the run with a huge 720 Indy off one of the vert ramps near the aquarium and quickly link it to a Special Grind over the bridge on the outer rail near the hippos. Hop off the grind and into a manual towards the vert ramp on the left and throw down a Special Trick while transferring to the other vert ramp. Revert into a manual and hop into a Special Grind on the one of the rails on the deck of the bridge. Transfer the grind across the gap to the other rail and ride it out on the other side.

GRIND THE 4 ZOO BANNERS

Location	On the roof of the stores by the bridge
Time	2:00
Awards	$250
How unlocked	Complete 'Nail the tricks they yell out'
Unlocks	Nothing

Bam Margera
"Hope you're not afraid of heights, ya little wuss! See if you can grind across all 4 of them Zoo banners."

It's time to grind on the banners that are strung up between the shops near the bridge. Although Bam went through the trouble of hauling some large quarter pipes up onto the rooftops, don't use them. This objective is best completed by carefully lining the skater up with each of the cables and the ollieing over the lip of the building into the grind on the cable. The skater begins the challenge perfectly lined up with **Banner Gap 1!** Hop over the edge and balance the grind across to the other side. Take your time and go back and forth between the roofs on the cables to score **Banner Gap 1!**, **Banner Gap 2!**, and **Banner Gap 3!**

BACK TO THE ROOF

If the skater misses a cable or just accidentally falls off the roof, head up onto the bridge and use the **Bridge Roof Grind** cable to get back up top. Since the grind is uphill, make sure to have plenty of momentum and ollie once or twice to help the skater stay on track.

The fourth and final banner hangs from the lower ledge of the building and is best reached from the ground. Head back towards the main entrance and pop off the sidewalk kicker into a grind on the green ledge. Hold the grind right onto the banner's cable and cross the street in the grind for **Banner Gap 4!**

LURE THE LIONS BACK TO THE CAGE

Location	On the truck near the lion's den
Time	2:00
Awards	$250
How unlocked	Complete 'Help the Lion Tamer escape'
Unlocks	Nothing

Lion Tamer
"The lions have escaped from their cages! I wonder what idiot let them out? See if you can lure them back! But be careful, they haven't eaten in days!"

Two lions escaped with the Lion Tamer during the earlier objective and it's up to you to lure them back to their den. They must have been in the mood for tuna because of them is standing guard outside the aquarium. Get each of the lion's attention and race off to the den to lure them back into their cage.

The most difficult part of this objective is getting their attention without getting killed. The best way to do this is to focus on the lions one at a time. Head off to the aquarium while hugging the rails near the rhinos and hippos. Loop in front of the lion while circling around the picnic table. The lion lunges at the skater but likely misses due to the quick circle. Nevertheless, she's interested and begins chasing down the skater. Avoid rails and objects that might confuse the lion; instead, simply skate as fast as possible back across the Zoo. Lead her right into the den to have her stay put.

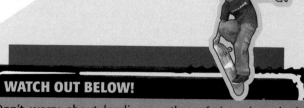

Lure the second lion back to the den in exactly the same manner. Circle around the picnic table near the lion so that she starts the chase and hold the Jump Button down for speed and zip off across the Zoo to reunite the pair in the confines of their den.

WATCH OUT BELOW!

Don't worry about landing on the safari truck parked outside the den. So long as the Special Trick is performed while hitting the **Lions Den Hop** gap, credit is given for completing the objective.

DO A SIT DOWN AIR OVER THE LION'S CAGE

Location	By the lion's den
Time	0:20
Awards	$250 and a Special Trick slot
How unlocked	Complete 'Beat Bob's 3 best combos'
Unlocks	Nothing

Bob Burnquist
"Ready to try my Special trick? Get Special and bust a Sit Down Air... but wait, let's make it hard! You have to do it while launching from on top of the lion house out over the cage wall."

Drop into the lion exhibit and go big off the ramp near the rocks while transferring onto the roof of the den. Make sure to get at least a 360 in and a pair of tricks so as to get the Special Meter maxed out. Reverting upon landing also helps do this. Either way, take that speed and air off the roof and over the fence. Tap into the Sit Down Air while clearing the fence to complete the objective.

Pro Challenges

GET THE SICK SCORE: 800,000 POINTS

Location	On the roof above the aviary entrance
Time	2:00
Awards	$500
How unlocked	Complete a Pro-Specific Challenge
Unlocks	ProSet5

Tony Hawk
"Cool! I didn't think you'd be able to find me. Up here there are some great places to go big. Throw down some huge combos and try to beat my Sick Score."

There are plenty of ramps to bang big tricks off of in this area, but what's really key to assembling this 800,000 point combo is the cable that runs through the trees and around the front of the shops. Make sure to pinpoint this cable's location before starting this string, as missing it blows the whole combo.

Get the combo started by tricking off the quarter pipe straight ahead—a 720 Double Back Foot Flip to Benihana works nicely. Revert into a Manual and Special Trick off the opposite ramp while spine transferring down to the roof below. Revert to a Nose Manual and ride into the alcove towards the brick quarter pipe.

Special Trick off the ramp, Revert and manual back to the opposing ramp and perform a Special Lip Trick on the coping. Revert out of the stall and ollie into a Special Grind on the cable leading off through the tree on the left. Hold the grind across the front of the stores to pick up the **Banner Gap 4!** bonus and hop into another Special Grind for variety. Continue the grind all the way to the monkey exhibits, around the octagonal roof, then trick down onto the street to end the lengthy chain.

COLLECT PRO C-O-M-B-O

Location	On the roof of the Zoo entrance
Time	2:00
Awards	$500
How unlocked	Complete a Pro-Specific Challenge
Unlocks	Nothing

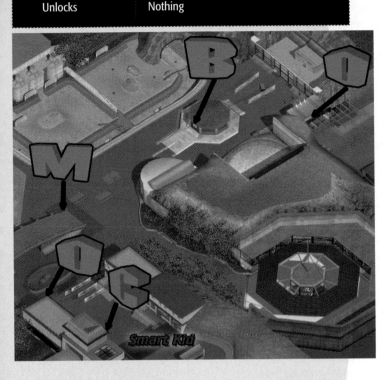

Smart Kid
"Okay, so you got all the C-O-M-B-O letters last time. But that was easy! I bet you can't do it now!"

Hop into a grind on the ledge above the information sign for the **z00r00fgAp** and carry it past the "C" and up onto the second ledge to snag the first "O". Ollie straight off the ledge into a manual and ride up the quarter pipe on the left side of the bridge and slide into a grind to the right. Ollie off the rail and over the demolished portion of the bridge. Manual across the bridge to the rail on the opposite side. Grind the rail for the "M" and manual all the way to the little ramp at the base of the Koala Café. Hop directly into a clockwise grind on the roof of the café to obtain the "B" and transfer it to either of the cables behind it. Grind across to the lions den and hop into a right-hand grind on the front of the lions cage. Ollie into a manual on the roof above the tram gate and air up off the ramp to get the final "O".

NO STOMPY, NO PROBLEM!

Those who have already unlocked the Pro Goals by completing a Pro-Specific Challenge have the option of completing this objective before sending Stompy on her bridge-bashing rampage. Although the strategy outlined below works equally well for those with a pre-rampage bridge, it's even easier to hold the grind onto the cable for the **Bridge Roof Grind** gap and manual across to the letter on the far rail.

TRANSFER OVER ELEPHANT ROCK

Location	In the elephant exhibit
Time	2:00
Awards	$500
How unlocked	Complete a Pro-Specific Challenge
Unlocks	Nothing

Bob Burnquist
"Let's see if you can transfer over Elephant Rock!"

The skater needs a ton of speed and hangtime to boost an air completely over Elephant Rock. Just as important, however, is the takeoff spot. Ride straight ahead into the halfpipe-moat and start tricking back and forth to max out the Special Meter. Keep the skater in a straight line about one or two board-width outside the drain in the floor. Once the skater is lined up properly and has sufficient speed, let loose with a huge air over the rock. Make the leap on a steep angle so as to get adequate height and hold hard to the Left on the controls.

GET KONG BACK IN HIS CAGE

Location	On the roof of the aviary entrance
Time	2:00
Awards	$500
How unlocked	Complete a Pro-Specific Challenge
Unlocks	Nothing

Zookeeper
"Kong has escaped from his cage! There are two switches inside the top of this chimney. If you can flip them both quick enough, he'll fall into his cage!"

There are two rails high up inside the chimney and the skater must lip trick on each of them long enough to open the trap doors below Kong. Before beginning, turn around and throw down some tricks on the quarter pipe opposite the chimney. Now, with plenty of speed, charge the banked brick wall in the chimney and Boneless into a lip trick. Hold the lip trick for 4 seconds to have the door below Kong open. Repeat this process on the other rail to cage the beast before he shows you his Stompy impersonation.

COMBO SCARE 40 BIRDS

Location	In the aviary
Time	2:00
Awards	$500
How unlocked	Complete a Pro-Specific Challenge
Unlocks	Nothing

Bam Margera
"All right these birds are pissing me off! They've been crapping all over the place. See if you can scare 40 of them in one combo."

Bam is right, these birds are making a major mess of the place! Give them a good scare by either lip tricking, airing, or grinding past their soft, feathered, underbelly.

Since it's going to take an awful lot of grinding around in a tight circle to scare 40 birds, try to scare as many as possible via airing and Spine Transferring off the ramps first. Once a half-dozen or so have been scared off in that manner, leap off the perimeter ramps into a grind on the rail ahead.

Take a lap around on the upper rail and, during one of the straightaways, carefully hop into a grind on the inner rail below. The skater picks up a lot of speed grinding this rail but it's possible to scare more birds in shorter amount of time this way. Ollie off the rail once the "fear of Bam" has been put into 40 birds.

SIDE MONEY

BUTT-HEADS

Time	N/A
Award	$100

Rhino Keeper
"Care to wager on these rhinos charging?"

Hop the moat to the rhino exhibit and choose which rhino, or both, drop when they ram one another. Choose correctly and the Rhino Keeper forks over $100!

THE MIRACLE OF BIRTH

Time	N/A
Award	$500

Whoa, there's a birds nest on the floor of the aviary! Skate up to it and press the Jump Button to inspect it.

Birdman
"Wanna help me collect eggs?"

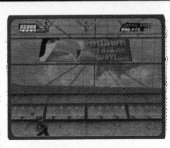

The three birds perched above are going to take turns laying eggs and it's up to you to catch them. Move the board-less skater back and forth under the birds to catch the eggs as they fall. Beware, the eggs start dropping a lot faster once the birds, ahem, loosen up. Quickly move back to the center after each catch so as to be ready for the next egg. The mini-game ends as soon as an egg is dropped or when all 10 are caught.

MONKEY MISCHIEF

Time	0:30
Award	$500

Go through the open door in the back of the giraffe pen and hit the red button under the "Release The Monkeys!" sign. Three monkeys appear and starting flinging feces that must be avoided for 30 seconds. Press Left and Right to keep out of the line of fire and collect $500.

Monkeyman
"Wanna play dodgeball with monkey feces?"

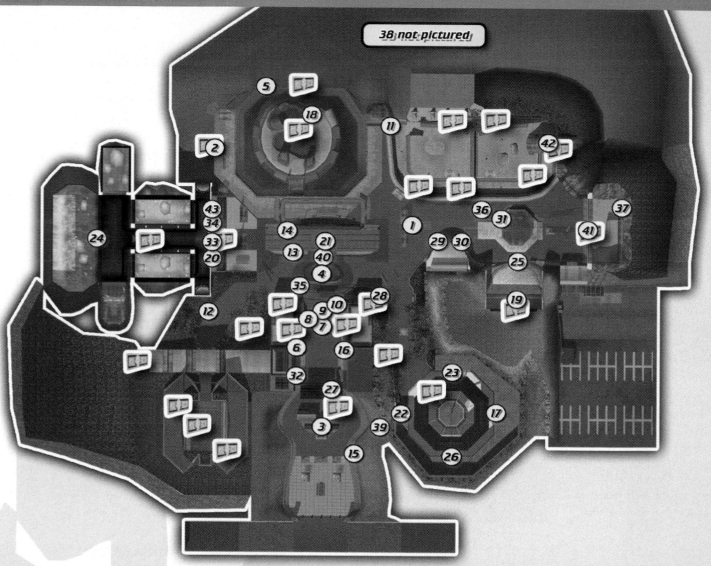

38 not pictured

GAP CHECKLIST

[1] PICNIC POP   **50 POINTS**
Transfer a grind between any two picnic tables.

[2] POP ROCK   **50 POINTS**
Grind the rail alongside the walkway to the left of the hippo exhibit and transfer the grind over the boulder that interrupts the rail.

[3] ALL EXHIBITS OPEN   **100 POINTS**
Transfer the two quarter pipes atop the ticket counters at the main entrance to the Zoo.

[4] ARF! ARF! ARF!   **100 POINTS**
Pop off the ledge running around the seal's pool and clear the entire pool.

[5] BACKWOODS PATH   **100 POINTS**
Link up a grind between all three logs on the hill behind the hippo exhibit. Grind the ledge near the moat to do it.

[6] BANK GAP   **100 POINTS**
Air off either of the kickers on the sidewalks nearest the main entrance. The leap must be off the uphill kicker and not the one closer to the bridge.

[7] BANNER GAP 1!   **100 POINTS**
Grind the Zoo banner nearest the main entrance.

[8] BANNER GAP 2!   **100 POINTS**
Grind across the Zoo banner second closest to the main entrance.

[9] BANNER GAP 3! 100 POINTS

Grind across the Zoo banner third from the main entrance.

10] BANNER GAP 4! 100 POINTS

Grind the Zoo banner nearest the bridge. This banner hangs lower than the others.

[11] BIG MOAT TRANSFER 100 POINTS

Air off the vert ramp between the hippo and rhino exhibits and land in the moat surrounding the rhinos.

[12] BIRDHOUSE RAIL 100 POINTS

Leave the aviary and grind the left-hand rail down to the aquarium.

[13] BRIDGE TRANSFER 100 POINTS

Spine Transfer over the bridge.

[14] GRIND OVER IT 100 POINTS

Grind from one end of the bridge to the other. This gap is still possible after the elephant destroys the bridge, just make sure to have enough speed to gap the area where there is no handrail.

[15] GRIND THE WHOLE PLANTER 100 POINTS

Grind the lower ledge running along the right and left sides of the walkway between the outside street (off the course) and the ticket booths. This is where Kenny the Koala is at the main starting point.

[16] HANDRAIL HOP 100 POINTS

Transfer a grind between any of the handrails near the shops by the entrance.

[17] HEAR NO EVIL 100 POINTS

Grind the railing near the monkey exhibit and transfer the grind across the brick quarter pipe in the center of the exhibit.

[18] HUNGRY, HUNGRY HIPPO POOL 100 POINTS

Grind the edge of the upper pool in the hippo exhibit.

[19] LONG NECK GAP 100 POINTS

Use the quarter pipes in the giraffe exhibit to gap over the doorway leading inside.

[20] LOW TIDE 100 POINTS

Lip trick on the lower white ledge on the walls near the aquarium entrance

[21] MANUAL OVER IT 100 POINTS

Manual up and over the bridge. This gap is still possible after the elephant destroys the bridge, just make sure to have enough speed to gap the area where there is no handrail.

[22] MOVE LIKE A MONKEY!

Wallie up into a clockwise grind on the wall above the monkey cages and transfer the grind to the cable running over the snack hut.

[23] SEE NO EVIL 100 POINTS

Grind the railing near the monkey exhibit and transfer the grind across the brick quarter pipe on the left side of the exhibit (as viewed from snack hut).

[24] SHARK TANK TRIP 100 POINTS

Head to the back of the aquarium and leap off the ramp and into a grind on the shark tank. Grind an entire lap around the shark tank to score the gap.

[25] SNACK BAR HOP 100 POINTS

Air up out of the giraffe exhibit to the roof of the Koala Café.

[26] SPEAK NO EVIL 100 POINTS

Grind the railing near the monkey exhibit and transfer the grind across the brick quarter pipe on the right side of the exhibit (as viewed from snack hut).

[27] WELCOME TO THE ZOO 100 POINTS

Ramp up to the roof of the ticket counters near the main entrance and ollie onto or over the roof of the ticket booths.

[28] WHAT A LONG PLANTER! 100 POINTS

Head down the hill near the main entrance and grind the planter on the right around towards the monkey exhibit. Transfer the grind past the snack hut towards the monkeys to score the gap.

[29] YOU BIG GORILLA 100 POINTS

Grind the ledge in front of the gorilla exhibit from left to right.

[30] YOU DRIVE ME APE! 100 POINTS

Grind from right to left along the ledge in front of the gorilla exhibit.

[31] YOU WANT FRIES WITH THAT? 100 POINTS

Grind a complete lap around the white counter on the Koala Café.

[32] ZOOROOFGAP 100 POINTS

Hop off the roof above the ticket booths and grind the ledge above Kong's cage and the Cash Points machine.

[33] AQUA SIGN GAP 500 POINTS

Leap into a lip trick on the rail that holds the aquarium's sign. This rail is just above the white ledge used in the **Low Tide** gap.

[34] BIG SURF 500 POINTS

Lip trick on the middle white ledge that's on the walls flanking the entrance to the aquarium.

[35] BRIDGE ROOF GRIND 500 POINTS

Grind the cable that leads from the roof above the shops down to the bridge.

[36] ELEPHANT HOP 500 POINTS

Ollie off the Koala Café and land on the head of the elephant on the road.

[37] HOLD ON! LIONS BELOW 500 POINTS

Lip trick atop the rocks at the rear of the lion's den.

[38] LOOP HOLE 500 POINTS

Gap the hole in the top of the loop during Bob's Pro Challenge.

[39] OVER THE HILLS 500 POINTS

Wallie into a clockwise grind on the wall above the monkey cages and ollie out of the grind, over the grass, and down to the ticket booths on the other side of the hill. Make the leap at the very last kink in the wall, just before the section that angles straight towards the snack hut.

[40] TAKE IT TO THE BRIDGE 500 POINTS

Transfer over the tunnel in the bridge via the quarter pipes on either side.

[41] LIONS DEN HOP 1000 POINTS

Air off the roof of the lion's den and over the fence to the street near the Koala Café.

[42] OVER ELEPHANT ROCK 1000 POINTS

Work the moat in the elephant exhibit like a halfpipe and let fly over the large rocks that form a loop with the moat.

[43] TIDAL WAVE 1000 POINTS

Lip trick on the uppermost white ledge on the walls of the aquarium entrance.

Carnival

Purchase from Secrets Shop for $15,000.

Whoo-boy, it's time for the Mullet County Fair! Folks are sure gonna have a whopper of a good time at this year's fair! The carnies have been working through the night to set up a lot of fun rides and attractions. Look for the Horror House, the Thunder Cups, the Rock'n Rock'itz, and a bunch of others, too! Oh, and the fair has plenty of farm animals—you haven't lived till you've gone pig chasin'! Folks who don't like to wrestle with pigs can test their strength on the Ding Dong or in the Wood Warriors competition. There's plenty of food to eat too! You do like the sweet tea, don'tcha?

LEVEL GOALS

Unlocked Objectives

Get a High Score: 750,000 points
Collect S-K-A-T-E
Amateur C-O-M-B-O letters
Hit the tricks and ring the bell!
Collect 6 souvenir photos
Do a 500,000 point combo
Try not to boot

Locked Objectives

Medal the Competition
Get a Sick Score: 1,500,000 points
Pro C-O-M-B-O letters
Help tear down the competition
Grind the whole coaster
Nail a 900 on the Rocket ride
Collect 10 Ride Tickets

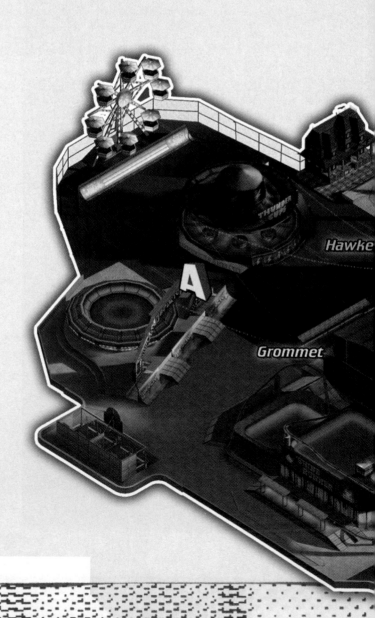

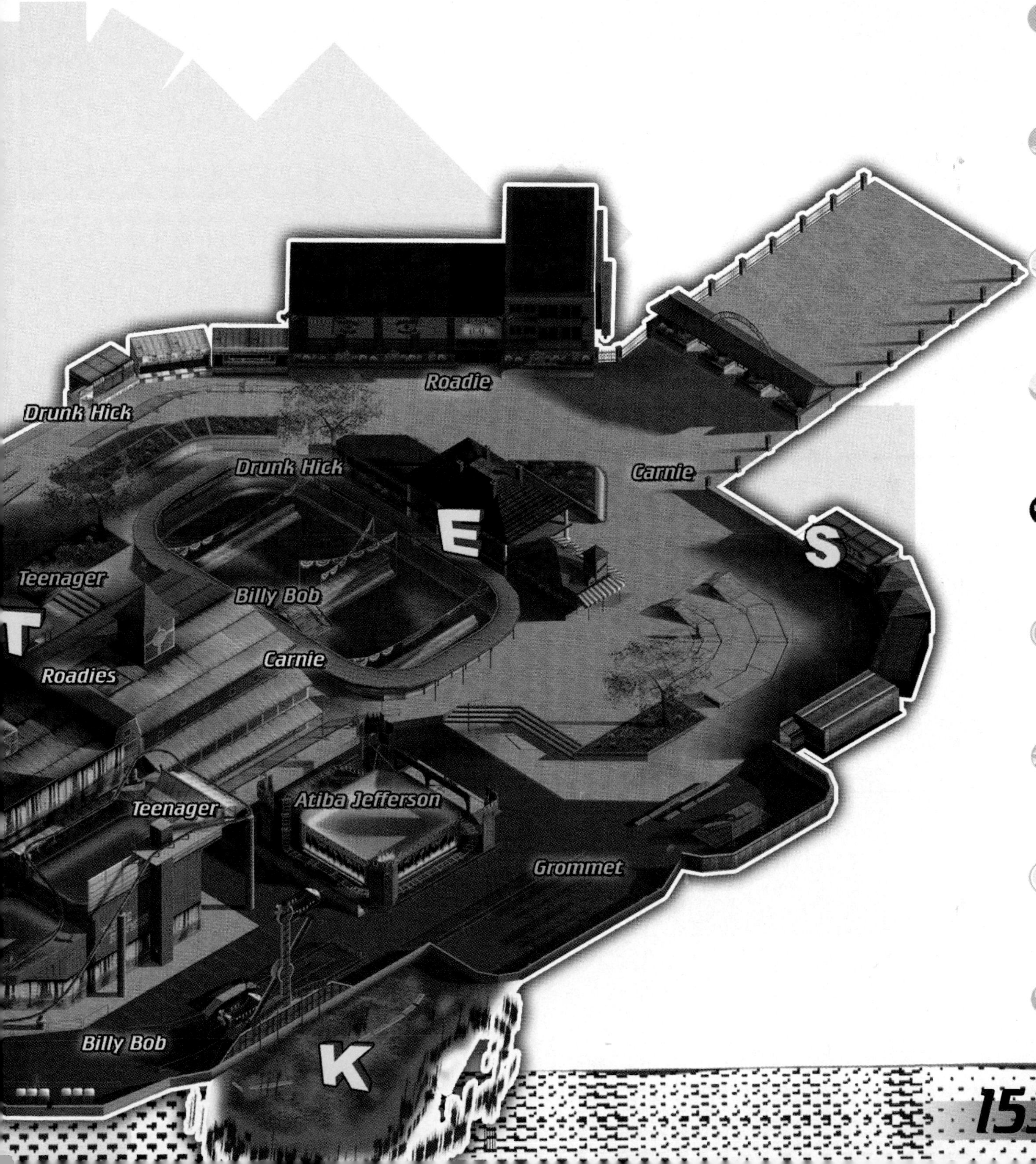

Drunk Hick

Roadie

Drunk Hick

Carnie

E

S

Teenager

Billy Bob

T

Carnie

Roadies

Teenager

Atiba Jefferson

Grommet

Billy Bob

K

Amateur Challenges

GET A HIGH SCORE: 750,000 POINTS

Location	Near the lumberjacks
Time	2:00
Awards	$500
How unlocked	N/A
Unlocks	ProSet2 and 'Get a Sick Score: 1,500,000 pts. '

Grommet

"This looks like a sweet spot to skate. Let's move all the tables out of the way. Oh, and I bet you can't beat my High Score!"

The Grommet set up a plethora of ramps to help make this challenge easier. The following line is worth between 750,000 and 1,000,000 points, depending on the number of multipliers mixed in. Keep in mind that it's easier to do if, during the opening aerials, the skater stays between the wall and the rail—don't transfer over the railing to the ramps near the Angry Dragon.

Start the run by tricking big with three or more tricks off the spine directly ahead. Revert the landing, and pull off a Special Trick on the ramp nearest the lumberjacks. Revert into a manual and roll past the spine to the ramp near the Rock'n Rock'itz ride and unleash another Special Trick. Link this with one more Special Trick on the ramp nearest the lumberjacks, then Revert into a grind on the center railing. Trick onto the Rock'itz ride and Special Grind up and over the ride and down onto the wall near the port-a-potties. Hold the grind the entire length of the wall to the Abductor, ollie into a Special Manual, and go big off the ramped face of the ferris wheel ride to end it.

COLLECT THE S-K-A-T-E LETTERS!

Location	Near the entrance
Time	2:00
Awards	$500
How unlocked	N/A
Unlocks	Nothing

Carnie

"Hey, bub—collect the S-K-A-T-E letters"

S Hop into a grind on the counter near the concessions straight ahead on the left.

K The "K" is between the logs in the swamp behind the Rock'n Rock'itz ride. Transfer a grind between the two for the **Gummy the Gator Gap**, or just manual across the dirt.

A Skate over to the Abductor and transfer the middle and right-hand ramps to pluck the "A" out of the air while snagging the **Ride and Puke** gap.

T The "T" is on the awning of the Wonder Barn directly across from the Horror House. Pop off the angled ledge in front of the sidewalk to access the awning.

E Hop into a grind on the outer edge of the rodeo ring's roof. Grind around toward the fancy white farmhouse to get the final letter.

AMATEUR C-O-M-B-O LETTERS!

Location	Near the rodeo ring
Time	2:00
Awards	$500
How unlocked	N/A
Unlocks	Pro C-O-M-B-O letters

Drunk Hick
"Hey, skater-person! Collect all the letters in C-O-M-B-O in one… combo!"

Grind the railing of the rodeo ring to snag the "C," then hop into a grind on the planter to the left to pick up the first "O" and the **Rail 2 Rail** gap. Manual straight across the street toward the lattice near the lumberjacks, and grind a clockwise loop on it to collect the "M". Manual off the end and angle toward the Angry Dragon ride. Hop the tracks and Wallride the castle wall up into a grind to grab the "B." Grind straight through the window and gap across onto the awning of the barn for the **Barn Hop** gap. Grab the final "O" while hopping off the end of the awning.

SPEED CONTROL

If the Wallride up to the "B" happens too quickly, or if the skater overshoots the final "O" when hitting the **Barn Hop** gap, it's because he's going too fast. If this occurs, don't hold down the Jump button during the lengthy lattice grind or when crossing the street from the first "O" to the "M."

HIT THE TRICKS AND RING THE BELL

Location	At the Ding Dong attraction
Time	1:00
Awards	$500
How unlocked	N/A
Unlocks	ProSet4

Hawker
"See if you can hit the tricks I yell out! To make it challenging, you have to ring the bell at the same time!"

Step right up and test your strength! Show those cute little ladies you've got the muscles to nail the tricks while gapping over the bell atop the tower!

Trick out the Special Meter and hit the ramps on either side of the Ding Dong to transfer up and over the bell. Perform the tricks that appear in the lower-left corner of the screen in the same jump in which the **Win a Prize** gap is awarded to clear them from the list. Use the spines in front of the Ding Dong to gain speed and to turn around, but don't worry about transferring between them, as that approach risks an unnecessary faceplant.

Those who are playing through the game in order should have maxed stats in all categories at this point in the game, so there shouldn't be a problem hitting the bell. In fact, you should have enough hangtime to perform two to three tricks per leap if the commands are input quick enough. Lastly, there are numerous gaps that will be awarded for transferring across the lower portion of the Ding Dong. These range from the **I've TRIPPED Higher Than That** gap at the bottom of the tower to the **Almost Neversoft** gap closer to the top.

COLLECT 6 SOUVENIR PHOTOS

Location	In front of the Fairgrounds HQ
Time	2:00
Awards	$500
How unlocked	N/A
Unlocks	Collect 10 Ride Tickets

Roadie
"All them souvenir photo cameras are set to work for free... You should go grab some before they start charging for 'em!"

Hop into a grind on the railing in front of the Duck Wrangler booth to get your photo taken as a strong man.

Grind the edge of the sidewalk behind the Ding Dong to get a photo of the skater as a space cadet.

Find the railing in front of the boarding station for the Shine Runner rollercoaster to get a shot dressed up as a superhero.

Grind the railing in front of the port-a-potties to pose for a picture as the winner of the 1974 Miss La Douche County beauty pageant.

Grind the railing on the sidewalk behind the Angry Dragon to take a picture in a full-blown Elvis costume.

Get a photo of the skater dressed like a carnie while grinding on the chicken pen.

DO A 500,000 POINT COMBO

Location	In the pool atop the Angry Dragon ride
Time	2:00
Awards	$500
How unlocked	N/A
Unlocks	Medal the Competition

Atiba Jefferson
"Alright man, cool! Now let's see you pull off one more big combo!"

This scoring line combines some big aerial tricks with a lengthy grind around the barn and onto the roller coaster. Before launching into the first trick, however, roll to the edge of the pool directly ahead of the skater and turn around to face the other direction.

Start the run by tricking off the wall of the pool near the Shine Runner sign, Revert to a manual, and launch into a Special Trick across the way. Revert and manual back across to the other side once again and perform another Special Trick. Revert the landing and slide into a counter-clockwise grind on the edge of the pool. Grind across the 2x4 and out through the window near the barn to hit the **Barn Hop** gap and land in a grind on the awning. Transfer the grind across the gap in the awning for the **Over the Barn Door** gap, and Special Grind the rest of the awning toward the roller coaster. Leap directly off the end of the awning and onto the coaster track for the **Thrill Ride** gap. Special Grind the track toward the big hill, then flip off the track and into one more Special Grind on the rail near the queue for the Rock'n Rock'itz ride. If you miss the railing, just land in a Special Manual instead and ride it out until you get the necessary point total.

TRY NOT TO BOOT

Location	In front of the Horror House
Time	0:07
Awards	$500
How unlocked	N/A
Unlocks	Grind the whole coaster

Teenager
"Hey man, I bet you can't eat a bunch of food then ride all the rides without losing your lunch!"

The sadistic teenager has a recipe for disaster: Let's see how much torture one stomach can take! Slurp down the food and drinks he calls for, and hit each of the main rides in the park. An additional seven seconds is added for each successful stop.

Head up the hill past the Horror House and grind the counter of The Meat Hut to pick up a greasy chili dog and fries.

Skate past the entrance and hop into a grind on the counter of the games and hold the grind past the Texas Justice shooting range and onto the Sweet Tea beverage trailer.

Now it's time to ride the ride. Head straight for the Rock'n Rock'itz ride and ollie over the Nokia banner to hit the ramp on the ride's loading platform.

Round the bend toward the loading station for the roller coaster and grind the track past the platform.

Feel like going for a spin? Pop off one of the kickers in front of the Abductor to transfer onto the roof of the UFO. Ride straight across the roof of the Abductor and hop off the back end to continue with the objective.

Line up with the ramp below the ferris wheel, and leap into a lip trick on one of the baskets as they rise up along the left side of the ride. Hold the lip trick to the top to snag the **Nice View Up Here** gap, then drop down off the ride.

Finally, the teenager wants to see you take a spin on the Thunder Cups. Ride up the base of the ride and grind the railing near the orange arrow to complete the objective.

MEDAL THE COMPETITION

Location	Inside the rodeo ring
Time	0:30
Awards	$500
How unlocked	Complete 'Do a 500,000 point combo'
Unlocks	'Help tear down the competition' and 'Nail a 900 on the Rocket ride'

Billy Bob
"Welcome to the fair! Round these parts I'm the best skater there is! Think you can beat me in a little competition?"

Billy Bob has set up some spines and quarter pipes inside the rodeo ring and wants to hold a little competition. Put the following two scoring lines together to show him that you don't have to be from 'round these parts to throw down some sick scores in a vert competition! It should be noted that the judges are more difficult to impress, so it will take 300,000 points or more to get a perfect score from them.

Since it's a vert competition, get the show started with a big flip-to-grab combo off the ramp below the red banner. Revert the landing and Spine Transfer over the spine straight ahead while linking a Special Trick and a Nosegrab together. Continue the string with another Revert and unleash another Special Trick off the ramp ahead. Now it's time for the second pass. Revert back to the spine in the center and transfer over it while performing another aerial Special Trick. Revert and manual toward the ramp where the string began and leap into a lip trick.

If there's one benefit to having the competition inside a rodeo ring, it's that there's an oval railing that you can use for near-endless grinding. Start this string out just like the previous one, but Revert into a manual when exiting the ramp at the opposite end. Hop into a Special Grind on the perimeter railing and go for a lap or two around the ring. Ollie off into a manual and tack on one more air trick before touching down with a perfect score.

GET A SICK SCORE: 1,500,000 POINTS	
Location	Across from the Abductor
Time	2:00
Awards	$500
How unlocked	Complete 'Get a High Score: 900,000 points'
Unlocks	ProSet1

Grommet
"Okay, this is it... Pull out all the stops and give it your best shot! I'll help the carnies finish setting up, and you can session the midway area to your hearts' content!"

PROSET SETUP

Fact: The following scoring line illustrates how to pull off a 1.5 million point combo at the Carnival. **Fact:** This combo is much easier to perform if ProSet2 has been turned off.

Start this lengthy scoring line by tricking out the Special Meter while transferring the Abductor ramps to the right for the **Ride and Puke** gap. Revert to a manual and hit the miniature quarter pipes across the street. Leap straight into the air and link up two high-speed Special Tricks, such as the Stalefish Backflip and the Semi Flip. Revert the landing and hit the **Ride and Puke** gap back in the other direction while performing another Special Trick. Don't land on the ramp though; instead, land in a grind on the rail on top of the ramp. Trick off the end of the rail and land in a manual near the clown. Two-wheel it past the basketball booth and into a left-hand Special Grind on the waist-high wall near the swamp.

The rest of the combo is all about linking up numerous grinds and manuals. Make sure you trick between the tricks to continue building the multiplier. Carefully balance the grind around the turns and up and over the Rock'n Rock'itz ride. Transfer the grind to the rail near the picnic tables and to the **Log**. Special Manual off the log and up toward the concessions. Hop into another Special Grind on the counter and hold it to the end of the wall near the main entrance. Manual over to the planter and transfer a grind onto the roof of the other set of concessions. Trick off the end of the concessions into a grind on the fence by the Horror House. Grind over the house and gap across to the Thunder Cups for the **Haunted Teacup Gap**. Trick down to the ground to end the string, thus completing the objective at around 30 or so seconds.

COMING UP SHORT

What's that? The combo only yielded 1.2 million and not 1.5 million? Well, chances are that's because you didn't sneak a quick flip trick in between all those grinds. It'll take some extra practice, but try to perform a quick Kickflip or Heelflip whenever getting on or off a rail or ledge. With a combo this lengthy, each Kickflip can be worth over 40,000 points depending on the base score. Multipliers are the key to success!

PRO C-O-M-B-O LETTERS

Location	Near Shave Ice Solutions stand
Time	2:00
Awards	$500
How unlocked	Complete 'Amateur C-O-M-B-O letters!'
Unlocks	Nothing

Drunk Hick
"Hey—you're good with that thing! Try to collect them C-O-M-B-O letters again… but this time it's gonna be much harder!"

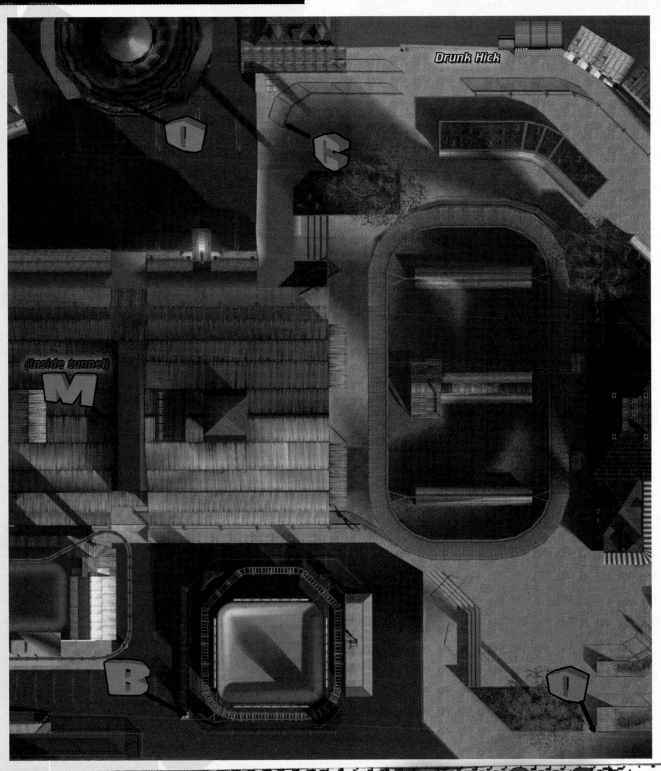

PROSET SETUP

Turn off ProSet4 for this challenge.

Grind the railing near the Horror House to pick up the "C," then transfer up and over the Ding Dong to **Win a Prize**. This also lines you up with the Thunder Cups. Revert the landing and manual toward the Thunder Cups. Go big off the front of the ride to pluck the "O" out of the air, and Revert into a manual toward the barn tunnel. Grind the right-hand ledge in the tunnel to collect the "M," then manual toward the far corner of the Angry Dragon. Ride up the ramp into a grind on the railing to gather the "B," and grind and manual over to the final letter on the planter by the pig pen.

HELP TEAR DOWN THE COMPETITION

Location	Next to the rodeo ring
Time	2:00
Awards	$500
How unlocked	Complete 'Medal the Competition'
Unlocks	Wonder Barn skating area

Carnie

"Hey… could you give us a hand? We gotta tear down these here banners but we ain't got no ladder. We'll loosen the poles, and then you go put some weight on 'em!"

The Carnie needs some help taking down the banners in the rodeo ring. Air up from each side of the spines and quarter pipes to lip trick on the banners. There are a total of four banners, and it takes a full five seconds of leaning on a banner to make it fall away. Approach the ramps straight on and leap into the air and press the Grind Button to avoid grinding on the banners. Make sure you press the Grind Button fast, though, as your skater may leap up and over the banner. The banners over the spine in the center crisscross, so make the leap near the sides of the ramp or else the banner may prove to be out of reach.

WONDER-FULL!

After completing this objective, the Carnie opens up the Wonder Barn for skating. Although there's not much inside other than a couple of rails, skaters with a lot of "ups" can Spine Transfer off the vert ramp in the back, through the hatch above, and onto the roof of the barn!

GRIND THE WHOLE COASTER

Location	At the top of the big hill on the coaster
Time	1:00
Awards	$500
How unlocked	Complete 'Try not to boot'
Unlocks	Nothing

Teenager
"Okay, you didn't hurl last time. Now, let's see you do a continuous grind all the way around the coaster track and I'll tape you! I'd say that if you get to the bottom of the big hill, you've gone far enough!"

UP *THERE!?*

Although it's possible to Spine Transfer out of the rooftop pools and up to the platform at the summit of the main hill, it's much easier to take the elevator. Ride through the orange door opposite the Rock'n Rock'itz ride and take the elevator to the top of the roller coaster.

While maintaining a grind for the entire length of the twisting roller coaster isn't necessarily *easy*, doing so with a maxed-out Rail Balance rating isn't terribly challenging. No, what makes this objective so difficult is trying to avoid the two roller coaster trains that are on the track as well.

Ultimately, this objective is all about timing. There's a very small window in which you can hop into a grind on the top of the coaster and lay down an uninterrupted grind all the way to the base of the big hill. Stand near the roller coaster track and wait for a train to crest the hill. Once the first car is over the hump, ollie into a grind and don't look back! It's important that you wait as long as possible, then start the grind; if not, the skater will catch up to the second train as it makes its way out of the station.

Balance down the coaster past the loading station and around the turn toward the hill. Gently tap to the left and right; too much "nervous" tapping could put the skater further out of balance. Keep grinding to trigger the **WHAT A TRIP!** Gap, then ollie down to safety.

NAIL A 900 ON THE ROCKET RIDE

Location	Next to Rock'n Rock'itz
Time	1:00
Awards	$500
How unlocked	Complete 'Medal the Competition'
Unlocks	Nothing

Billy Bob
"I bet you can't nail a new Special Trick on the Rock'n Rock'itz ride!"

The rockets on the Rock'n Rock'itz ride come complete with mini-halfpipes inside them, just perfect for launching Special Tricks at incredible heights! Wait behind the second yellow line and perform some flatland tricks to get the Special Meter maxed out while the rockets descend from overhead. Wait for the rocket to begin to move past the loading platform, then hop off the ramp and onto the rocket.

While onboard the rocket, line up with the center of the halfpipe and trick back and forth *without rotation* until the Special Meter lights up (if it isn't already). Upon reaching enough height, launch straight into the air and input the commands for a 900. Keep a straight line and land back inside the rocket to complete the objective.

COLLECT 10 RIDE TICKETS

Location	On top of the Wonder Barn
Time	0:30
Awards	$500
How unlocked	Complete 'Collect 6 souvenir photos'
Unlocks	ProSet5

Roadie
"Collect 10 o' them ride tickets! Now hurry up, man!"

PROSET SETUP

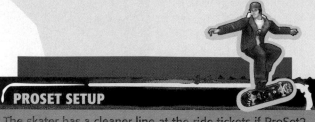

The skater has a cleaner line at the ride tickets if ProSet2 is turned off.

There are 10 ride tickets to collect and only 30 seconds to do it. Follow this quick and relatively pain-free line to ride the 'Shine Runner all night long!

From the starting location on top of the Wonder Barn (transfer up from inside the barn, or grind the coaster over to reach the Roadie), Spine Transfer over the pairings of quarter pipes and ride off the roof and into a grind on the coaster track below. After snagging the fourth ride ticket, hop

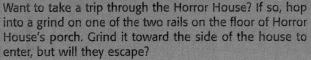

off the tracks and into a grind on the wall behind the port-a-potties to pick up the next ride ticket. Grind the wall toward the Rock'n Rock'itz ride, grind over the ride, then switch the grind to the rail on the left. Grab the eighth ride ticket near the corner of the Angry Dragon, and turn around and charge the kicker near the ride's sign. Grab the ninth ticket out of the air while gapping into the bowl on top of the ride. Skate across the bowl toward the 'Shine Runner, and air up to the final ticket hovering above.

SPEAKING OF RIDES...

Want to take a trip through the Horror House? If so, hop into a grind on one of the two rails on the floor of Horror House's porch. Grind it toward the side of the house to enter, but will they escape?

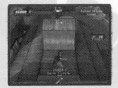  

SIDE MONEY

WOOD WARRIORS COMPETITION

Time	First to cut 5 logs wins
Award	Bragging rights

Lumberjack
"Hey! Skater-person! Wanna join the Wood Warriors invitational?"

Skate up to the unmanned saw and tell the Lumberjack you want to compete. Press back and forth on the controls in a smooth motion to cut the log. Press the Jump Button to place another log on the chopping block to continue cutting. The first to cut five logs wins.

TEXAS JUSTICE

Time	10 shots
Award	$15 - $30 per target

Carnie
"Hey! You! Wanna get in some target practice?"

Take the air rifle from the Carnie and prepare for some target practice. Watch the red crosshair move around the screen, and press the corresponding button when it gets in front of a target. The targets are worth various point totals (5 points for stationary targets, 10 for moving ones), and your score after 10 shots determines your ranking. More importantly, each shot can be worth up to $30! The lantern, jug, and cross are all worth $15 while the cowboy and the vulture are each worth $30! Be patient and only shoot when the crosshair is directly over the symbol matching the button on the controller!

SQUEAL LIKE A PIG

Time	First to catch the pig wins
Award	Good karma

Pig Lover
"That pig over there sure has a purty mouth! See if you can catch him before my cousins do!"

Oh brother, one can only imagine what those guys are gonna do with that poor little pig in the rodeo ring. Skate after the pig and rescue it from the pig lover's cousins. Knock the cousins to the ground by slapping them.

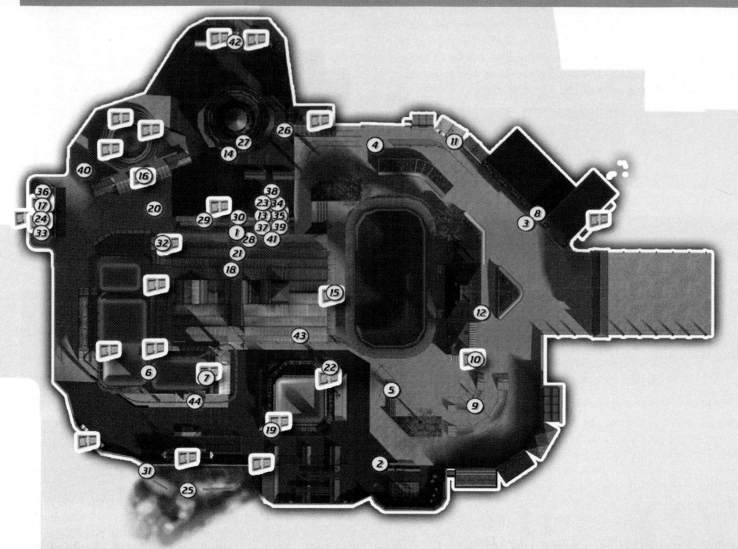

GAP CHECKLIST

[1] LEDGE HOP   **25 POINTS**

Transfer a grind across the main concrete ledge behind the Ding Dong attraction. Be sure to gap the entrance to the barn tunnel.

[2] LOG   **25 POINTS**

Transfer a grind onto the logs lying in the street near the lumberjacks.

[3] PLANTER POP   **25 POINTS**

Transfer a grind across the planters in front of the Fairgrounds HQ building.

[4] RAIL 2 RAIL   **25 POINTS**

Transfer a grind between any two adjacent rails.

[5] STAIR HOP   **25 POINTS**

Ollie down the stairs near the entrance to the Angry Dragon ride.

[6] 'SHINE BOWL TRANSFER   **50 POINTS**

Spine Transfer between any of the rooftop pools near the main roller coaster.

[7] BACK PORCH LIP GAP   **50 POINTS**

Lip trick on the roof of the old shack near the uppermost pool near the main roller coaster.

[8] BILLY GOAT GAP   **50 POINTS**

Air up and over the goat near the Fairgrounds HQ building via the banked planters on either side of the door.

[9] CHICKEN SHI.. MANUAL   **50 POINTS**

Manual through the curving chicken pen near the snack vendors.

[10] COCK TO LEDGE   **50 POINTS**

Grind the inside ledge of the curving chicken pen and transfer the grind to the red and white striped awning.

[11] COUNTER GRIND   **50 POINTS**

Grind the counter on the three vendors nearest the Horror House.

[12] GRIND THE SHINY LIGHTS 50 POINTS

Grind the strand of white lights that extend from the fancy white house near the main entrance all the way to the lumberjacks.

[13] I'VE TRIPPED HIGHER THAN THAT! 50 POINTS

Transfer the ramps on the Ding Dong strength test so low that the board barely gets off the ramp.

[14] LOW LIP GAP 50 POINTS

Lip trick on any of the awnings or lower edges of the rides such as the Abductor or Thunder Cups.

[15] OVER THE BARN DOOR 50 POINTS

Grind the awning

[16] RIDE AND PUKE 50 POINTS

Transfer between the large "Abductor" quarter pipes .

[17] RIM ROCKIN' 50 POINTS

Lip trick on any of the backboards in the foul shooting game.

[18] 3 COW MANUAL 100 POINTS

Hop into a manual on the troughs inside the barn tunnel and roll past each of the cows' heads.

[19] ANGRY WINDOW 100 POINTS

Grind the edge of the bowl atop the Angry Dragon and carry the grind over the 2x4 and out the window near the swamp. Land in a grind on the wall running alongside the swamp.

[20] BANNER UP! 100 POINTS

Grind the flags from the Wonder Barn to the top of the Abductor.

[21] BARN HOLE MANUAL 100 POINTS

Manual all the way through the tunnel in the barn from the entrance near the Abductor across towards the Angry Dragon.

[22] BARN HOP 100 POINTS

Grind off the bowl of the Angry Dragon, through window in the "castle" and over to the awning of the Wonder Barn.

[23] CONGRATS ON YOUR FIRST OLLIE 100 POINTS

Transfer the ramps on the Ding Dong strength test with extremely low altitude.

[24] FROM THE CHARITY STRIPE 100 POINTS

Transfer one from one basketball booth to one directly next to it.

[25] GUMMY THE GATOR GAP 100 POINTS

Transfer a grind on the logs out in the swamp near the Rock'n Rock'itz ride. Watch out for the gator!

[26] HAUNTED TEACUP GAP 100 POINTS

Skate down the hill from the snack vendors and grind the fence up and onto the roof of the Horror House. Ollie off the end and land in a grind on the edge of the Thunder Cups ride.

[27] HIGH LIP GAP 100 POINTS

Lip Trick on any ledge that's above a **Low Lip Gap** such as the Thunder Cups sign or the upper balcony on the building near the entrance.

[28] HIGH WIRE ACT 100 POINTS

Grind the flags from the very top of the Wonder Barn to the upper edge of the Thunder Cups ride.

[29] MIDWAY MANUAL 100 POINTS

Manual along the pink ledge behind the Ding Dong (between the awning support poles) and transfer the manual across the gap where the tunnel entrance is and continue on in a manual on the other ledge.

[30] MIDWAY TRANSFER 100 POINTS

Use ProSet2 to transfer across the tunnel in the barn. Air up from the ramp adjacent the Ding Dong and land on the ProSet2 ramps.

[31] SWAMP ESCAPE 100 POINTS

Grind the logs in the swamp towards port-a-potties and kick up and over the wall back to safety.

[32] THRILL RIDE 100 POINTS

Grind the awning of the barn past the Thunder Cups ride and towards the roller coaster and ollie off the edge of the awning and into a grind on the roller coaster track.

[33] FOOT ON THE LINE 200 POINTS

Transfer one from a basketball booth to one two booths down.

[34] LIMP NOODLE 200 POINTS

Transfer the ramps on the Ding Dong strength test very low to the ground.

[35] YOU CALL THAT AIR? 250 POINTS

Transfer the ramps on the Ding Dong strength test very low to the ground.

[36] FROM DOWNTOWN 300 POINTS

Transfer from the basketball booth on either end of the attraction to the one on the far end.

[37] SHOULDA SKIPPED THAT CHILI DOG 300 POINTS

Transfer the ramps on the Ding Dong strength test without getting over head high off the ground.

[38] NICE VIEW, BUT ITS NO PENTHOUSE 350 POINTS

Transfer the ramps on the Ding Dong strength test without getting more than half way up the meter.

[39] ALMOST NEVER SOFT 450 POINTS

Transfer the ramps on the Ding Dong strength test. Get moderate height, but not high enough to ring bell.

[40] ABDUCTOR LIP MANUAL 500 POINTS

Hop into a manual on the steps running behind the Abductor and two-wheel it from one end to the other.

[41] WIN A PRIZE 500 POINTS

Transfer the ramps on the Ding Dong strength test as high as possible, thus causing the bell to ring.

[42] NICE VIEW UP HERE 1000 POINTS

Lip trick onto one of the baskets in the ferris wheel and hold the lip trick to the very top of the ride.

[43] ROOF DRAGON GAP 1000 POINTS

Ollie off the roof of the Wonder Barn into the pool atop the Angry Dragon ride.

[44] WHAT A TRIP! 1000 POINTS

Grind from the top of the big hill on the roller coaster all the way down the track, past the loading station, and up the start of the large hill. See the 'Grind the Whole Coaster' objective for tips.

Chicago

Purchase from Secrets Shop for $15,000.

Here's an opportunity to sample one of the awesome courses from *Mat Hoffman's Pro BMX™ 2*! Set in the downtown area of the city, this course contains has some pedestrian and a lot of vehicular traffic to look out for. But dealing with the crowds is worth it to sample the numerous ramps and rails tucked away in every corner of the level. Skaters will find plenty of scoring opportunities, whether it's down by the river, near the museum, or even across the river by the fountain. And it's a good thing, too, as this level boasts the most difficult scoring challenges in the game!

LEVEL GOALS

Unlocked Objectives

Get a High Score: 900,000 points
Collect S-K-A-T-E
Amateur C-O-M-B-O letters
Deliver the Pizzas
The Bridge Challenge
Grind 5 Fire Hydrants
Put Bugs on 5 Mafiosos

Locked Objectives

Get a Sick Score: 1,500,000 points
Pro C-O-M-B-O letters
Nail the tricks they yell out
Knock Over 10 Ballplayers in one combo
Do a 100,000 point combo on the ledge
900 off the bridge to the ferry's top deck
Distract the Guards

S Skater Kid

Skater Kid

A

K

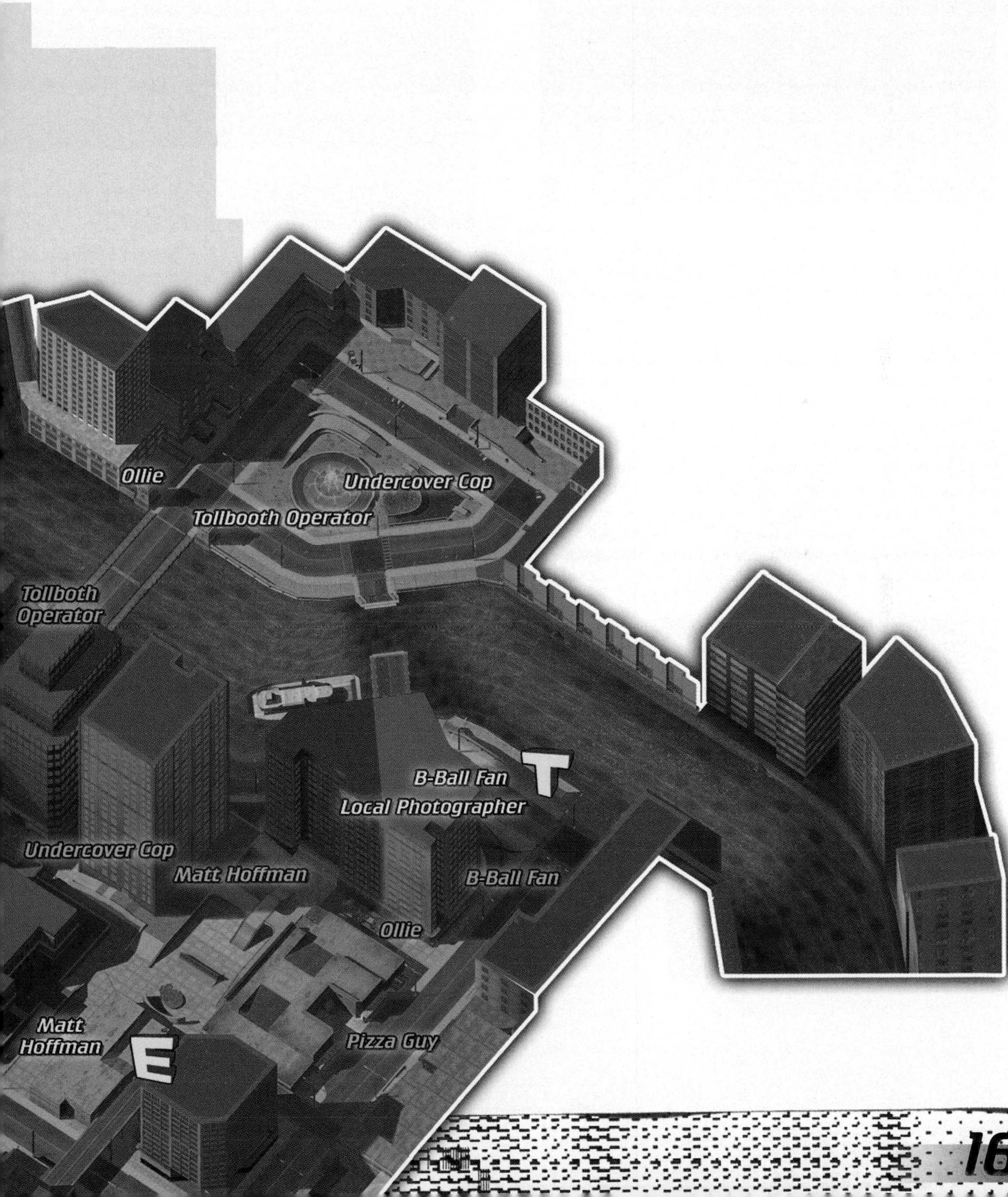

Ollie

Undercover Cop

Tollbooth Operator

Tollboth Operator

B-Ball Fan
Local Photographer

Undercover Cop

Matt Hoffman

B-Ball Fan

Ollie

Matt Hoffman

Pizza Guy

Amateur Challenges

GET A HIGH SCORE: 900,000 POINTS

Location	On the bridge in the plaza
Time	2:00
Awards	$500
How unlocked	N/A
Unlocks	Get a Sick Score: 1,500,000 points

Mat Hoffman

"Yo! Chicago's a pretty big city, with a lot of stuff to bust out. You think you can beat my High Score?"

Unlike the previous scoring objectives, the line detailed here requires some light travel. Head past Mat and trick down the stairs leading to the large transfer to the right of the bus. Trick out the Special Meter with some flatland tricks and wait across the street from the pair of quarter pipes until traffic calms down.

Start the run by Special Tricking across the **Heartattack Transfer**. Revert into a manual across the street and pop off the planter and land in a grind on the ledge of the upper walkway for the **Planter-2-Ledge** gap. Trick across the break in the ledge and land in a Special Grind for the **Ledge-2-Ledge** gap. Continue the Special Grind a clockwise lap around the large brick concert hall across from the bus, picking up several **Ledge-2-Ledge** gaps in the process. Try to land in a different Special Grind after each gap and, on the second lap, ollie down into a manual on the street near the coffeehouse. Ollie the short wall near the bus stop and go big off the large concrete spine with a Spine Transfer to Indy 900 to put an exclamation point on this 7-figure combo!

COLLECT S-K-A-T-E

Location	In front of the museum near the coffeehouse
Time	2:00
Awards	$500
How unlocked	N/A
Unlocks	Nail the tricks they yell out

Skater Kid

"All right, you know the drill. Try to hunt down all of the S-K-A-T-E letters!"

They've saved the most difficult batch of S-K-A-T-E letters for last, by far. Not only are these letters spread throughout the entire city, but they're very well hidden.

S Transfer onto the roof of the coffeehouse and air off the kicker in the front to snag the "S".

K The "K" is on what seems to be an unreachable windowsill on the concert hall. Cross the street near the bus and enter one of the three arches in the building to be teleported to the opposite side of the building. Turn around and enter the middle archway in the back to be teleported to the window where the "K" is.

A Head up the ramp near the bus towards the pizza place and ollie off the kicker to the right to land in a grind on the railing near the "A". This also scores the **Planter-2-Rail** gap.

T Head clockwise around the city and down along the waterfront. Pass the benches on the right and ride up the vert ramp straight ahead to slide into a left-hand grind on the ledge. Carry the grind onto the power line and up to the letter atop the utility pole.

E Continue looping around town and enter the area under the El. Follow the tracks as they curve to the left and Wallride the wall to the left of the trees to get the hard-to-find "E".

AMATEUR C-O-M-B-O LETTERS

Location	Around the corner from the starfish
Time	2:00
Awards	$500
How unlocked	N/A
Unlocks	Pro C-O-M-B-O letters

Ollie the Bum
"I lost my letters, can you go find C-O-M-B-O for me? And you gotta do it in one combo too!"

Hop into a grind on the planter straight ahead to pick up the "C" and manual towards the steps ahead. Grind the right-hand ledge up to the "O" and ollie down the other side into a manual. Grind the curved ledge on the corner for the "M" and take to another manual. Turn to the right and ollie over the red railing in the street to snag the "B". Be sure to land in a manual and hit the **Heartattack Transfer** to pick up the second "O".

DELIVER THE PIZZAS

Location	Near the red brick building across from the theatre
Time	0:15
Awards	$500
How unlocked	N/A
Unlocks	Do a 100,000 point combo on the ledge

Pizza Guy
"Could you do me a favor and deliver these pizzas for me? You'd better hurry though, I have 45 seconds to deliver them all or I don't get paid. And don't drop 'em!"

The Pizza Guy needs some help delivering his pizzas to the local businesses. The red arrow at the top of the screen helps guide the skater to each drop-off. Look for the pizza box and skate through it to get 10 seconds added to the clock. There's not a lot of time so be sure to grind ledges and rails for extra speed.

The first delivery is neat the boarding platform for the El. Cross the street and use the ramp to leap up onto the tracks. Follow the tracks around to the left and ollie onto the platform to make the first delivery.

The second delivery is to the coffeehouse. Take off down the street and aim straight for the door on the right of the shop.

Continue the clockwise loop around the city towards the bridge at the corner. The third pizza goes to the office building on the corner opposite the bridge.

Grind the yellow rails in the alleyway, pass the Undercover Cop, and head up the rampway to the back of the concert hall. The final pizza box is near the arches.

THE BRIDGE CHALLENGE

Location	On the corner near the bridge
Time	2:00
Awards	$500
How unlocked	N/A
Unlocks	900 off bridge to the ferry's top deck

Wanna convince the Tollbooth Operator to lower the bridge? Well, you must land 3 combos while gapping across the river first! Although the bridge is relatively easy to gap across for the first trick, the Tollbooth Operator is going to raise it with each successful jump.

The first leap across the **BridgeGap** can be done with an unlit Special Meter. Ride up the incline and perform the specified triple flip trick (Right + Flip, Flip, Flip Button) while in the air. Land it cleanly to get credit for the jump.

The bridge is a little steeper for the second jump, but it can still be done from a standstill and without a fully lit Special Meter. Charge up the ramp, perform the grab (Up/Left + Grab Button) and flip (Down + Flip Button) tricks the Toll Booth requests and land it for **BridgeGap 2!** Land the combo smoothly so as to ensure that the Skater has a maxed out Special Meter for the third attempt.

The bridge is nearly vertical for the final attempt, but the added oomph from having a lit Special Meter makes it doable. This jump also feature a combo of tricks. Hit the initial grab (Up/Right + Grab Button) right away so as to leave time for the flip trick (Down/Right + Flip Button).

GRIND 5 FIRE HYDRANTS

Location	Across from the starfish
Time	0:30
Awards	$500
How unlocked	N/A
Unlocks	Knock over 10 ballplayers in one combo

There are 5 fire hydrants scattered around the city and you've got just 30 seconds to "Kiss the Rail" on each of them. Be sure to grind everything in sight to increase the skater's speed and hop over the fire hydrant while tapping the Grind Button.

From the starting point, hop into a grind on the yellow rail to pick up speed. The first fire hydrant is just beyond this rail.

Take the inside route around the corner to grind the rail on the building on the corner and continue towards the museum. The next fire hydrant is on the left side of the road, just past the El.

The next fire hydrant is near Mat's tour bus. Circle around the bus stop towards the blue "Windy City" awning to locate it.

Continue down that street towards the bridge, but keep to the left. The fourth fire hydrant is just before the corner.

Time will be starting to run out, so make the turn at the bridge quickly and grind the rail and benches on the right to pick up even more speed. The final hydrant is on the right side of the road, just past the first yellow rail.

STOPPAGE TIME

While some objectives end precisely when time runs out, this is one of those challenges that lets the skater continue on the quest until their last combo is finished. So, if time is running out on you, just hop into a grind or a manual and grind that final fire hydrant after time expires.

PUT BUGS ON 5 MAFIOSOS

Location	Beside the large brick building
Time	2:00
Awards	$500
How unlocked	N/A
Unlocks	Distract the guards

How to put this delicately? Chicago is known for having many *family-run businesses*, and well, sometimes they do things that anger the police. Help out the pimpin' copper and his investigation by seeking out the five well-dressed Mafiosos and flip tricking over them. Each of the Mafiosos can be found casing the various businesses around town.

Skate away from the Undercover Cop towards the street with Mat's bus and head towards the bridge. Make a right just before the bridge and hug the building on the inside of the turn. The first **Mob Hit!** can be made right there.

Follow the road by the river to the starfish. The next Mafiosos is Under the roof by the white columns.

The next Mafioso to hit is near the museum entrance. Hit the ramps beside the steps to leap up and over his head.

Head down the alley towards the plaza behind the concert hall and ride up the walkway of the white building on the left. The next target is near the door on the steps above the Undercover Cop!

Follow the upper walkway in the plaza to the helipad and gap across the **Roof Topper** gap via the wooden ramp. The final Mafioso is on the upper part of the next building's roof.

GET A SICK SCORE: 1,500,000 POINTS

Location	On the roof across from the helipad
Time	2:00
Awards	$500
How unlocked	Complete 'Get a High Score: 900,000 points'
Unlocks	Nothing

DÉJÀ VU?

The bulk of the Sick Score combo outlined here is the same as the line given for the High Score. Why mess with a proven winner? Where the two differ, and where the extra 600,000 points comes into play, is the beginning and end of the run. Nailing this line takes some practice—consider it your final training before taking on the world in the multiplayer mode!

Those who managed to pull off the Sick Score combo laid out in the 'Carnival' chapter already know that the keys to a huge combo are Special Grinds and lots and lots of quick flip tricks to boost the multiplier. Those rules are reinforced here in the more spacious Chi-town.

Start the run by flip tricking into a grind on the cable leading to the concert hall and hold that same grind across the ledge of the building towards the street. Toss a Triple Impossible while gapping down into the street and land in a Special Manual. Pull off a quick flip trick on the vert ramp near the steps, Revert the landing, and manual back across the street towards the planter. Special Trick off the planter into a manual on the concert hall walkway and quickly hop into a Special Grind on the outer ledge.

Now it's time to grind the daylights out of that concert hall ledge. Flip trick across the gap near each of the three staircases and land in a different Special Grind while grabbing the **Ledge-2-Ledge** bonus multiple times. Be extra careful near the front of the building as the ledge curves a lot there. Keep up the grinding for a full lap and a half around the building. Hop down onto the street when passing the museum a second time and manual towards the ramps near the coffeehouse.

Flip trick over the little wall near the edge of the street and manual into a Spine Transfer over the concrete spine. Mix in a quick Special Trick during the transfer, Revert the landing, and manual into yet another Special Trick off the back ramp. Revert back towards the spine and finish the string with

one last, conservative trick such as a brief lip trick just to get the extra multiplier.

MAGIC MATH

One of the side effects of playing *Tony Hawk's Pro Skater 4* is that you can become very good at making quick mathematical calculations in your head. Let's face it, there's nothing worse than bailing and only then realizing you had more than enough points to complete the scoring challenge. For those who are computationally challenged, here's a tip: look for a base score of 50,000 points and a multiplier of 30. Those are the magic numbers for this combo and equal the necessary 1.5 million points!

PRO C-O-M-B-O LETTERS

Location	Across the bridge
Time	2:00
Awards	$500
How unlocked	Complete 'Amateur C-O-M-B-O letters'
Unlocks	Nothing

Ollie the Bum

"I lost 'em again! Collect the C-O-M-B-O letters in one combo for me! I won't ever ask again!"

This is it, the final C-O-M-B-O challenge in the game! Enter the alcove near Ollie and leap off the quarter pipe nearest the bridge to snag the "C". Revert the landing and quickly hop into a grind on the ledge leading up towards the blue awning. Air over the awning and onto the following ledge to grab the "O" (or land in a manual on the sidewalk) and transfer the grind to the curving ledge in the corner near the mailbox. Manual to a grind on the right-hand ledge near the staircase. Pick up the "M" while hitting the **Ledge-2-Ledge** gap at the top of the steps and manual towards the granite vert ramp in the corner. Grind off the top of the vert ramp onto the ledge to the right to gather up the "B" and ollie down onto the ledge by the river to find the final letter.

NAIL THE TRICKS THEY YELL OUT

Location	At the coffeehouse
Time	1:00
Awards	$500
How unlocked	Complete 'Collect S-K-A-T-E'
Unlocks	Nothing

Skater Kid
"Nail the tricks that get yelled out!"

Use the concrete spine to the right of the coffeehouse and the large ramp against the back wall to perform each of the tricks as they appear. This final Falling Tricks challenge is made difficult by the numerous diagonal-button presses that are required, as well as by the mixing in of lip tricks. Try to get in two of the air tricks with each leap and wait for two of the lip tricks to "stack up". Ride up the ramp and into one lip trick and ollie directly into the second to take them out faster. It's even possible to clear out a simple Kickflip or Heelflip on the way back down onto the ramp.

KNOCK OVER 10 BALLPLAYERS IN ONE COMBO

Location	Across the street from the starfish
Time	2:00
Awards	$500
How unlocked	Complete 'Grind 5 fire hydrants'
Unlocks	Nothing

B-Ball Fan
"There are a bunch of second rate ball players hanging out by the river. See if you can knock over 10 of them in one combo!"

There are four pairs of b-ball players standing near the railing along the river walk. Grind and manual past them to slap them to the ground. They get back to their feet after a few seconds, giving you a chance to hit them again! Take out 10 of them in one combo to complete the challenge.

Descend the walkway and turn around just past the first pair of ball players. Hop into a grind on the rail and quickly leap down into a manual. Use the vert ramp to turn around and Revert into a grind on the railing. Take out the pair of ball players as they clamber back to their feet and continue grinding the rail. Ollie across each of the gaps for the **Rail-2-Rail** gap and clobber all of the ball players standing by the river. If any slipped by without getting nailed, ollie off the rail into a manual and use the vert ramp at the other end of the walkway to turn around just as before. Make

the grinding return trip back towards the starting point and hop down off the rail the moment 10 ball players have been knocked down.

DO A 100,000 POINT COMBO ON THE LEDGE

Location	On ledge above starfish
Time	2:00
Awards	$500
How unlocked	Complete 'Deliver the pizzas'
Unlocks	Nothing

Local Photographer
"Yo, I hope you've been practicing your flat ground circus act. Now let's see you if you can do a big combo on this ledge."

Scoring 100,000 points in flatland tricks is pretty hard when there's no room to roll around in a manual. The key to pulling it off is to slightly roll up against the side of the building and start the combo next to it so that the skater stays still. Tap into a manual and start linking multiple flatland tricks together. Incorporate each of their variants such as the Wrap Around and Handflip and add plenty of Pivots and Truckspins too! Once the multiplier has grown to over 7, flip trick into a Special Manual and balance it in place for a while. Switch back to the flatland tricks, increase the multiplier some more, and end the string with another Special Manual to give the base score a boost.

900 OFF BRIDGE TO THE FERRY'S TOP DECK

Location	Near the fountain
Time	1:00
Awards	$500
How unlocked	Complete 'The bridge challenge'
Unlocks	Nothing

Tollbooth Operator
"Do a 900 from this bridge onto the upper deck of the ferry!"

One small step for the Tollbooth Operator, one large leap for skating-kind! There's a reason why that second bridge was never lowered, and this is it! Grind around the fountain to max out the Special Meter and skate up the left side of the bridge as fast as possible. Bank hard to the right at the last moment and fly off the right-hand edge of the bridge. Input the commands for the 900. Quickly straighten out the skater if needed and wait to see where you land. The skater must land on the upper deck of the ship to score the **Jump Ship!** gap and to complete the objective.

DISTRACT THE GUARDS

Location	Near the fountain
Time	1:00
Awards	$500
How unlocked	Complete 'Put bugs on 5 Mafiosos'
Unlocks	Nothing

Undercover Cop

"I'm trying to get into mob headquarters, but there are 4 guards blocking the entrance. See if you can distract 'em by setting off the alarms on their cars."

The Undercover Cop is one step closer to bustin' the mob. Help him get into their headquarters by grinding on the four cars parked outside the large building across from the fountain. Start in the corner near the curved gray ledge and quickly skate and grind across all four cars. The car alarms on the cars only sound for a few seconds so you have to be quick about it. The Undercover Cop can only bust into their base if all four cars' alarms are going off at once!

CASH ICONS / PRO SETS / GAPS

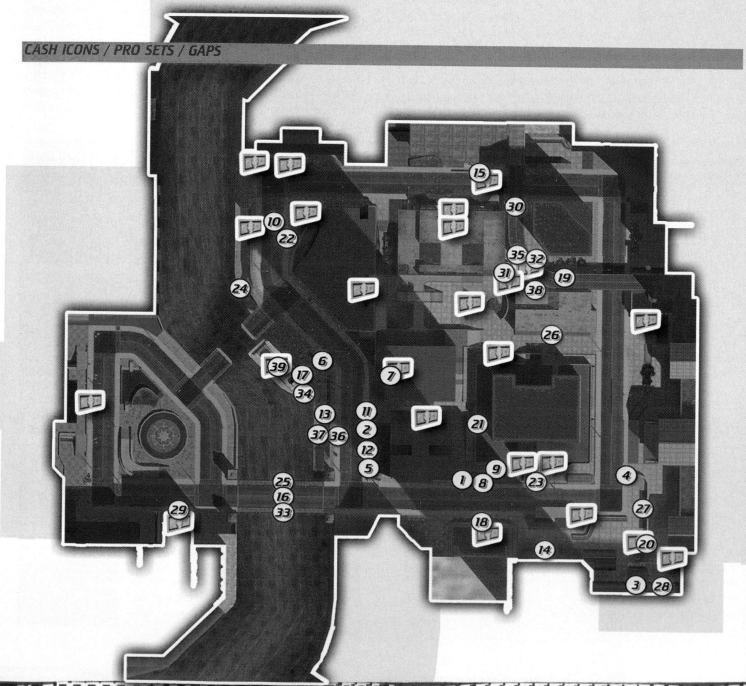

GAP CHECKLIST

[1] BENCH-2-PLANTER   25 POINTS
Transfer a grind from one of the park benches to a planter.

[2] BENCH-2-RAIL   25 POINTS
Transfer a grind from a bench to a rail.

[3] FROTHY LIP   25 POINTS
Lip trick on the quarter pipe atop the coffeehouse.

[4] LEDGE-2-PLANTER   25 POINTS
Grind a ledge and ollie into a grind on a planter.

[5] LEDGE-2-RAIL   25 POINTS
Grind a ledge and ollie into a grind on a rail.

[6] LIGHT RAIL   25 POINTS
Grind the rail over the planters on the river walk.

[7] LIP EXTENSION   25 POINTS
Leap into a lip trick on the rail above the vert ramp facing the river.

[8] PLANTER-2-BENCH   25 POINTS
Transfer a grind from one of the planters to a park bench.

[9] PLANTER-2-LEDGE   25 POINTS
Transfer a grind from one of the planters onto a ledge.

[10] PLANTER-2-RAIL   25 POINTS
Grind a planter and transfer it to a rail.

[11] RAIL-2-BENCH   25 POINTS
Transfer a grind from one of the rails onto a park bench.

[12] RAIL-2-LEDGE   25 POINTS
Transfer a grind from one of the rails onto a ledge.

[13] RAIL-2-PLANTER   25 POINTS
Transfer a grind from a rail onto a planter.

[14] UP TO AWNING   25 POINTS
Grind the blue "Wise Guy" awning near Mat's bus.

[15] BENCH-2-BENCH   50 POINTS
Transfer a grind between two benches.

[16] BRIDGE GAP 1!   50 POINTS
Complete the tricks specified in the first part of the 'The Bridge Challenge'.

[17] FERRY PRINCESS   50 POINTS
Transfer a grind from the railing by the river walk onto the railing on the ferry.

[18] HEARTATTACK TRANSFER   50 POINTS
Transfer over the staircase in front of the Beer Palace via the two large vert ramps on either side.

[19] JUMPING TRACK   50 POINTS
Transfer a grind between two adjacent rails on the El's tracks.

[20] LATTE-2-GO   50 POINTS
Fly off the kicker atop the coffeehouse and land in a grind on the wall in front of the museum.

[21] LEDGE-2-LEDGE   50 POINTS
Transfer a grind between any two adjacent ledges.

[22] MODERN GAP   50 POINTS
Transfer a grind onto or off of the starfish statue near the river.

[23] PLANTER-2-PLANTER   50 POINTS
Transfer a grind between any two adjacent planters.

[24] RAIL-2-RAIL   50 POINTS
Transfer a grind between any two adjacent rails.

[25] BRIDGE GAP2!   100 POINTS
Complete the tricks specified in the second part of the 'The Bridge Challenge'.

[26] GRASSY MANUAL   100 POINTS
Manual the lengthy of the very long planter that leads out of the plaza towards the museum.

[27] HIGH ART TRANSFER   100 POINTS
Transfer between the quarter pipes in front of the museum, near the coffeehouse.

[28] LATTA MOCHA AIR   100 POINTS
Gap between the vert ramps on either side of the coffeehouse.

[29] OVER BLUE AWNING   100 POINTS
Cross the bridge and grind the ledge on the left. Kick off the kink in the ledge, transfer over the blue awning, and land in a grind on the ledge on the other side.

[30] OVER THE EL   100 POINTS
Hit the kicker across the street from the barbershop and gap up and over the El's tracks in a single leap.

[31] ROOF TOPPER   100 POINTS
Gap from the roof of the building with the helipad to the building next to it via the wooden ramp in the corner.

[32] YELLOW-2-YELLOW   100 POINTS
Transfer a grind between the two low-lying yellow rails under the El.

[33] BRIDGE GAP 3!   200 POINTS
Complete the tricks specified in the third part of the 'The Bridge Challenge'.

[34] FERRY TO SURFACE STREETS   200 POINTS
Boneless off the ramp at the bow of the ferry and land on the street above the river walk.

[35] JUMPING TWO TRACKS!   200 POINTS
Grind the outer rail on the El's tracks and ollie across to a grind on the rail on the opposite edge. Best done at the curve.

[36] RIVER BARRIER MANUAL   200 POINTS
Hop into a manual on the concrete barrier near the street above the ferry. Manual the entire length of the barrier from one bridge to the other.

[37] RIVER-SIDE MANUAL   200 POINTS
Manual the entire length of the river walk, from one vert ramp all the way to the other. Seriously.

[38] TIGHT LEDGE MANUAL   200 POINTS
Manual the skinny ledge leading out of the plaza and under the El's tracks.

[39] JUMP SHIP!   5000 POINTS
Land the 900 on the upper deck of the ferry in the '900 off bridge to the ferry's top deck' objective.

CASH PRIZES

Find every gap in the game to receive $1500

LEVELS

The Secret Levels each contain 14 objectives that range from moderately difficult to extremely challenging. A complete walkthrough for each of these levels can be found in the main 'Skate-Thru' section of the book.

LEVEL	PRICE
Carnival	$15,000
Chicago	$15,000

SKATERS

SKATER	PRICE	
Secret Skater 1	$9,000	
Secret Skater 2	$9,000	
Secret Skater 3	$9,000	
Secret Skater 4	$15,000	Available after Career Mode is 100% complete.

MYSTERY SKATER #1: METAL HEAD

STARTING STATS		SIGNATURE TRICKS	
Air	5	Stage Dive!	1000+ points
Hangtime	5	Headbangers Unite	500+ points
Ollie	4	Bloody Eddie	1000+ points
Speed	5		
Spin	7		
Switch	4		
Flip Speed	5		
Rail Balance	6		
Lip Balance	5		
Manual Balance	4		

MYSTERY SKATER #2: STAR WARRIOR

STARTING STATS		SIGNATURE TRICKS	
Air	7	Jump Jet	1200+ points
Hangtime	7	Grapple Grab	1200 points
Ollie	3	Quick Draw	500+ points
Speed	7		
Spin	7		
Switch	3		
Flip Speed	5		
Rail Balance	3		
Lip Balance	3		
Manual Balance	5		

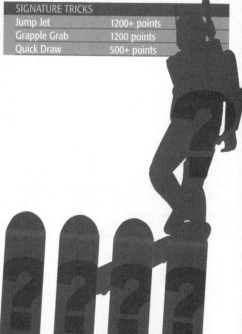

MIKE VALLELY

World's Toughest Pro Skater

STARTING STATS	
Air	6
Hangtime	6
Ollie	4
Speed	4
Spin	5
Switch	4
Flip Speed	5
Rail Balance	5
Lip Balance	5
Manual Balance	6

SIGNATURE TRICKS	
Elbow Smash	500+ points
Ho Ho Street Plant	1500+ points
Flamingo	1000 points

CHEATS

Cheats can be activated via the in-game Options Menu.

CHEAT	PRICE	DESCRIPTION
Cheat 1	$1,500	Make Special Moves even more special!
Cheat 2	$1,500	Gorilla Mode
Cheat 3	$1,500	Kid Mode
Cheat 4	$1,500	Big Head Mode
Cheat 5	$1,500	The future of skateboarding
Cheat 6	$1,500	More your speed
Cheat 7	$1,500	Party Time
Cheat 8	$1,000	Now you see me. Now you don't.
Cheat 9	$1,500	Bloodier than a…
Cheat 10	$1,500	Hot! Hot! Hot!
Cheat 11	$1,500	Sim Mode. Make the game no fun.

CLOTHES AND GEAR

The following items can be purchased through either the 'Secret Gear' selection under the 'Clothes and Gear' menu, or via the 'Clothes' selection in the 'Spend Cash' menu.

ITEM	PRICE
O.D. Head	$400
Ollie Head	$400
Kenny Head	$400
Metal Head	$300
Clown Head	$300
Eraser Hair	$250
Clown Hair	$250
Paper Bag	$300
King Glasses	$100
O.D. Shirt	$250
Ollie Coat	$250
Kilt	$250
Smile Boxers	$150
Heart Boxers	$150
Ollie Pants	$250
Clown Pants	$250
Clown Boots	$150

DAISY

Hot Chick

STARTING STATS	
Air	6
Hangtime	5
Ollie	6
Speed	4
Spin	5
Switch	5
Flip Speed	5
Rail Balance	4
Lip Balance	6
Manual Balance	4

SIGNATURE TRICKS	
Banana Board Splits	1500+ points
Sunbathing	1000+ points
Hula Hoopin'	500+ points
Ahhh Yeahhh!	1400+ points

MOVIES

Highlight videos of each of the professional skaters are unlocked whenever a Pro Challenge is completed. Also, the Pro Bails 1 video is unlocked by completing the Create-A-Skater's Pro Challenge at the Shipyard.

MOVIE	PRICE	DESCRIPTION
Homies Skatin' 1	$800	Yes, we can skate. Barely.
Homies Skatin' 2	$800	More Neversoft skills in action.
Pro Bails 2	$800	You gotta be tough to get good!
Kona Old School	$800	Back in the day…
Outtakes	$800	Making games, looking like fools doing it.

Online Multiplayer

This portion of the guide applies primarily to playing online with the PS2. Nevertheless, all of the game descriptions and tips are applicable for use during System Link play with the Xbox. Please refer to official *Tony Hawk's Pro Skater 4* user's manuals regarding Internet and System Link connectivity instructions.

GETTING STARTED

GET A KEYBOARD!

Although it isn't necessary, a big part of playing online is interacting with other people, and that means communicating. While the in-game typing interface is satisfactory for infrequent chatting, those who plan to play online a lot should invest in a USB keyboard.

The very first thing the player needs to do when going online is make a skater selection. This decision is based completely on aesthetics as all skaters are automatically given maxed stats online. This is a great reason to put the Create-A-Skater tool to use; as much as everyone admires the pro skaters included in the game, it's always more fun to skate with individually styled skaters. After selecting a skater, take the time to edit the trick settings if necessary and select "Ready" and choose either LAN or Internet depending on your system configuration.

The next screen is the Internet Options screen. Here, you are given the opportunity to upload and download parks built in the Park Editor, save their settings, and even create an online user profile that can keep track of your "Homies" for you. When ready to actually take to the streets, select the 'Play Online' option to get a list of the available servers. From there you can select a specific region or family of servers and enter its lobby. Once inside, a list of current games will be displayed, as well as the options to chat, add people to your "Homies" list and even join or host a game. Select a game to see the number of players, your ping to that server (the lower the better), and other information such as skill level and course.

HOW TO BE A GOOD HOST

The benefit of being a host is that the host decides what games to play and on what courses to play them. By selecting the hosting option from the lobby, you'll be taken to the Server Options screen. Give your game a name ("Neversoft" is the default name), select the starting level, the maximum number of players, a skill level, and whether or not teams

or observers are allowed. Those wishing to only play with friends can assign a password to the game, preventing strangers (and friends who forget the password) from joining your game.

While there are obvious benefits to being a host, there is also a good deal of responsibility. Ultimately, the host's actions dictate whether or not people have a good time. The following list shows the do's and don'ts of online skating.

- Give the game a descriptive name so people know what to expect before joining. "Graffiti at London" is an example of a way to do this.
- Don't ever end a game prematurely unless everyone agrees that it's time for a change.
- Take requests. People like it when the host is courteous, so ask the other skaters what game or level they want to play on.
- Keep an eye on the balance of abilities between teams and request for some switching of teams if things are too lopsided.
- Give credit where it's due. Let people know they are playing well or encourage those who are struggling to keep trying.
- Allow observers. Just like real skateboarding, newbies can only learn how to play better if the more advanced players allow them to watch.
- Don't put up with nonsense. No matter how friendly and positive you try to make it, there are going to be occasions when someone needs to be booted from the game in order to ensure that everyone else continues to have a good time.
- Don't quit the game without warning. Everyone has to log off eventually, ask if anyone wants to take over hosting duties before you go.

- Don't turn on collision unless it's requested. This is a very touchy issue with people and many will leave the game if collision is turned on. Be sure to ask for a quick vote before switching it one way or the other.

- Unlock all levels. Avoid starting a game as the host if you haven't yet unlocked all of the courses in the game. Spend some more time with Career Mode or just let other people host until later.

GOT SKILLZ?

Players can expect to find the "Noobs" and "Pros" servers in addition to the various region-based servers. While the level of competition is sure to vary on a day-to-day basis, these servers are meant for people on the extreme ends of the learning curve. The Noobs server is the perfect place for those with little skater experience to have some friendly sessions together. On the other hand, the Pros server will likely feature highly competitive games between veteran skaters. It is recommended that people use the numerous regional servers to gauge their abilities. Those who continually struggle on the regional servers may desire to move down to the Noobs server, whereas those who continuously win should consider moving up to the Pros server.

PLAYING NICE

While the host has the final say in who plays what games, it's up to each and every gamer to make sure that a friendly atmosphere is maintained. Consider the following suggestions before going online.

- Keep it positive. No matter what the outcome of the game is, it's always a nice gesture to type "gg" or "good game" or to use the taunt commands to dish out some "Props".

- Don't flood the screen. If you have something to say, by all means type it in. But don't type it in 10 times in a row!

- Keep profanity to a minimum. There are ways to request a game or course change without using expletives. Most people will prefer you keep it clean.

- Don't quit mid-game unless it's an emergency. Most games only last a couple of minutes so try to stick it out until the end. Everyone will thank you for waiting till the game is over.

- Obey the host's wishes. If the host asks you to switch teams to balance things out, go ahead and do it. There's no online ranking system or stat-keeping to worry about. Give the new team a try and if you don't like it, switch back afterwards.

- Don't cheat. This one needs no explanation.

THE COURSES

This section of the chapter contains maps of all Capture the Flag bases as well as some recommendations for finding success on each of the 9 courses in the game.

COLLEGE

Red Base

Blue Base

Green Base

Yellow Base

King of the Hill	Use the elevator to ride up to the roof of the Fine Arts building and jump into a grind on the cable that leads to the roof of the Engineering building. This cable is easy to miss and often allows the "King" to sit out of reach while the others fall back to ground level.
Graffiti	There are numerous ledges inside the parking garage that are easily overlooked in favor of the ones out in the open. Link up a big grind combo with the ledges and grind the cables towards the clock tower to make them unstealable.
Goal Attack	Try selecting the 'Race the Inline Skater' goal as the only objective and have everybody wait near the Philosophy Building to have a mass start. It's not skating, but the occasional race is always good for some fun.

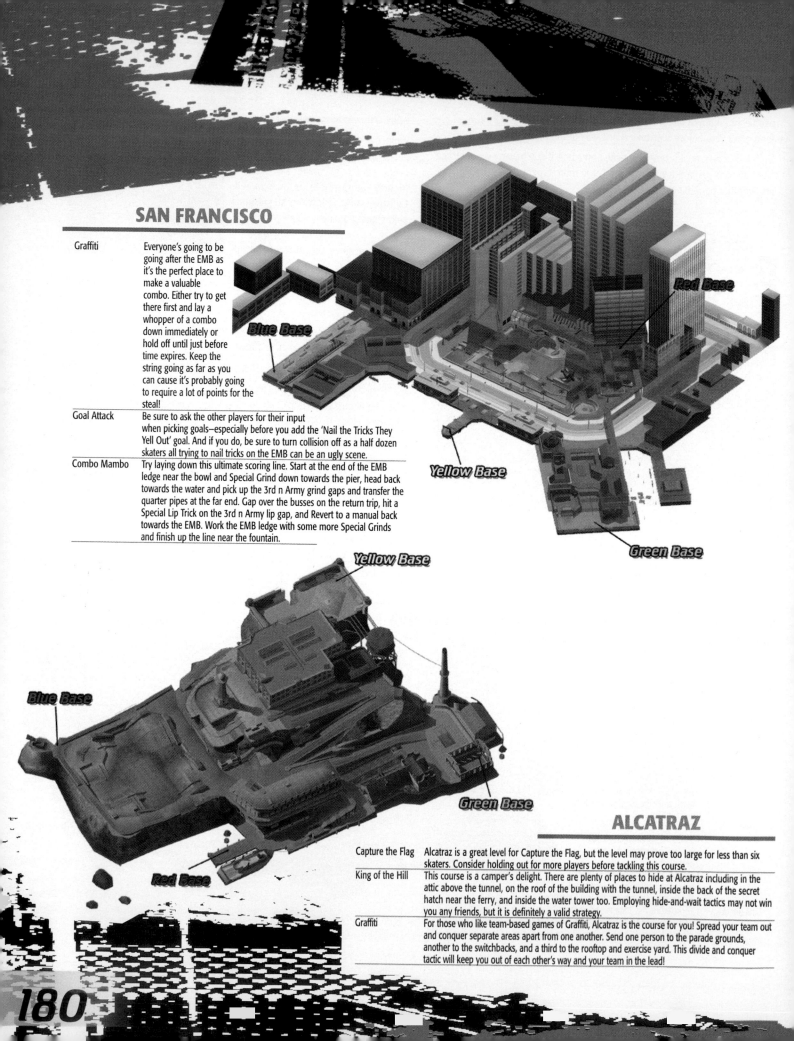

SAN FRANCISCO

Blue Base

Red Base

Yellow Base

Green Base

Graffiti	Everyone's going to be going after the EMB as it's the perfect place to make a valuable combo. Either try to get there first and lay a whopper of a combo down immediately or hold off until just before time expires. Keep the string going as far as you can cause it's probably going to require a lot of points for the steal!
Goal Attack	Be sure to ask the other players for their input when picking goals—especially before you add the 'Nail the Tricks They Yell Out' goal. And if you do, be sure to turn collision off as a half dozen skaters all trying to nail tricks on the EMB can be an ugly scene.
Combo Mambo	Try laying down this ultimate scoring line. Start at the end of the EMB ledge near the bowl and Special Grind down towards the pier, head back towards the water and pick up the 3rd n Army grind gaps and transfer the quarter pipes at the far end. Gap over the busses on the return trip, hit a Special Lip Trick on the 3rd n Army lip gap, and Revert to a manual back towards the EMB. Work the EMB ledge with some more Special Grinds and finish up the line near the fountain.

Yellow Base

Blue Base

Green Base

Red Base

ALCATRAZ

Capture the Flag	Alcatraz is a great level for Capture the Flag, but the level may prove too large for less than six skaters. Consider holding out for more players before tackling this course.
King of the Hill	This course is a camper's delight. There are plenty of places to hide at Alcatraz including in the attic above the tunnel, on the roof of the building with the tunnel, inside the back of the secret hatch near the ferry, and inside the water tower too. Employing hide-and-wait tactics may not win you any friends, but it is definitely a valid strategy.
Graffiti	For those who like team-based games of Graffiti, Alcatraz is the course for you! Spread your team out and conquer separate areas apart from one another. Send one person to the parade grounds, another to the switchbacks, and a third to the rooftop and exercise yard. This divide and conquer tactic will keep you out of each other's way and your team in the lead!

KONA

Slap!	Kona is perhaps the best course in which to play Slap! as it's wide open design allows players to see skaters off in the distance. Fans of Slap! may even find it suitable for games with less than 3 people.
Goal Attack	This is another great game to play at Kona as the design is conducive to having numerous people trying to collect items at once. Also, seeing several people attempt the snake run simultaneously is quite comical!
Score Challenge	Those who enjoy playing Score Challenge with target scores in excess of 10,000,000 points are going to really like Kona. This course offers the most variety and is the most likely to allow scores of 100,000,000 points. Then again, target scores over 10,000,000 points should be reserved for team-based games… unless, of course, you're not going anywhere for a while.

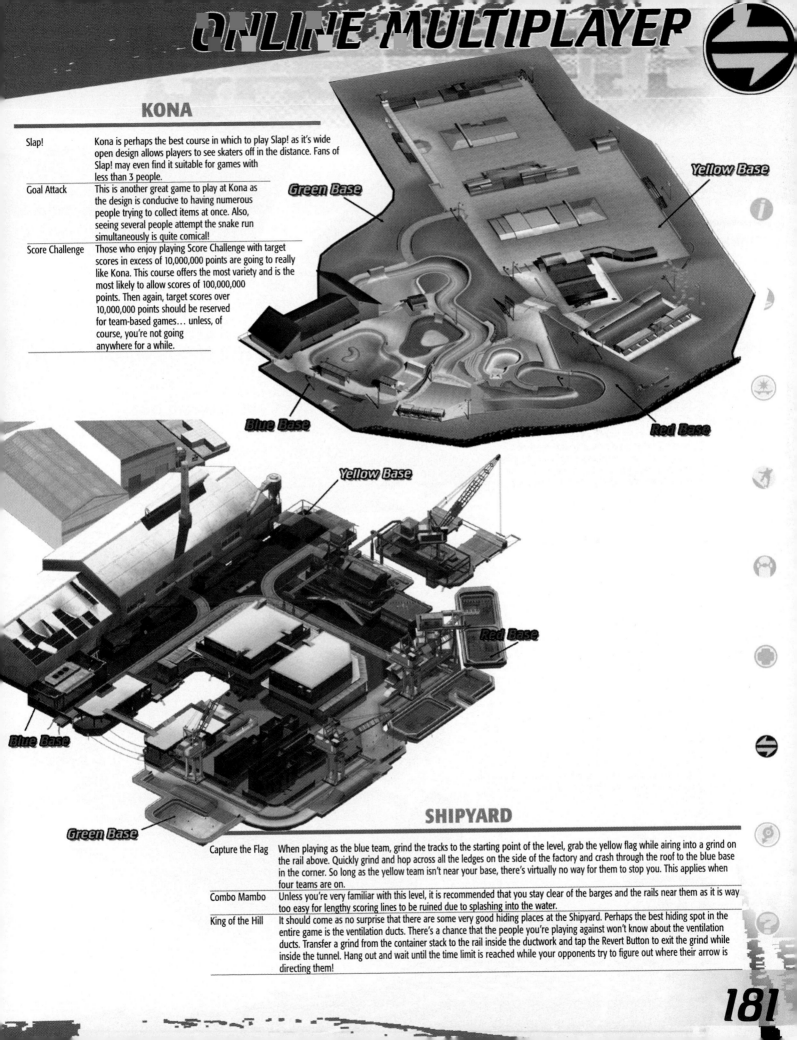

Green Base

Yellow Base

Blue Base

Red Base

Yellow Base

Red Base

Blue Base

Green Base

SHIPYARD

Capture the Flag	When playing as the blue team, grind the tracks to the starting point of the level, grab the yellow flag while airing into a grind on the rail above. Quickly grind and hop across all the ledges on the side of the factory and crash through the roof to the blue base in the corner. So long as the yellow team isn't near your base, there's virtually no way for them to stop you. This applies when four teams are on.
Combo Mambo	Unless you're very familiar with this level, it is recommended that you stay clear of the barges and the rails near them as it is way too easy for lengthy scoring lines to be ruined due to splashing into the water.
King of the Hill	It should come as no surprise that there are some very good hiding places at the Shipyard. Perhaps the best hiding spot in the entire game is the ventilation ducts. There's a chance that the people you're playing against won't know about the ventilation ducts. Transfer a grind from the container stack to the rail inside the ductwork and tap the Revert Button to exit the grind while inside the tunnel. Hang out and wait until the time limit is reached while your opponents try to figure out where their arrow is directing them!

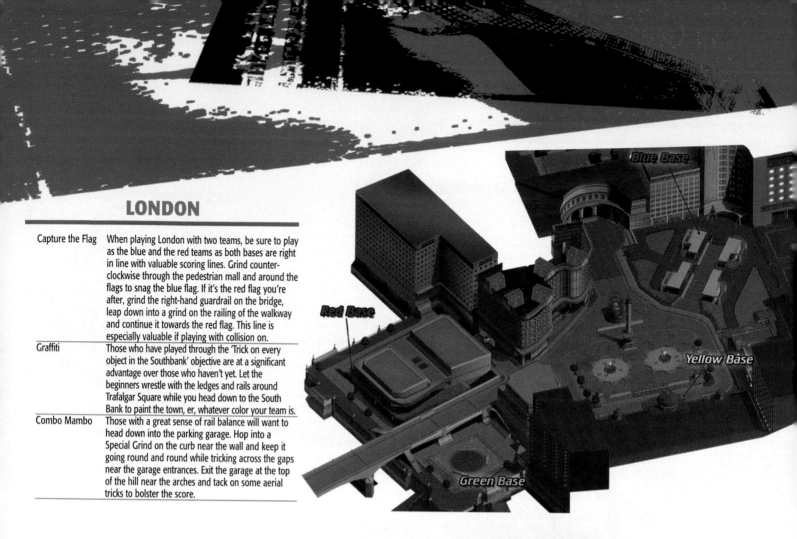

LONDON

Capture the Flag	When playing London with two teams, be sure to play as the blue and the red teams as both bases are right in line with valuable scoring lines. Grind counter-clockwise through the pedestrian mall and around the flags to snag the blue flag. If it's the red flag you're after, grind the right-hand guardrail on the bridge, leap down into a grind on the railing of the walkway and continue it towards the red flag. This line is especially valuable if playing with collision on.
Graffiti	Those who have played through the 'Trick on every object in the Southbank' objective are at a significant advantage over those who haven't yet. Let the beginners wrestle with the ledges and rails around Trafalgar Square while you head down to the South Bank to paint the town, er, whatever color your team is.
Combo Mambo	Those with a great sense of rail balance will want to head down into the parking garage. Hop into a Special Grind on the curb near the wall and keep it going round and round while tricking across the gaps near the garage entrances. Exit the garage at the top of the hill near the arches and tack on some aerial tricks to bolster the score.

ZOO

Capture the Flag	When playing with four teams of three or more skaters apiece, always try to be on the yellow team. The yellow flag is in the upper hippo pool and is not only easy to miss, but hard to get to safely. With this location, the yellow team only needs to leave one person defending the bridge across the water while the other teammates take to offense. Just make sure to cross the bridge when returning an enemy flag as falling in the water will cause it to be returned to their base.
Score Challenge	The Zoo is home to some mighty big halfpipes as well as some of the longest grinds in the game. Get a team together and have some members session the elephant moat while the others work the rails near the hippo exhibit and inside the aviary.

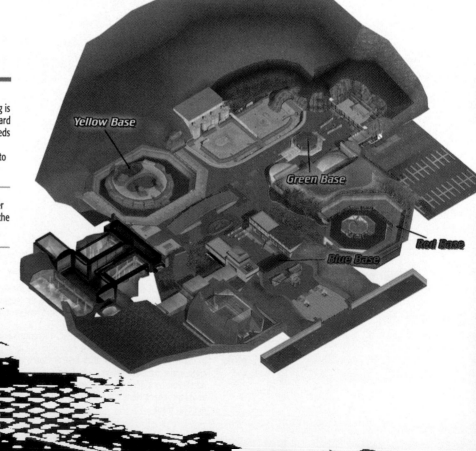

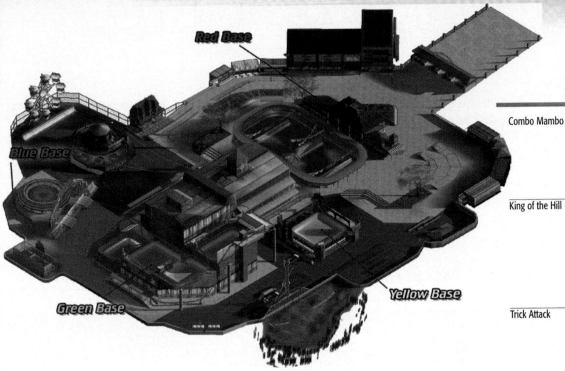

Red Base

Blue Base

Green Base

Yellow Base

CARNIVAL

Combo Mambo	Be sure to get a good combo going on the cinder block wall that runs from the Abductor over to the Angry Dragon. From there, trick into a grind on the logs and the counters to loop it all the way around to the entrance of the fairgrounds.
King of the Hill	A King can find lots of ways to outrun opponents at the Carnival. Not only are there lengthy walls and rails everywhere to grind for speed, but the clever King can ride the elevator to the top of the roller coaster and hop into a grind on the tracks. This is a great way to guarantee at least fifteen straight seconds of uninterrupted royalty!
Trick Attack	Someone challenge you to a game of Trick Attack? If so, put the scoring line provided for the 'Get a Sick Score' objective to use here. Hit it once and return to the start and do it again in a switch stance and with different Special Tricks.

Green Base

Blue Base

Red Base

Yellow Base

CHICAGO

Capture the Flag	All of the bases are on the perimeter of the town and you can bet that's where most of the traffic will be. Cut across the center of the map when going diagonally and try to use the rooftop ramps, the El's tracks, and even the doorways that lead through the concert hall.
Combo Mambo	Let the other guys roam around town hitting sporadic rails and ramps. You know better than that. Trick off the ramps near Mat's bus and hop into a Special Grind on the lengthy ledge wrapping around the concert hall. Trick across the gaps in the ledge and continue on in a Special Grind. Keep it going until balance all but runs out and trick down into a Special Manual in the street.
Graffiti	String a big combo together on the ledge around the concert hall and use the points gained to make some of the lesser rails and benches near the street all but unstealable. Also, don't forget to head across the bridge to the area near the fountain. There's an abundance of small ledges to score there!

Neversoft Never Quits

There's no denying that *Tony Hawk's Pro Skater 4* is the deepest and most sophisticated installment in this storied series. With nearly 200 different objectives to complete, and each of them being obtained through fully-voiced NPCs, some may even go so far as to say that this skateboard series is blurring the boundaries between sports and role-playing games. Not an unfair statement either, given that the trick system has steadily evolved to a complexity seldom seen outside of fantasy-based magic systems. Yet, no matter how great the improvements are, there is always a stigma associated with a series that sees more than one or two sequels. This is especially true when there *seems* to be nothing left to improve upon. Well, as you'll see in this chapter, Neversoft has found lots of ways to improve upon every game in the series, no matter how perfect their fans thought they each were.

TONY HAWK'S PRO SKATER THROUGH THE YEARS

CHARACTER SELECT	BOARD SELECT	EDIT STATS	LEVEL SELECT	GOLD MEDAL

Could not edit stats!

TONY HAWK'S PRO SKATER (1999)

Like all great stories, this one began a long, long, er, 3 years ago. A little-known company by the name of Neversoft had gotten the green light from Activision to develop a 3D skateboarding game. Skating games have been around almost as long as gaming itself, but none have ever truly succeeded outside of the arcades. That was all about to change.

Not only did Neversoft have a very capable engine running their game, but they signed skating's living legend Tony Hawk to lend his name and credibility to the title. Nine other professional skateboarders signed on as well, thereby allowing the ambitious developers to add a variety of skating styles and signature tricks to the title. And if that wasn't enough to grab the attention of gamers around the world, an ultra-cool soundtrack, including music from bands such as Primus, Goldfinger, and the Suicidal Tendencies, was eventually added as well.

While the name recognition of Tony Hawk was no doubt responsible for some of the early hype the title received, it was ultimately the enjoyable, addictive gameplay that propelled *Tony Hawk's Pro Skater* to the top of the sales charts. For the first time ever, gamers and skaters alike were able to enjoy some of the hottest skate spots around the country without leaving their living room. Players were able to perform Kickflips, Smith Grinds, and even special tricks such as the Dark Slide and Christ Air. In short, the game allowed people to play as real skaters, performing real tricks, at real skate spots. It was the game that everyone was waiting for.

Appeared on PlayStation, Nintendo 64, and Dreamcast consoles, as well as the PC.

FUN FACTS

Courses	Warehouse (Woodland Hills), School (Miami), Mall (New York), Skate Park (Chicago), Downtown (Minneapolis), Downhill Jam (Phoenix), Burnside (Portland), Streets (San Francisco), and Concrete Conspiracy (Roswell).
Skaters	Tony Hawk, Bob Burnquist, Kareem Campbell, Rune Glifberg, Bucky Lasek, Chad Muska, Andrew Reynolds, Geoff Rowley, Elissa Steamer, and Jamie Thomas.
Special Tricks	Each skater only had 3 Special Tricks, except Tony Hawk who had 4.
Multiplayer	Graffiti, Trick Attack, and HORSE were included in the original.

MEMORABLE MOMENT

There are many memorable moments in the original *Tony Hawk's Pro Skater*, but it's hard to beat the thrill that came from *finally* snagging the Hidden Tape at the Downhill Jam course. Skaters had to grind across a dam onto a narrow ledge and then quickly air off a tiny ramp to soar onto a rock spire in the center of the level to pick up the tape.

Tony Hawk's Pro Skater was released just a short while after Tony landed his legendary 900 at the X-Games. Soon after, fans everywhere were able to drop into their digital halfpipes and pull "The 900" at will.

AUTHOR'S NOTE

The original *Tony Hawk's Pro Skater* was responsible for single-handedly rekindling my interest in gaming. It was so captivating that I recall playing the demo (Skate Park course) for nearly five hours straight. That's over 150 two-minute sessions on the same course without stopping!

TONY HAWK'S PRO SKATER 2 (2000)

The original game was such a success that it is still considered one of the top Playstation games of all time. Given the amount of praise the game was given, not to mention its permanent home in the best-sellers list, a sequel was inevitable. And Neversoft didn't disappoint.

While Neversoft was able to revel in relative obscurity during the creation of the original game, that was certainly not the case for the sequel. Not only did they have their own lofty standards to live up to, but there was now a large fan base with equally high expectations. As it turns out, everyone's wish list was fulfilled, and then some. Gamers not only received a much larger and complex Career Mode that contained eight courses with ten objectives each, but players were even treated to an unlockable secret course! Other additions to the game's primary gameplay mode included a gaps checklist and a money system that allowed players to purchase new decks, special tricks, and stat points.

While a bigger and deeper Career Mode was to be expected, few anticipated the introduction of the Create-A-Skater and Park Editor tools. These additions increased the long-term replayability of the game, and sent a clear message to the fans of the series and the industry as a whole: the *Tony Hawk's Pro Skater* series is here to stay!

Appeared on PlayStation, Nintendo 64, Dreamcast, and Xbox consoles, as well as the PC.

FUN FACTS	
Courses	Hangar (Mullet Falls, MT), School II (Southern Cali), Quiksilver Pro Bowl Jam (Marseille, FR), NY City (NY), Venice Beach (CA), Plywood Paradise (Ventura, CA), Philadelphia (PA), Bullhorn Brawl (Mexico), and Skater Heaven.
Skaters	Steve Caballero, Eric Koston, and Rodney Mullen all signed on for the sequel.
Trick Linking	The Manual and Nose Manual were first introduced in Tony Hawk's Pro Skater 2. Before the manual, tricking into and out of grinds was the only way to string tricks together.
Multiplayer	Graffiti, Trick Attack, and HORSE were joined by the multiplayer games Tag and Free Skate. Of the five, Tag is the only one not to see a repeat appearance, it has since been resurrected as Slap!

MEMORABLE MOMENT

Tony Hawk's Pro Skater 2 had many memorable moments, and one of them was going through the loop at the Bullhorn Brawl course. Skaters were able to get completely inverted with this over-the-top ramp. Pun fully intended.

AUTHOR'S NOTE

When I think of *Tony Hawk's Pro Skater 2*, the first thing that comes to mind is the music. To this day, the soundtrack from *Tony Hawk's Pro Skater 2* is still my favorite. What other game gives you Bad Religion, Anthrax, Rage Against the Machine, and Naughty By Nature?

TONY HAWK'S PRO SKATER 3 (2001)

The time between *Tony Hawk's Pro Skater 2* and its successor was the longest period between installments yet seen in the series, but it was for good reason. *Tony Hawk's Pro Skater 3* was the first in the series to make the jump to the new generation of consoles. Not only did the game have to look better than ever before, but the higher processing power of the newer hardware allowed for much larger courses and a greater level of interactivity. So, not only did Neversoft have to deal with the learning curve associated with a new console, but they had to ensure that their fans felt the wait was worth it.

When it released in the fall of 2001, *Tony Hawk's Pro Skater 3* was proven to be worth the wait, indeed. Although the money system used in *Tony Hawk's Pro Skater 2* (and *Tony Hawk's Pro Skater 4*) was dropped from the Career Mode, the addition of skater-specific trick goals and multiple locations for Stat Points, S-K-A-T-E letters, and Decks more than made up for it. Another temporary tradeoff was the removal of the gaps checklist. Although the "completists" out there may never know if they found each and every gap, Neversoft found ways to hide over 500 in the game!

While the enormous courses and the cinematic elements drew the most attention from fans and magazines, the biggest step forward for the series came from the evolution of the trick system. Players were given the opportunity to map various tricks to any button combination they desired. "Hidden Combos" allowed skaters to combo specific tricks together while maintaining a greater sense of flow. In addition, flatland tricks made their debut in this release, and manualing has never been the same since.

Appeared on the PlayStation, Playstation 2, Gamecube, Xbox, and the PC.

FUN FACTS	
Courses	Foundry, Canada, Rio Ruckus, Suburbia, Airport, Skater Island, Los Angeles, Tokyo, and a Cruise Ship.
Skaters	Although Bob Burnquist temporarily lost his faith in 2001, the addition of Bam Margera and his patented Jackass trick were a welcome addition.
Trick Linking	Tony Hawk's Pro Skater 3 gave gamers the Revert, which made it possible to link aerial tricks into a scoring line. Together with the manual, it was now possible to link tricks across almost any terrain.
Multiplayer	All the multiplayer games from Tony Hawk's Pro Skater 2 were brought back with the exception of Tag, which was reborn as Slap! Additionally, King of the Hill was first introduced in Tony Hawk's Pro Skater 3 as well. Aside from the variety of multiplayer games, what really stood out with this installment was the ability to play online (PS2 only) against other gamers. Unfortunately, Neversoft was a year ahead of its time and console gaming wouldn't be truly ready for the online world until 2002.

AUTHOR'S NOTE

The beauty of *Tony Hawk's Pro Skater 3*, to me, was the freedom to really go after the big combos. The addition of the Revert made it possible to score point totals that were previously absurd to even think about. I'll never forget linking together my first million-point combo on the Cruise Ship!

MEMORABLE MOMENT

Tony Hawk's Pro Skater 3 added a lot to the series, especially the introduction of scripted events to the gameplay. Of these, none are more memorable than triggering an earthquake in Los Angeles. Watching the course deform before your very eyes was a defining moment.

TONY HAWK'S PRO SKATER 4 (2002)

If you're reading this book, then there's a great chance that you already know the next story in this chapter! In just one year, Neversoft has not only reworked the game engine from the ground up, but they have expanded upon the game in an unprecedented fashion. Consider the facts: the number of objectives has doubled, 8-player online functionality has been added, and the trick system has again been enhanced. Given this, it's safe to say that the guys and gals behind the *Tony Hawk's Pro Skater* series are most certainly *never soft*.

Interviews

TONY HAWK

Favorite level in THPS series
Downhill Jam (THPS1)
Favorite Special Trick in THPS series
360 Varial McTwist
How long have you been skating?
25 years

What is your favorite skate park?
Durban
Favorite song from any version of THPS
Toy Dolls "Dig That Groove" (THPS4)

Tony Hawk hanging out at Neversoft, checking out the status of the game.

MICK WEST

THPS online name
Mick NS
Job title
Technical Director
Date of birth
3/28/67

Years in game industry
15
All-time favorite game
Zelda
Games you have worked on in the past
Too many to list

Favorite level in THPS series
Los Angeles (THPS3)
Favorite special trick in THPS series
Coffin Grind

BOB BURNQUIST

Favorite level in THPS series
Marseille, France (THPS2)
Favorite Special Trick in THPS series
Blunt slides
How long have you been skating?
15 years

What is your favorite skate park?
My backyard!
Favorite song from any version of THPS
[no answer]

Bob Burnquist getting pictures taken for his model reference.

DAVE COWLING

THPS online name
'Top Bloke'
Job Title
Lead Programmer - Xbox
Date of birth
09/20/1970

Years in game industry
9
All-time favorite game
3D Ant Attack (ZX Spectrum – long, long time ago)

Games you have worked on in the past
Apocalypse, Spider-Man, THPS3
Favorite level in THPS series
Alcatraz (THPS4)
Favorite special trick in THPS series
The Jackass

STEVE CABALLERO

Favorite level in THPS series
School (THPS1)
Favorite Special Trick in THPS series
Hang Ten Nose Wheelie Grind
How long have you been skating?
Since 1976 (over 25 years)

What is your favorite skate park?
Vans Milpitas Skatepark
Favorite song from any version of THPS
The Faction "Skate & Destroy" (THPS4)

Steve Caballero preparing to record his voice over.

PAUL ROBINSON

THPS online name
'Pooper'
Job Title
Programmer (GameCube)
Date of birth
02/16/1973

Years in game industry
12
All-time favorite game
Tetris
Games you have worked on in the past
Jurassic Park (SNES), Viewpoint (PS1),

One (PS1), Army Men 3D (PS1), THPS3 & 4 (GameCube)
Favorite level in THPS series
Foundry (THPS3)
Favorite special trick in THPS series
Faction Guitar Slide

KAREEM CAMPBELL

Favorite level in THPS series
New York (THPS2)
Favorite Special Trick in THPS series
Ghetto Bird
How long have you been skating?
11 years

What is your favorite skate park?
Belgium Skatepark
Favorite song from any version of THPS
Kareem Campbell "Time for Some Axion" (THPS3)

Kareem Campbell autographing some items for Neversoft.

STEVE GANEM

THPS online name
'Kraken'
Job title
Programmer (Network)
Date of birth
10/11/76

Years in game industry
6
All-time favorite game
Warcraft 2
Games you have worked on in the past
Toonstruck, Golden Nugget 64, Nox, THPS3

Favorite level in THPS series
Alcatraz (THPS4)
Favorite special trick in THPS series
Rowley Darkslide

RUNE GLIFBERG

Favorite level in THPS series
Cruise Ship (THPS3)
Favorite Special Trick in THPS series
The Human Dart
How long have you been skating?
16 years

What is your favorite skate park?
Marseille, France
Favorite song from any version of THPS
KRS One "Hush" (THPS3)

Rune Glifberg thinking about what his Special Tricks should be.

KEVIN MULHALL

THPS online name
'Guilt Ladle'
Job title
Producer
Date of birth
07/10/75

Years in game industry
9 (1993)
All-time favorite game
Bubble Bobble
Games you have worked on in the past
THPS4, THPS3, Spider-Man, Wu-Tang: Shaolin Style, Thrill Kill.

Favorite level in THPS series
Cruise Ship (THPS3)
Favorite special trick in THPS series
American Tribute

ERIC KOSTON

Favorite level in THPS series
Southern California School (THPS2)
Favorite Special Trick in THPS series
Spidey Flip
How long have you been skating?
16 years

What is your favorite skate park?
Girl Skatepark
Favorite song from any version of THPS
[no answer]

Joel Jewett preps Eric Koston before recording some voice over.

JOEL JEWETT

THPS online name
'Angus'
Job title
President Neversoft Entertainment
Date of birth
1963

Years in game industry
Nine
All-time favorite game
Pool, darts, quarters or golf.
Games you have worked on in the past
All Neversoft games.

Favorite level in THPS series
Pretty much like them all.
Favorite special trick in THPS series
The Jackass is tough to beat.

BUCKY LASEK

Favorite level in THPS series
College (THPS4)
Favorite Special Trick in THPS series
Misty Flip
How long have you been skating?
17 years

What is your favorite skate park?
Skate Park of Tampa (SPOT)
Favorite song from any version of THPS
[no answer]

Bucky Lasek checking out the latest version of the game.

CHAD FINDLEY

THPS online name
Usually just 'Chad'
Job title
Senior Designer
Date of birth
10/16/71

Years in game industry
8 or 9 years
All-time favorite game
Spy Hunter
Games you have worked on in the past
Mechwarrior 2, Mech 2: Ghost Bear's

Legacy, Apocalypse, Spider-Man (PSX), Tony Hawk 3
Favorite special trick in THPS series
360 Varial McTwist or Misty Flip

BAM MARGERA

Favorite level in THPS series
Airport (THPS3)
Favorite Special Trick in THPS series
Triple Backside Kickflip
How long have you been skating?
14 years

What is your favorite skate park?
FDR (Philadelphia)
Favorite song from any version of THPS
CKY "96 Quite Bitter Beings" (THPS3)

Bam Margera talking to Scott Pease about special trick design.

SCOTT PEASE

THPS online name
'Janky Cracka Foo'
Job title
Pro-Ducer
Date of birth
You don't need to know that

Years in game industry
[no answer]
All-time favorite game
AutoDuel
Games you have worked on in the past
Pitfall 3D, Apocalypse, THPS series, and Maximum Surge starring Yasmine Bleeth

Favorite level in THPS series
The Freeway
Favorite special trick in THPS series
Somi Spin

RODNEY MULLEN

Favorite level in THPS series
Venice (THPS2)
Favorite Special Trick in THPS series
Gazelle Underflip
How long have you been skating?
Began 1-1-77 (25 years)

What is your favorite skate park?
Skate Park of Tampa (SPOT)
Favorite song from any version of THPS
Motorhead "Ace of Spades" (THPS3)

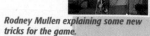

Rodney Mullen explaining some new tricks for the game.

CHRIS WARD

THPS online name
'Neversoft_Leeds'
Job title
Art Director
Date of birth
07/19/68

Years in game industry
Too @#%$## many
All-time favorite game
Defender - Arcade /Elite - BBC home computer
Games you have worked on in the past
Cliffhanger, Apocalypse, Spider-Man, THPS series. Oh, and too many cancelled games.

Favorite level in THPS series
All the levels yet to do in THPS5
Favorite special trick in THPS series
Any one I can pull off, I have two

CHAD MUSKA

Favorite level in THPS series
Downhill Jam (THPS1)
Favorite Special Trick in THPS series
Ghetto Blaster!
How long have you been skating?
14 years

What is your favorite skate park?
The streets of the world
Favorite song from any version of THPS
Any of the Muskabeatz (THPS4)

Chad Muska recording some voice over for the game.

PETE DAY

Job title
Animator
Date of birth
12 April 1962
Years in game industry
10

All-time favorite game
Half Life
Games you have worked on in the past
THPS4 & 3, Spider-Man, Skeleton Warriors, Croc 1 & 2, FX Fighter, CreatureShock

Favorite level in THPS series
Carnival (THPS4)
Favorite special trick in THPS series
JangoJumpJet

ANDREW REYNOLDS

Favorite level in THPS series
Warehouse (THPS1)
Favorite Special Trick in THPS series
[no answer]
How long have you been skating?
14 years

What is your favorite skate park?
Huntington Beach Skatepark
Favorite song from any version of THPS
Ramones "Blitzkrieg Bop" (THPS3)

Andrew Reynolds taking a call before his voice over session.

DARREN THORNE

THPS online name
'DDT'
Job title
Lead Artist
Date of birth
04/13/67

Years in game industry
9
All-time favorite game
DOOM 2
Games you have worked on in the past
Comanche 3, F22 Raptor

Favorite level in THPS series
Not sure.
Favorite special trick in THPS series
Lazy Ass Manual, Coffin Grind

GEOFF ROWLEY

Favorite level in THPS series
London (THPS4)
Favorite Special Trick in THPS series
Ferret Fight
How long have you been skating?
13 years

What is your favorite skate park?
[no answer]
Favorite song from any version of THPS
Motorhead "Ace of Spades" (THPS3)

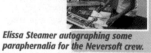

Geoff Rowley discussing special tricks with Scott Pease.

ELISSA STEAMER

Favorite level in THPS series
Warehouse (THPS1)
Favorite Special Trick in THPS series
[no answer]
How long have you been skating?
14 years

What is your favorite skate park?
Huntington Beach Skatepark
Favorite song from any version of THPS
Ramones "Blitzkrieg Bop" (THPS3)

Elissa Steamer autographing some paraphernalia for the Neversoft crew.

JAMIE THOMAS

Favorite level in THPS series
Warehouse / School (THPS1)
Favorite Special Trick in THPS series
American Hero Grind
How long have you been skating?
16 years

What is your favorite skate park?
Barcelona
Favorite song from any version of THPS
Dead Kennedy's "Police Truck" (THPS1)

Jamie Thomas getting set to record some voice over for the game.

6 WORLD TITLES, NEVER THE SAME WAVE TWICE.

Visit 13 of the most popular surf spots from around the globe.

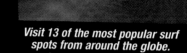

9 modes of play including 2 player PUSH™ mode.

SURFING WILL NEVER BE THE SAME

Drop in with **6-time World Champion Kelly Slater** or one of 8 other top pros in the ultimate surf experience, Kelly Slater's Pro Surfer®. Play a total of **30 levels** at the **most challenging surf breaks from around the globe.** Pull off big air and fantasy tricks like **Rodeo Flip, Knack Knack** and **Hangman** that let you take surfing to a whole new level. Surf in a constantly changing wave environment – **you'll never see the same wave twice.**

KELLY SLATER'S PRO SURFER®

PlayStation 2

KELLY SLATER'S PRO SURFER

Surf on waves populated with other surfers.

ACTIVISION
O2

SPORTS REVOLUTION

ACTIVISIONO2.COM

by Doug Walsh

BradyGames Publishing
An Imprint of Pearson Education
201 West 103rd Street
Indianapolis, Indiana 46290

ISBN: 0-7440-0187-0

Library of Congress Catalog No.: 2002094849

Printing Code: The rightmost double-digit number is the year of the book's printing; the rightmost single-digit number is the number of the book's printing. For example, 02-1 shows that the first printing of the book occurred in 2002.

05 04 03 02   4 3 2 1

Manufactured in the United States of America.

BradyGAMES Staff

Publisher
David Waybright

Editor-In-Chief
H. Leigh Davis

Creative Director
Robin Lasek

Marketing Manager
Janet Eshenour

Licensing Manager
Mike Degler

Assistant Marketing Manager
Susie Nieman

Credits

Senior Project Editor
Ken Schmidt

Screenshot Editor
Michael Owen

Book Designer
Doug Wilkins

Poster Designer
Carol Stamile

Production Designers
Bob Klunder
Billy Huys

About the Author

Doug Walsh has been an avid gamer and board sports junkie throughout most of his life. As luck would have it, he found a way to blend these hobbies into a career over the past two years as the strategy guide author for Activision's O2 lineup. This book marks Doug's 16th Official Strategy Guide and his 8th in the Activision O2 series. The author lives with his wife, Kristin, and their two Siberian Huskies in the Puget Sound area.

Acknowledgments

First off I want to thank Kevin Mulhall of Neversoft for the tremendous assistance he provided and for inviting me to join in Neversoft's online skate sessions. To Ken Schmidt, Leigh Davis, Doug Wilkins, Mike Degler, and Michael Owen at BradyGAMES, I want to say thank you very much for putting forth such a great effort on this book. Lastly, I want to thank my lovely wife Kristin for always being there and for never getting bored of listening to me talk about my Sick Scores.

BradyGames would like to thank the entire staff at Neversoft and the following people at Activision: David Pokress, Mike Chiang, Stacey Drellishak, Lindsey Hayes, Mike Ward, Greg Deutsch, David Anderson, Stacy Rivas, Joe Favazza, Marilena Rixford, Matt McClure, Ben DeGuzman, Lee Cheramie, Jesse Shannon, Aaron Justman, Steve Peterson, Clint Baptiste, John Rosser, Brad Arnold, and Activision's Strategy Guide Producer Justin Berenbaum